"*Loving and Working* is a groundbreaking book that combines a sense of solidarity among women and critical analysis of the American workplace with spiritual rootedness and a passion for public concerns. After describing the conflicts faced by professional women with children, it offers a biblically-rooted 'integrative spirituality' that can strengthen both men and women in their service of the common good."
— **Sally Cunneen, Associate Editor,** *Cross Currents*

"Drawing on the actual experiences of women professionals who are trying to combine career and family, Barciauskas and Hull have provided accessible, clear, and intellectually rigorous arguments to help women and men analyze the nature of prevailing assumptions about work and family. At the same time they suggest an alternative work ethic derived from a careful and sensitive analysis of the relational ethic lying buried within Western religious and cultural traditions. Unlike many critical examinations of significant social issues, this book does not aim simply to expose problems. Through the examples of such remarkable women as the biblical Deborah and the nineteenth-century publicists Angelina and Sarah Grimke, the authors offer us emotional encouragement and practical suggestions for risking the changes necessary to incorporate women's values and experience into the prevailing normative structures shaping love and work."   — **Rose Gatens, Assistant Director for Programs, North Carolina Humanities Council**

"*Loving and Working* illuminates in a fresh way the conflict between self-sacrifice and self-realization which persists as an obstacle to professional advancement and personal fulfillment for women who seek to achieve both. The empirical assumptions and the nature of inquiry in Psychology and Theology are often themselves in conflict. Here, they have been skillfully combined to reflect the complex reality of women's experience and to create a unique historical context for its examination. This is a 'must read' book for women who accept and explore the spiritual dimension of their lives even as they pursue a secular ambition. It will be especially important in the university classroom where information and values are transmitted to the next generation."
— **Jeanne Neff, Vice President for Academic Affairs, Susquehanna University**

"Rosemary Curran Barciauskas and Debra Beery Hull have collaborated in the writing of a very ambitious book about a significant aspect of the American woman's life. They have taken up the question of woman's place in the contemporary setting and infused their study with a rich documentation and a fascinating report of the status of women in the home and the workplace. What makes their contribution so compelling is the particular blending of insight and information drawn from their respective fields — sociology and theology. They have written with intelligence and in a highly accessible style. Moreover, they have combined a variety of sources, including interview responses, short narratives of significant historical figures, and biblical text. If I was a hair skeptical about how well the authors could integrate all of this diverse material after reading their introductory remarks, I soon discovered that they were more than capable of doing so — and with clarity and excellent summary statements at the end of each chapter.

"The thesis of the book is an important one. The authors have interpreted the problem of individualism in American life through the lens of women's studies. They have argued that the separation of persons into private and public spaces according to gender is thoroughly dysfunctional, serving neither family nor civic community. They present a remarkably comprehensive account of the tensions and realities of gender division and conclude their study with an inspiring set of recommendations for social change.

"The book promises to be a highly useful one because it pulls together materials and arguments that have been presented in earlier studies in bits and pieces. I commend the study to readers who have puzzled over the connection between women's struggle to be recognized in their public contribution and the social studies of contemporary individualism and citizenship." — **Clare Benedicks Fischer,**
Aurelia Henry Reinhardt Professor of Religion and Culture,
Starr King School for the Ministry, Berkeley, Calif.

LOVING and WORKING

LOVING and WORKING

Reweaving Women's Public and Private Lives

Rosemary Curran Barciauskas
and
Debra Beery Hull

MEYER
STONE
BOOKS

Published in the United States by Meyer-Stone Books,
a division of Meyer, Stone, and Company, Inc.,
2014 South Yost Avenue, Bloomington, IN 47403.
Telephone: 812-333-0313

Cover design: Carol Evans-Smith

Typesetting output: T_EXSource, Houston

Manufactured in the United States of America
93 92 91 90 89   5 4 3 2 1

Library of Congress Cataloging in Publication Data

Barciauskas, Rosemary Curran, 1948-
    Loving and Working : reweaving women's public and private lives /
Rosemary Curran Barciauskas and Debra Beery Hull.
      p.   cm.
    Bibliography: p.
    ISBN 0-940989-48-4
    1. Women — United States — History. 2. Women in the professions —
United States. 3. Work and family — United States. 4. Women in the
Bible. 5. Feminism — Moral and ethical aspects. I. Hull, Debra
Beery, 1951- . II. Title.
HQ1410.B37   1989
305.4'0973 — dc20   89- 9308
                                             CIP

To our children,
David and Katie
and
Joel and Aimee,
in hopes that this book
will make a difference
in the lives of their generation.

Contents

Part II   *New Virtues for a New World*

Acknowledgments

There are a great many people to whom we owe a debt of gratitude for making this book possible. Foremost among them are the 174 women and men who responded to our initial survey and the 40 women who participated in our interview sessions. Their forthright sharing of their lives and concerns provides the heart and flesh of this book.

The success of former Academic Vice President of Wheeling College, Jeanne Kammer Neff, in securing a Myrin Pew grant for faculty research provided an initial impetus to our work. We are grateful for her encouragement to us in those early stages of work, as well as her willingness to read and comment on the completed manuscript. We are also thankful to many other members of the faculty and staff at Wheeling College who were supportive of our research and writing in a variety of ways.

Special mention should be given to two of our colleagues. Eugene Lauer gave us good advice when we decided to publish our research and also read our manuscript. Rose Gatens participated in our initial research, talked over key ideas with us, and provided invaluable editing help at several stages of our work. Her clear thinking and encouraging words played an important role in bringing this book to completion. Joseph and Sally Cunneen also provided constructive advice and help at several stages of our writing. We thank them and other colleagues who kindly read and commented on our manuscript. As our editor, John Eagleson was mercifully light-handed and yet always helpful and available.

We would also like to thank members of our extended families who offered space, childcare, and insight when we needed it most.

Finally, we offer our deepest thanks and love to our husbands, John Hull and Jonas Barciauskas, who not only offered us professional help, critique, and encouragement, but also shared housekeeping and parenting tasks in an unusually equitable way. At times their own professional work was put aside to allow us extra time. They have helped us to realize the dream of reweaving our own public and private lives.

LOVING and WORKING

Introduction

More than anything else, we hope this book will lead to a greater feeling of solidarity among women. There are immense differences that separate us from one another, and solidarity is far from automatic. Some of us are poor, some rich. Some of us are homemakers, some work outside the home in traditionally feminine fields, and others work in nontraditional fields. Some of us are single, others married. Many of us have children. Some of us are younger, some older, some politically conservative, some liberal, others apolitical. We are a rainbow of colors and cultures and religious traditions.

The listing of differences could go on and on. And yet, beyond the differences there are fundamental bonds between us, bonds we feel need to be identified and strengthened. The bonds we feel with other women are rooted in the affection we feel for our mothers, our sisters, our daughters, and our friends. Sometimes these tender ties are strained when we discover growing differences between us — differences brought on by maturity, education, change of lifestyle, divergences in value systems, religious or ideological conversions. As women we often experience a great deal of anguish trying to maintain relationships with other women to whom we feel some kind of natural or affectional commitment. One goal of this book is to help us see why it is important that these bonds of commitment lead us on to a sense of care and responsibility for all women. In the religious vision that informs this book, human communion — care for and responsibility toward all humans — is surely an ultimate goal. We focus on solidarity among women, not in any way to exclude our solidarity with the men in our lives, but simply because of the particular needs of this historical moment in our society and in our world. We care very much about the lives of our own sisters, friends, and daughters. Is there any reason to care less about the lives of other women's daughters — women and daughters whom we do not personally know, but with whom we inevitably share some common struggles, some common feelings, and some common dreams.

This book began with the kind of natural affinity and search for solidarity of which we are speaking. We were drawn to each other immediately — two women with preschool children and a deeply held

1

commitment to our work as scholars. Because we have always felt a responsibility to use the gifts we have been given for others, and because much of our fulfillment as human beings comes from the work we are able to do in our professions, we are highly invested in our careers. At the same time, we are absolutely committed to loving and nurturing our children in a secure and happy family. We were brought up in established churches and either worked in professional ministry or seriously considered doing so. Both of us chose our husbands carefully, consciously looking for men who would share fully the care of the family and the nurturance of children. We want both our careers and our marriages to reflect our faith and the spiritual values we hold dear.

All was not well with us, though. The practicalities and psychic energy needed to balance our dual commitments to career and family and integrate our secular and our religious values caused daily conflicts for us. We began to wonder if we really could do it all. For us the turning point came when one of our employers sent us a memo implying in rather strong terms that professional people should expect to work fifty to sixty hours a week. That expectation as well as other aspects of the work world seemed to make it impossible for us to participate fully and mutually in our careers and in our families. As we began to talk with other women, we found that we were not alone.

These discoveries led us to the only course of action for scholars; we began to study the problem in a systematic way. The fact that our collaboration allowed us to combine the disciplines of social science and theology broadened and enriched our work. We began by conducting a survey/interview study of three hundred professional women.[1] Then we reflected on our results in the context of religious, cultural, and historical perspectives.

Our survey required about forty-five minutes to complete. Fifty-three percent of the women we contacted returned the survey to us, and about forty travelled to group interviews we held around our state. Their willingness to take a chunk of time out of their already overburdened lives, and the heartrending personal stories they told us, assured us that we were studying an area of critical importance in the lives of many women and men. What we found in our research and in the writings of others is summed up by this participant.

> I would say that it's my gut reaction that I can't do either job the way I'd like to. I can't do my career the way I'd like to do it. I can't be the wife and mommy the way I'd really like to do it. Because I'm trying to do both, I'm giving up a little of each.

The focus of our research was on professional and managerial women and their families. We chose to study these women partly because they are the group who share most closely our own experiences. But in many respects, we believe that all women have similar stresses and will benefit from changes in our culture that allow for the greater integration of public and private life. The impetus for this change necessitates leadership from women in all sorts of positions. Those who are in places of educational, political, and financial influence have a particularly serious responsibility to become facilitators of change.

It will be obvious that this book is an interdisciplinary effort. One of the differences that we as co-authors had to work with was the difference in mentality and style between a social scientist and a theologian, even when our fundamental viewpoints were very much the same. But we felt that there was a need for a book that could hold current reality and a hopeful, spiritual vision in tension. On the one hand we have tried to clearly identify women's concrete situations and the attitudes we hold about our situations, based on careful empirical research. We have also *reflected* on those conditions and attitudes from the viewpoint of a committed faith within the Judaeo-Christian tradition. In other words, we wanted to be able to move from *what is* to *what could and should be.* Much of what we say would be agreeable to any humanist. But we believe that the resources of the Jewish and Christian traditions, while they must be read by women with special caution and care, provide both clear ethical imperatives and wonderful models for women who seek a spirituality for the new shape of their lives.

Our fundamental assumption in this book is that women have the right to work and to participate with full equality in the public sphere of life, but that they also have the right to have children and to nurture them. We do not believe that these two aspects of life are mutually exclusive, either for women or for men.

The realities of the current situation can be summarized briefly. Despite some progress, many women continue to bear *a disproportionate burden* of family care and to experience discriminatory effects that discourage their full participation in public work. Most women express the desire for a life in which *family and career* can be successfully *integrated,* but as yet American women have not reached consensus on societal/structural changes that would support this integration. *Women's specific* experiences, strengths, and life patterns, as well as the changing life patterns of men who share family responsibilities, must be established as *"normal" rather than exceptional* and fully supported in workplace practice and in public culture.

When we began our research we suspected that the difficulty women have had in reaching a consensus on needed changes had its roots in deep-seated ethical and spiritual attitudes held by women. We found this, indeed, to be the case, but the relationship between these attitudes and women's behavior in both public and private life was much more complex than we had first imagined it to be. Women in our culture have been influenced by *two conflicting ethics* — an ethic of self-sacrificing love, deemed especially appropriate to women and to family life, and the American ethic of individualism predominant in the male-oriented work world. Relegating the Judaeo-Christian ideal of *agape* love to the traditionally feminine sphere of home and family has negatively affected our culture in several ways: (a) it has fostered an unhealthy neglect of self-development and care for the self on the part of women; (b) it has allowed the individualistic ethic to reign supreme in the public realm, unmitigated by any altruistic concern for others and for the common good; (c) it has created an abyss for caring men and women between the other-centered ethic that they embrace in the private sphere, and the self-enhancing ethic of the workplace; and (d) it has left women and men with no generally understood motivation for giving of themselves in the pursuit of beneficial social change.

Much of women's dividedness and ambivalence on issues of concern to them can be traced to the conflict of these two ethics. We feel that the challenges of women's life at the end of the twentieth century call for a new spiritual basis. An integrative spirituality draws forth the best from each of these ethics, and rejects that in each ethic which is debilitating to women, both personally and as a social group. Central biblical themes such as *self-worth*, *social communion*, and *calling* are the foundations of this renewed spirituality. Such a spirituality would commit us to a care for the public realm — to consider the good of other women, and of other women's daughters and sons, even when their needs are different from our own. It would help us to pursue, among other things, a better integration of love and work for both women and men, based on a more relational ethic.

Part I of this book, then, is descriptive. In the first chapter we note the dilemmas facing the contemporary woman who tries to combine work and family. In order to see this dilemma in proper perspective, we trace the history of women and work in this country from colonial times to the post–World War II period. In the second chapter, we again take an historical approach, but this time our focus is on the women's movement. We are particularly interested in noticing why the most recent phase of the women's movement has failed to give priority to family issues, and thus failed to enlist the support of many homemaking women. In chapter 3 we review our research results in the light of other recent research on working women. We discuss the various motivations that lead women to continue to work in the public sphere, despite its burdens, and we present profiles of the two conflicting ethics that we found among our participants.

The second part of this book is a search for resources in Judaism and Christianity that can help us to create a new and more fruitful spirituality. In chapter 4 we look at the fundamental Jewish and Christian virtue of self-giving love, as expressed in the Greek term *agape*. We note why it has been a troublesome virtue for us women, and we suggest how it can be incorporated into a "public spirituality." Chapter 5 develops more fully the notion of a public spirituality as a counterbalance to the individualism that has come to color much of the public life of modern America. In chapter 6 we turn to Hebrew and Christian Scripture. Given the oppressive effects on women's lives of a fundamentalist reading of certain scriptural texts, we emphasize the tools and methods of careful scholarship that must precede our approach to these 2000–3000-year-old texts. With these tools in hand, we examine some of the texts that have been particularly troubling to women, as well as some of the texts that herald women's full liberation. Chapters 7, 8, and 9 are meant to provide new images and models for us in the lives of our foremothers. Chapter 7 focuses on women in Scripture and in early Christian history whose extraordinary lives exhibited virtues that are particularly relevant to us today — virtues such as self-esteem, courage, intelligence, and mutual support. Chapter 8 takes up the biblical notion of "calling," examines its importance for women and men today, and then presents women from Scripture and the medieval period who lived out a calling to full participation in the public culture of their era. The notion of a divine or inner impulsion to work in the public world is also evidenced in the lives of the four nineteenth-century women whom we meet in chapter 9.

Part III of our book is meant to bring us back to our own concrete situations, fortified with new spiritual resources. Chapter 10 makes it clear that our full liberation requires mutual interchange and solidarity with the men in our family and work lives, as well as with other women. Chapter 11 gives some practical guidelines for creating a more just and caring culture both for ourselves, and as our legacy to our sons and daughters.

Part I

Women and Work

Chapter 1

Careers and Families among American Women: Can We Do Both?

Those of use who reached maturity in the 1970s were expected to clone the male competitive model in the labor market while raising our children in our spare time. . . . Mere mortals such as I end up trapped between the demands of the earthmothers and the hard-nosed careerists, and because these demands are incompatible and contradictory, we are ultimately unable to satisfy either. —Sylvia Hewlett

We have talked with countless women in the past two years who are trying to nurture families and contribute to public life through their work. Many of them have great talents to share, creative solutions to real-life challenges, and indefatigable energy. Yet not one woman we talked to, ourselves included, has been entirely successful in integrating life. From our discussions, we have come to realize that the practical difficulties women still face may persist because of certain deep-seated beliefs and attitudes by which we live. Many of these beliefs and attitudes are, in fact, our strengths. Most of us wish to live in intimate relationships with others, and we work hard and give generously of ourselves in those relationships; we prefer harmonious human relations, and we are reluctant to act aggressively against others; we are open to our own feelings and sensitive to those of others; we recognize that our individual egos are not of primary importance; and finally, we desire to integrate love and work. But these strengths, which serve us well in the private realm of family and friends, can betray us in the traditional public realm of work, where ambition is often rewarded more than altruism, aggressiveness more than nurturing, and calculation more than openness about our feelings. Our expectations for ourselves seem incompatible. As economist and author Sylvia Hewlett has put it,

> Those of us who reached maturity in the 1970s were expected to clone the male competitive model in the labor market while raising our children in our spare time.... We were also expected to raise these children according to wildly inflated notions of motherhood. In essence, I belong to that "lucky" generation of superwomen who got to combine the nurturing standards of the 1950s with the strident feminism of the 1970s. Mere mortals such as I end up trapped between the demands of the earthmothers and the hard-nosed careerists, and because these demands are incompatible and contradictory, we are ultimately unable to satisfy either.[1]

A central theme of this book is that when we move into the public realm we need to re-think what constitutes virtue — both for ourselves and for our male partners and co-workers. We believe and hope that feminine strengths can transform the workplace if we ourselves are willing to re-evaluate what we have to give. We need to find a spirituality that fits our public lives as well as our private lives. As a contemporary author has said,

> The God who cares about our private lives is concerned about our public lives as well.... We need to see that in a healthy society the private and the public are not mutually exclusive, not in competition with each other.... They work together dialectically, helping to create and nurture one another.[2]

Today a growing number of women and men are seeking a reconciliation of family and work values. Their efforts rest on the heritage that is ours to discover in the lives of those who went before us.

The relationship between a woman's private family/spiritual life and the way she shapes public culture through her professional work has varied over time and in different areas of the country. In the next part of this chapter, we will discuss the current situation for those attempting to achieve a career/family balance. In the latter sections of the chapter we will trace the work lives of women in North America from the colonial period to the present time, concentrating on factors that allowed the greater or lesser integration of work and family.

The Current Situation

Throughout history there have always been women with independent spirits who resisted social and media pressure, prevailed in the face of the vast discrimination against them, and entered the work force. In about 1920, Ida Withers Harrison wrote,

The way women have responded to their opportunities to enter new and wider fields of labor, the efforts they have made to prepare themselves for it, the difficulties they have overcome in achieving it, show that they felt it was a higher call to a fuller and nobler life.[3]

The cost of such a call was very dear, for it often forced women to choose between a career and a family.

Like so many other women social scientists, [Elsie Clews] Parsons [social reformer, feminist, and anthropologist in the nineteenth century] found in science a vehicle for transcending the restrictions of her sex, but that vehicle set her apart from the world in which she had been bred — the world of womanhood, idealism, and social reform.[4]

She, like many others, was forced to coexist in two worlds. At work she entered a world that valued rationality, competition, and personal achievement; at home, on the other hand, values of aesthetics, cooperation, and nurturance were paramount.

The Cost of Choosing Children

No doubt because of the difficulties inherent in maintaining two disparate value systems, professional women have always been less likely to marry and have children than other women. A study of eminent women in psychology, past and present, showed that only 76 percent had married and only 38 percent of those (or 29 percent of the total group) had born children. (Averages that are fairly stable over time show that 95 percent of all women marry and 90 percent have children.) Those who did marry delayed their marriages until they were, on the average, twenty-nine years old. The comparable national average age for women to marry was twenty-one.[5] These days the pattern is much the same. A study of women in the Harvard Business School class of 1973 showed that ten years after graduation, only 60 percent of the women were married, and 46 percent had children.[6]

Besides the number of women who decided not to marry, not to have children, or to delay marriage and children until their careers were well established, there are also numerous examples of talented women who gave up promising careers either temporarily or permanently for the sake of their families. One woman's life, described in an article on this phenomenon, went like this:

A thirty-three-year-old advertising executive with an M.B.A. from Columbia University juggled work and home life after the birth of

her first child. But she quit her job...when her second child was
born....[She] found she could not work, commute, nurse her new
baby and tend to her family. When something had to give, it was
her job.[7]

The necessity of choosing between family and career never has extended
equally to men. A study of a large number of university professors
showed that 100 percent of the men but only 37 percent of the women
were married.[8] A *Wall Street Journal* survey of male and female senior
executives showed that only 48 percent of the women were married and
only 39 percent had children, while 96 percent of the men were married
and 97 percent had children.[9]

   The greater percentage of professional men than women who have
children probably reflects the fact that men do not share equally in the
day-to-day rearing of the children. One woman describes a conversation
she had with a father when she asked him to bake brownies for his
son's school.

> "Me?" he asks incredulously. After twelve years of fatherhood, [he]
> has apparently never been asked to make brownies, never been a
> Room Mother. Perhaps he is a father who spends "quality time"
> with his children on weekends or evenings, but he did not sound
> like a man who knew his way around the kitchen. That's where
> mothers generally conduct their "quality time," helping children
> with homework while making dinner and taking phone calls.[10]

Single career women earn significantly greater salaries and professional
honors than married career women, yet married career men earn greater
salaries than single men,[11] and men with children have higher salaries
and rank than men without children.[12] Married career women have less
time than married career men for talking over professional issues and research ideas with their colleagues,[13] two activities necessary to remaining
current in one's field, and hence to career advancement. In the field of
psychology, women have been found to be less professionally productive
than their husbands;[14] and in the field of sociology they have a lower job
classification than their husbands.[15] One of the participants in our study
who is a sociologist said this:

> I wish I would have paid someone to do my Christmas shop-
> ping...all those hours in the mall. I would have much rather
> invested that time in my job. If our salaries were more in line
> with where our [male] counterparts are of our same age and in our
> same profession, we would have more options.

When women apply for jobs, they are advised by career counselors not to mention marital status or motherhood because it might work against their job candidacy. Men, on the other hand, are advised to include such information because it enhances their qualifications. In a recent study of psychology job applicants, 51 percent of men, but only 17 percent of women listed their marital status on their résumé. Of the applicants who mentioned marital status, 73 percent of the men indicated they were married, but no women did. Twenty-five percent of the men reported the number of children they had; no woman did.[16] Clearly, being married and having children is a career asset for men, but a career liability for women.

Even though they don't mention it on their résumés, the number of women attempting to combine career and family is increasing. A study of male and female Ph.D.'s from the classes of 1950, 1960, and 1968, showed that only 60 percent of the women in the classes of 1950 and 1960 were married. But in the class of 1968, 70 percent of the women married.[17] The number of traditional families has declined greatly in the past several years, though the number of such families was never as great as popular myth would have it. In 1955, when "Leave it to Beaver" and "Father Knows Best" exemplified the ideal American family, 22–23 percent of families actually consisted of a working father, housewife mother, and two or more school-age children. By 1985, only 7 percent of U.S. families fit that description. In 1986, 70 percent of women with children six to seventeen years old, and 54 percent of mothers with children under six were working.[18] More than 75 percent of divorced mothers are in the paid labor force,[19] and 89 percent of single-parent families are supported by the mother.[20]

The Challenges to Living an Integrated Life

Significant and growing numbers of women with children are committed simultaneously to nurturing a family and contributing to the larger world through their professions. But the practical constraints and emotional energy necessary to fulfill this mutual commitment make life very difficult for many women. Careers have been defined as "jobs which are highly salient personally, have a developmental sequence, and require a high degree of commitment."[21] Our employer was correct about expectations for professional people. Professional careers require time commitments of fifty to eighty hours a week, especially for those who wish to advance.[22] As the 1987 film *Baby Boomer* vividly demonstrated, in addition to the sheer number of hours of work required, the pattern of commitment to a demanding career does not mesh well with family life.

It is not uncommon for employers to require that apprentice lawyers, doctors, and business executives work hours that absolutely preclude active participation in domestic life. The years between 25 and 35 are often the years in which professionals are challenged to demonstrate their ability to take the "fast-track" to the top.... Yet these are precisely the years in which many couples have young children and the heaviest household responsibilities.[23]

Like us, a great many women feel a strong desire to have both a meaningful work life and a family, to integrate their private and public lives, and to share them fully with the men they love. Often women feel torn between a deep sense of a call to contribute their talents through work and to fulfill their deepest needs for human connection through family. One professional woman with young children said to us:

People ask me how I do it. I tell them I cheat! I cheat at home with my kids and my spouse, and I cheat at work, and I cheat with my friends. Do I feel good about it? No! But it's the only way I can survive.

Women are beginning to recognize that after twisting themselves into pretzels for years, it is time for something besides themselves to change.

In later chapters we will reflect on how our religious roots can be resources for living fully, justly, and generously in this new situation. But first we believe that an accurate understanding of our current condition requires reflection on the history of American women's work and social struggle. In general, the historical description presented here is the story of the northeast and mid-Atlantic regions of the country. The same basic pattern was played out in frontier areas as well, although several years later. Some special circumstances made the southern experience somewhat different.

A History of the Work Lives of Women in America

The Colonial Period

In colonial times work and family were closely integrated. Because the country was relatively undeveloped and settled mostly by men, the labor supply was limited and women were few in number. Children, another source of needed labor, were valued as an economic asset, but the infant mortality rate was high. Women were frequently pregnant and many died in childbirth.

Everyone had to work; idleness was considered a sin. Work was not mechanized or highly specialized, but instead centered on the individual family's life-maintenance efforts. The work women did — weaving cloth, making clothes and shoes, growing and preserving food, making soap, candles, and medicines — was essential to the survival of the family and the community.

The roles of men and women were less compartmentalized and dependent on gender than they came to be later in history, so that women enjoyed a certain status in the community:

> The pioneer family existed as a self-sufficient unit that took pride in its ability to provide food and clothing for themselves and their children. As a result, women found themselves on far more equal footing.[24]

Women were frequently in situations where they heard and participated in political discussions. In some areas of the country women retained control of their dowries after marriage, and in their husband's absence were able to act in his behalf in financial and legal matters. When they became widows, women often continued to run the family business and to manage independently the family assets.

And yet the social and economic status a woman enjoyed came solely through her father or husband. She had no guaranteed educational or political rights and could not vote. Single women rarely lived alone; career women were almost nonexistent; few women functioned in the world as fully independent human beings. As Abigail Adams so clearly pointed out to her husband John,

> I cannot say, that I think you are very generous to the ladies; for whilst you are proclaiming peace and goodwill to men, emancipating all nations, you insist upon retaining an absolute power over all wives.[25]

Pre-Civil War Period

Following the Revolutionary War, America became more independent from its English/European roots in social and economic as well as political realms. American democracy provided for a more egalitarian society, at least with respect to the rights of men. In the new country a man's position in the community came increasingly from his ability and initiative rather than from his inherited status. As we shall see in later chapters, this "rugged individualism" has left its mark on American society even today.

The adolescent nation was on an economic roller-coaster ride, thrilling but barely under control, with economic growth characterized by specialization, diversification, speculation, and industrialization. To maximize competitiveness in the emerging capitalistic society, production had to be moved out of the family unit. No longer the economic center, the home came to be seen as a respite from the business world, the family a center of order, tranquility, and moral righteousness. The worlds of work and family, so closely intertwined in the colonial period, were split apart, the spheres of influence for men and women separated according to gender, an attitude well-captured in these lines from Tennyson's "The Princess."

> Man for the field and woman for the hearth;
> Man for the sword and for the needle she;
> Man with the head and woman with the heart;
> Man to command and woman to obey;
> All else confusion.[26]

As professional life developed in America, formal education or licensing became entry requirements. Since very few women had access to higher education or training programs, many areas in which they once worked (such as health care) were now closed to them. Two exceptions were teaching and nursing. Employment of women teachers, especially on the frontier, reflected the fact that there was a shortage of teachers and that women worked for little money. Thirty to fifty percent of what male teachers earned was considered appropriate pay for women.[27] And although women continued to be employed as nurses, nursing was most often considered a natural and unpaid extension of the duties of the housewife or unencumbered female relative.

New blue-collar jobs created by the industrial expansion were frequently filled by male immigrants. Yet among immigrants and the native poor work force were some women. These impoverished, usually unmarried young women followed their previously home-based work (weaving cloth, making clothes and shoes) into the factory or domestic service, to low-paying, sometimes dangerous jobs where advancement was rare. The lead character Julie and her friend Carrie in the musical "Carousel" are probably typical of the working girls of this time, toiling away in the mill, hoping to get married.

The commonly-held ideal of womanhood though was not a woman who supported herself, but one who didn't have to. "Working girls" contrasted sharply with "ladies." Ladies devoted themselves to home and family, creating pure and pious environments that displayed their husbands' wealth. Idleness went from being a sin to a status symbol. The definition of women's virtue was changing.

> The most rudimentary education was considered all that was necessary for a woman. Anything beyond that was considered indelicate and unwomanly, and was supposed to unfit her for the sphere to which God had assigned her.[28]

Higher education and any work other than supervising the domestic scene was considered too taxing for the weaker female sex, especially for adolescent girls who, it was thought, needed to save their strength for the challenges of puberty, pregnancy, and childbirth. The prevailing medical view was that intercourse sapped brain strength, reflected a base human (mostly male) need, and was for procreation only.

Gentlemen tried to focus on higher thoughts and didn't bother their wives for sex too frequently. If necessary, they sought sexual release outside the home.

In the South, female slaves were often forced to satisfy the sexual needs of their white masters. The mulatto children who resulted were a source of embarrassment to white women, further alienating them from their husbands. Undoubtedly, as men and women became more and more consigned to separate spheres, the closeness they had felt for one another during the colonial period waned. Men and women who separated from each other during the day became strangers at home, no longer sharing basic human experiences. On the other hand, families who continued to work together, especially slave and farm families, were able to maintain a sense of shared purpose and intimacy.[29]

The Period Surrounding the Civil War

The considerable talents and energy of many "ladies" could not be suppressed by their constraint in the home. Bored in their idleness, these women turned their attention to education. As a result of their efforts, women's colleges with curricula patterned after all-male schools began to open their doors in the East. In the Midwest, women were admitted first to Oberlin, in the 1830s, then to other formerly all-male schools.

Simultaneously, women turned their attention to missionary work. Spreading the gospel and providing medical care and education for impoverished women and children in this country and abroad became their goals.[30] But nineteenth-century church women soon discovered that while the already-established, male-dominated church mission societies were happy for women to raise money and turn it over to the men to spend, they were not willing to give women decision-making power within their organizations. In his Sunday sermon, one pastor

> threw cold water on women organizing for general missionary work for preaching the gospel, and exhorted them rather to turn their attention to dress reform and to caring for their own homes and children.[31]

But many of the men who opposed women's social reform groups were distracted by the war or away from home fighting. The women who were left behind found that they could manage the farm or business, make financial decisions, and act independently in areas previously controlled by men. Women who entered the paid work force during the Civil War had their own source of income for the first time. Together, these women controlled enough money to have a decision-making impact on the country.

Consequently, women began to form their own mission societies and civic organizations. The founder of one such organization, the Christian Woman's Board of Missions in the Christian Church (Disciples of Christ), Carolyn Neville Pearre, describes her call to work beyond the sphere of home and family:

> On the ninth day of April, 1874, after my private devotions, about ten o'clock in the morning, the thought came to me to organize the women of the church for missionary work. No one has the right to say nay to a movement that [I] and the other women of the church believe to be of God.[32]

In its constitution, the Christian Woman's Board of Missions explicitly stated that all affairs, money, and property were to be controlled by women members.

Other independent women's missionary organizations were established by the Congregationalists, Methodists, Presbyterians, Episcopalians, and Baptists in the period between 1868 and 1874. Women's civic organizations formed at about the same time were the YWCA, Women's Christian Temperance Union, and the American Red Cross. Through all these organizations, women found that they could organize themselves, work together, raise money, and help to shape worlds far beyond the confines of their homes.

It became increasingly apparent to educated and religious women that they needed the vote to be able to carry forth the reforms they had worked so hard to secure. To avoid being seen as an assault on the family, suffrage was presented as a way for women to bring their "natural" moral and spiritual leadership to bear on the government.[33] (See chapter 2 for a more thorough discussion of the cooperation between suffragists and social reformers.)

Many of the struggles surrounding the early work on women's suffrage paralleled the recent fight for the Equal Rights Amendment. The battle for suffrage, like the ERA, was fought largely by educated middle- and upper-class women, working-class women being fully occupied trying to provide a decent life for their families. Efforts by middle- and upper-class women were not always unified, frequently marred by controversy and division. Some women abolitionists felt that the rights of blacks, especially to vote, would be endangered by other women insisting on the vote for women. Undeterred though, many women did continue to struggle into the next century for the right to vote.

The World Wars

World War I again brought women out of their homes and into the paid work force. Women's work (in the factories, as nurses, in the Red Cross, in the business community) was so instrumental to the war effort, that the vote, recommended by President Wilson and finally granted in 1920, was seen by some as a reward given to women for their war-time service. After World War I, some women, especially those working in factories, returned home, but the percentage of women, especially young women working in blue-collar positions, continued to rise. A small percentage of women was able to enter professions other than nursing or teaching, but they were generally either unmarried or wealthy enough to hire full-time domestic help.

During the depression, many "average" women needed to work to help their families survive, but there was a subtle attitudinal change that made this period of time different from the colonial era. In the 1920s and 1930s women did not work at the behest or with the support of the community. Even though their husbands could no longer support their families, working women were chided for being selfish, for taking jobs away from men, and for stigmatizing their own husbands, illustrating the power of Victorian ideals even in the face of economic realities. To cope with community criticism, working women were forced to begin the long tradition of apologizing for their work, limiting their accomplishments, and downplaying their achievements relative to those of their husbands.

As the economy began to grow out of the depression in the years just before World War II, women were encouraged to return to the home, the proper sphere of influence for them. But attitudes about home life were changing as well. Rather than oppose the evils of society by providing a safe haven as they had done during the Victorian period, women were supposed to concentrate on meeting the psychological needs of individual family members:

> Laundering had once been just laundering; now it was an expression of love. The new bride could speak her affection by washing tell-tale gray out of her husband's shirts. Feeding the family had once been just feeding the family; now it was a way to communicate deep seated emotions. Diapering was no longer just diapering, but a time to build the baby's sense of security; cleaning the bathroom sink was not just cleaning, but an exercise for the maternal instincts, protecting the family from disease.[34]

By this time, many women were college educated. Typically they majored in education so they could work until marriage and have something to fall back on should the marriage not work out; or in home economics, so they could be proper wives and mothers. Mostly male-edited women's magazines encouraged their readers to study proper hygiene, nutrition, and care of the sick child. But the wife and mother, chiefly responsible for the fulfillment of the family's psychological well-being, found that she herself was not fulfilled. The age at first marriage rose; the divorce rate rose. Women who were able to support themselves were less willing to tolerate poor marriages.

The advent of World War II was accompanied, as always in times of war, by a need for large numbers of women in the work force to help maintain the gigantic war effort. This time married women entered the work force in large numbers, and, by and large, societal institutions supported their efforts. Women who worked outside the home were seen as good patriots. Child-care assistance was provided by governmental agencies, by older relatives, or by cheap domestic help. A few communal kitchens and laundries made home maintenance chores easier.

After World War II, with the influx of a large number of male (formerly military) workers back into an economy gearing down from the war, women were strongly encouraged to return home. The film *Rosie the Riveter* documents the pervasiveness and power of the media efforts directed at women during this period. Spending time with the children, followed closely by the purchase and consumption of material goods, became the chief responsibilities of women. New domestic technology was developed for the individual nuclear family, in many cases contributing to the isolation of women in the home, raising housekeeping standards to unreasonable levels, and increasing the time women spent tending to the care of their families:

> As families move up the economic and social ladder...the wife stops working; the house becomes neater; new rooms are added; the children wear ready-made clothes; they stay in school longer, take piano and ballet lessons; slenderizing becomes a passion; nails must be manicured; choices must be made between muslin and percale sheets, double-oven or single-oven stoves, wool or nylon carpets.[35]

In chapter 2 we discuss more fully the lives of women in the 1950s and early 1960s and the factors that enabled women to return to public work. Central to this discussion is the role of feminism in shaping current views of the family.

Chapter 2

The Women's Movement and Family: A Historical View

The true woman is as yet a dream of the future.
— Elizabeth Cady Stanton, 1888

On January 12, 1987, the California Supreme Court ruled that a woman had a right to job security following maternity leave.[1] The next day, as we were interviewing a group of women who agreed to help us discuss the career and family concerns of professional women, an older woman spoke about this decision, voicing her ambivalence. At first, her face softened and her voice took on a wistful quality as she thought of her own career-oriented daughters who want to have children. Rulings like this would make it easier for them to have children without having to give up their careers. But as she began to think about her job as a supervisor, her posture stiffened and her voice hardened. As a supervisor, her reaction was negative:

> I have four women working for me, all of childbearing age. What would we do if one of them got pregnant, let alone more than one? It would be very difficult and expensive to replace them with temporary help.

This woman's concerns are very real, and her ambivalent feelings painful to her. She, like many others we spoke to, separated the concern she felt for her own daughters, for her sense of family, from the concern she felt about doing a good job as a supervisor. The fact that the good of the community, and family life in general, might be served by a situation that would be expensive and difficult for her as a supervisor did not occur to her. Nor did the potential long-term benefits to companies like hers (such as retention of experienced, committed workers) enter into her thinking. She was obviously a caring person who was troubled by her

21

reaction. And yet she had no language, no experience, no social support for connecting the concern she felt for her daughters with concern for the daughters of other women she encountered in the workplace. For her, the family and the workplace were dichotomous, non-integral aspects of life.

This woman is not unique in her experience of the sharp line delineating concerns of the workplace from concerns of the family. Economist Sylvia Hewlett, in her book *A Lesser Life*, says:

> Modern women are squeezed between the devil and the deep blue sea, and there are no lifeboats out there in the form of public policies designed to help these women combine their roles as workers. For the United States has the least adequate family support system in the Western world. The bottom line is that American women (and often their children) are in bad shape. They are squeezed between the modern and the traditional forms of economic security to an extent which is unknown in other countries. Women elsewhere simply do better, as wives and mothers and as workers.[2]

Many American women understand first-hand what Hewlett means. No-fault divorce laws and the hesitancy of courts to grant alimony take away the traditional forms of economic security available to women as wives and homemakers, leaving a growing number of displaced women with no means to support themselves. Working women are paid between 60 and 70 percent of what their male counterparts earn. Single mothers and their children make up the largest poverty group in the United States. All working mothers, married or not, care for their children without much help from their government or their employers, and many do so with little help from their husbands. Women continue to bear the burden of care for elderly relatives — their own and their husband's.

How did these conditions develop in the most prosperous country in the world? Why is it that American women are so ambivalent about insisting on the supports they need? And why are women and the men who love them so reluctant to join with others who actively seek changes that would help the family? One way to understand the difficulty women have in achieving a consensus for change in the workplace is to recognize the extent to which they have accepted a male pattern of work and the ethic that accompanies it as the only alternative. The deepest and most elusive discrimination is the way in which women's experience, women's life-patterns, and women's style of valuing are considered "abnormal" and problematic in the current workplace.

It is our contention that in the past, most feminist efforts were directed at being "let in" to the traditional male culture of public life and work. These efforts, critical to the development of women, nevertheless resulted in a lower priority being given to family concerns. In short, for women to be taken seriously as the equals of men, they were forced to abandon that which is most closely identified as the female experience. We will begin by tracing the history of the relationship between feminism and the family in the United States. We will note how closely this history has been tied to the moral expectations and religious lives of women. We conclude with a discussion of a new feminist agenda that seeks a greater integration of what is specifically female into public culture, and that calls for new understanding of biblical virtue on the part of all of us.

A History of Feminism and the Family in the United States

Seneca Falls

The beginning of the women's movement in the United States is most often traced to July 19, 1848, in Seneca Falls, New York. There Elizabeth Cady Stanton and Lucretia Mott, a recognized Quaker preacher and orator, organized the first large convention devoted to women's rights, based on the principle that "woman is man's equal, was intended to be so by the Creator, and the highest good of the race demands that she should be recognized as such."[3]

The depth of commitment expressed by early leaders of the women's rights movement is illustrated by the words of Lucy Stone, who married Henry Blackwell rather late in life, keeping her birth name "in more than symbolic fear that to become a wife was to die as a person."[4]

> From the first years to which my memory stretches, I have been a disappointed woman. When, with my brothers, I reached forth after sources of knowledge, I was reproved with "It isn't fit for you; it doesn't belong to women...." In education, in marriage, in religion, in everything, disappointment is the lot of women. It shall be the business of my life to deepen this disappointment in every woman's heart until she bows down to it no longer. I wish that women, instead of being walking show-cases, instead of begging of their fathers and brothers the latest and gayest new bonnet, would ask of them their rights.[5]

Several historical factors converged in setting the stage for the birth of the women's movement in the United States, and for its emphasis on granting women rights that would give them legal, economic, and political equality with men.[6] As we have seen, the industrial revolution brought with it working conditions that were harmful to the lives of workers. In addition to working in dangerous places like mills and garment factories, women were often paid much less than their male co-workers, concentrated in especially unpleasant jobs, and infrequently promoted or advanced to supervisory positions. The injustice of this situation and the harm it wreaked in the lives of women and children did not escape well-educated, socially-prominent, reform-minded women who adhered to the goals of nineteenth-century liberalism.

Not surprisingly, these political impulses also encouraged the growing movement to abolish slavery. Slaves, like women, were a clearly disadvantaged group.

> [Slaves] could own no property and indeed themselves were treated as property. They had no legal rights to their own children, no right to vote, no right to payment for the work they performed for their masters, no redress against abuse or violence, and no access to education, skilled work, or independent social status of any kind. It could scarcely have escaped the attention of the married women working for abolition that despite their relative comfort and security, precisely the same restrictions applied to them.[7]

Sarah Grimke said exactly this about her own experience:

> It was when my soul was deeply moved at wrongs of the slave that I first perceived distinctly the subject condition of women.[8]

The moral outrage that fueled the anti-slavery movement led women like Stanton, Mott, and the Grimke sisters, all active abolitionists, to push for women's rights as well. Stanton and Mott met in 1840 when they attended the World's Anti-Slavery Convention in London. Their dedication to women's rights resulted in large part because no female delegate to this convention was allowed to participate in discussions or to vote. About her experience, Stanton wrote,

> My experiences at the World's Anti-Slavery Convention, all I had read of the legal status of women, and the oppression I saw everywhere, together swept across my soul, intensified now by many personal experiences.[9]

Other women, not previously identified with the abolition cause, were brought directly into the women's rights movement by such notables as Susan B. Anthony.

The declaration that resulted from the Seneca Falls Convention asked for women many of the same legal rights that were being asked for black men:

> ...[the] right to personal freedom, to acquire an education, to earn a living, to own their property and wages, to make contracts, to sue

and be sued, to testify in court, to obtain a divorce for just cause, to have joint ownership of their children — and to have equal political rights with [white] men.[10]

In addition to political liberalism, the position of some Protestant churches encouraged women to assert their rights.

As much as orthodox Protestantism insisted on customary gender differences as a bedrock of social and religious order and strove to limit woman's proper role to a certain circumscribed benevolence, the proselytizing churches elevated and endorsed women's moral character and social role. Evangelical Protestantism in the nineteenth century supported the notion that women were morally superior to men and thus encouraged women to value themselves and their own contribution to social life. Quakerism and more antinomian varieties of Protestant belief, with their stress on the equal importance of all human beings before God, inspired some of the most eloquent and powerful nineteenth-century spokeswomen for equal rights and freedoms.[11]

Notice that the emphasis of the Seneca Falls Declaration was on granting women legal and political rights. These rights would enable women to act independently and in behalf of their children in the public (mostly male) culture, especially in the event of their husband's death or desertion. Issues that are important to us today, such as child care, parental leave, and health care benefits, were not of concern to early women's rights leaders, even though many were wives and mothers. For the vast majority of women, combining a career and a family was inconceivable. Working mothers worked solely to help the family survive. The few professional women there were generally did not marry or have children. Even women's rights leaders saw motherhood and homemaking as the chief responsibilities of women. Early feminists had no language or experience for concepts like equal partnership marriage or shared parenting. The views of Elizabeth Cady Stanton on marriage reflect conditions of the time. She said,

...[marriage] makes man master, woman slave: whenever the interests of husband and wife conflict, as they must, those of the husband are gratified and those of the wife sacrificed because the husband has the legal and economic power over the wife.[12]

A summary of the positive and negative factors in the goals of the nineteenth-century women's rights movement shows that,

The liberalism that formed the underpinnings of American society provided the rationale for mid-nineteenth century feminism:
women, like other citizens, had the right to such civil liberties as
education and admission to the professions; and they should retain legal rights after marriage. Insofar as they went, these ideas
were in women's interests, but they did little to promote changes in
male/female role relationships and nothing for changes in family
patterns.[13]

Those working for women's rights early in our nation's history depended
on two types of rationale. As we have discovered, one was based on the
philosophy of political liberalism — that all human beings are equal and
deserve the same rights and opportunities. Elizabeth Cady Stanton, in
an address before the New York State Legislature in 1854, put it this
way,

> Here, gentlemen, is our difficulty: When we plead our cause before
> the lawmakers and savants of the republic, they can not take in the
> idea that men and women are alike. . . . We ask for all that you have
> asked for yourselves in the progress of your development, since
> the *Mayflower* cast anchor beside Plymouth rock; and simply on
> the ground that the rights of every human being are the same and
> identical.[14]

The other rationale resulted from the view that equal rights would allow women better to use their traditional talents and proclivities, as
mothers and guardians of public morality. Writing in the reform journal *The Lily*, Jane Frohock, a contemporary of Stanton's, summed up this
position.

> It is woman's womanhood, her instinctive femininity, her highest
> morality that society now needs to counter-act the excess of mas-
> culinity that is everywhere to be found in our unjust and unequal
> laws.[15]

Maren Lockwood Cott explains,

> It followed from that articulation of womanhood that both sexes
> would benefit if women were to gain *equal* access to education,
> work, citizenship, so as to represent themselves and balance society
> with their characteristic contribution.[16]

As will become clear in later chapters of this book, our position rests on
the work of the early feminists and the rationale they articulated. Surely

women and men, equal in the eyes of their creator, can be nothing less in the eyes of their peers. Our society will be best served when women are allowed, encouraged, and empowered to shape public culture by the infusion of their own characteristic life experiences and virtue. Merely being let in to a male culture that continues as is will not lead to full human development for any of us.

Suffrage

In the decades following Seneca Falls, some of the rights women had declared for themselves were granted. By 1870 women's rights activists turned their attention almost exclusively to working toward the most important political right still denied women, the right to vote. As we saw in the last chapter, a number of highly educated, socially-prominent, reform-minded suffragists were also active in the temperance movement and in efforts to gain voting rights for black men. Although certain rifts developed between those whose primary allegiance was to women's suffrage, black suffrage, or temperance, these groups of women were able to form alliances in working together for social change.

Many of the temperance and black suffrage workers were brought into the women's suffrage movement because of their inability to get the laws they wanted through various state and federal legislative bodies. These women found that they needed the right to vote in order to give a powerful political voice to their concerns.

One example is found in the life of Zerelda Wallace, an ardent temperance worker and faithful church member. The frustration that Wallace and others felt trying to further their social reform goals led them to demand full political rights for women. Their assumption in backing suffragists was that women's natural moral orientation would lead them to vote as a bloc for social reform programs, outnumbering the hesitant men. To this end, Wallace helped establish the International Congress of Women, a coalition of social-reform minded women, in 1888. At the founding of this organization, Wallace said that women from various movements were working together in order "to plead for freedom for themselves in the name of and for the good of humanity."[17]

The long struggle for women's suffrage finally ended in 1920 with the passage of the nineteenth amendment to the Constitution. In the seventy-two-year fight for the vote, "the women of this country were forced to conduct 56 campaigns of referenda to male voters, 480 campaigns to get legislatures to submit suffrage amendments to voters, [and] 277 campaigns to get state party conventions to include women suffrage planks."[18] None of the women who worked so hard for suffrage were allowed to vote. Few of their daughters voted. But as a result of their efforts, we do.

The Mid-Twentieth Century

Between 1920 and the early 1960s, the women's rights movement did not occupy a prominent place in the political life of America. Temperance efforts continued. Some women worked with Margaret Sanger to secure birth control rights for women, and with other leaders who were working for protective legislation for female and child workers. Pacifists began actively to oppose the rise of Nazism in Europe. Although all these efforts had the potential to be of benefit to women, none was directly identified as a feminist cause.

As a matter of fact, Sanger's birth control movement gained its greatest success once she and her followers turned away from the radical political (feminist) protest that resulted in their being jailed for distributing birth control devices, to an emphasis on the importance of birth control in improving child care. "Sanger [was more successful when she] shifted her emphasis from women's control of their bodies to eugenic reasoning about better babies."[19] With this change in emphasis came support from more conservative groups such as Mother's Clubs and the League of Women Voters.

Labor and union activists continued to emphasize women's characteristically high level of morality and aesthetic appreciation. Lines from a poem written by James Opperheim and later recorded by Judy Collins, commemorating the woolen mill strike in Lawrence, Massachusetts, in 1912 express the dual commitment and the desires of women active in labor reform:

> As we come marching, marching, we battle too for men,
> For they are Women's children, and we mother them again,
> Our lives shall not be sweated from birth until life closes.
> Hearts can starve as well as bodies:
> Give us Bread and give us Roses...
> The rising of the women means the rising of the race.[20]

Modern Feminism

In the early 1960s, women's rights activists again became a distinct, broadly-based, easily-recognized part of American political life. The re-emergence of feminism began in small, informal groups throughout the country, usually centered around large cities or institutions of higher education. In consciousness-raising groups, women of the modern generation began to confront the values of their past, to recognize oppression, and to explore alternate ideas, values, and lifestyles. In their groups, women discussed the works of such feminists as Kate Millet, Simone de Beauvoir, and Betty Friedan. These authors called to task the 1950s model of womanhood in which women gave up their educational dreams for marriage, full-time motherhood, and homemaking. Friedan wrote about the life of women in the 1950s.

> Why did so many American women, with the ability and education to discover and create, go back home again, to look for "something more" in house work and rearing children?...Why, with the removal of all the legal, political, economic, and educational barriers that once kept women from being man's equal, a person in her own right, an individual free to develop her own potential, should she accept this new image which insists she is not a person but a "Woman," by definition barred from the freedom of human existence and a voice in human destiny?[21]

Simone de Beauvoir was even more pointed in her critique of motherhood and homemaking:

> It is fraudulent to maintain that through maternity woman becomes concretely man's equal....She can never find salvation in her [house] work itself; it keeps her busy but it does not justify her existence, for her justification rests with free personalities other than her own. Shut up in the home, woman cannot herself establish her existence; she lacks the means requisite for self-affirmation as an individual; and in consequence her individuality is not given recognition.[22]

The words of Emma Goldman reflect the Marxist emphasis among radical feminists of the sixties:

> The institution of marriage makes a parasite of woman, an absolute dependent. It incapacitates her for life's struggle, annihilates her social consciousness, paralyzes her imagination, and then imposes its gracious protection, which is in reality a snare, a travesty on human character.[23]

Consciousness-raising groups provided a safe and supportive environment for women exposed to these ideas to make changes in their lives. Psychologist Phyllis Chessler says,

> Some women started living together; some started living alone for the first time....Some women left their husbands; others began to live with a man....Women stopped going to beauty parlors and began to value their time; they needed fewer adornments to "make up" for being female.[24]

Despite the obvious value of consciousness-raising groups in the lives of individual women, Hewlett criticizes them for concentrating on individual rather than political structural change:

> The problem is that consciousness raising tends to shift the burden for change away from society and toward the individual women. It encourages women to look to themselves, or to that small group of women with whom they share consciousness, as the source of their "liberation." In short, consciousness raising is an approach that de-emphasizes broad-based social action in favor of personal redemption.[25]

Nevertheless, women did organize themselves for political activity. Unfortunately, it was the more flamboyant among them who garnered most of the media attention. Radical feminists were reported to have publicly burned their bras, although it is doubtful that this ever actually occurred; picketed the Miss America pageant, crowning a sheep; and advocated parenthood without men through the use of artificial insemination from existing sperm banks.

   Many more women were quietly, less colorfully, forming political action groups. One prominent organization was the National Organization for Women.

> NOW was formed in October 1966 by Betty Friedan and a few other women activists. It revived and carried forward the nineteenth-century tradition of equal rights feminism, and its stated purpose was "to take action to bring women into full participation in the mainstream of American society *now*, exercising all the privileges and responsibilities thereof in truly equal partnership."[26]

The purpose of NOW sounds very similar to the goals of the early women's rights leaders in Seneca Falls 118 years earlier. Similar too are other groups formed somewhat after NOW — the National Women's Political Caucus and the Women's Equity Action League. All these organizations tended to reject traditional feminine behavior, concentrating instead on gaining additional legal, economic, and political rights for women, especially for women working outside the home.

   Anne Bowen Follis, founder of Homemakers for Equal Rights, responds to this emphasis:

> When women's liberation came upon us in the late sixties, many of us didn't know how to react. It was the feminist movement that brought attention to the gross inequities between men's and women's wages.... The movement also pointed out the rampant

discrimination that made it difficult for women to get into such professions as law, medicine, journalism, and broadcasting. But the
women's movement seemed to be saying something else that made
a lot of people uneasy. It seemed to say, essentially, that the woman
who didn't work outside the home was an exploited fool.[27]

Follis became active in the struggle for passage of the Equal Rights
Amendment, and helped to organize homemakers who supported the
ERA. At the same time, she remained a powerful voice with a significant
following, pointing out the desertion many homemakers and mothers felt
by certain of their feminist sisters during this time.

The Equal Rights Amendment and Abortion

Equality of rights under the law shall not be denied or abridged by
the United States or by any state on account of sex.[28]

The Equal Rights Amendment was proposed shortly after passage of the
nineteenth amendment in 1920. In 1971 it was passed by the House of
Representatives, and in 1972, by the Senate. The majority voting in favor
of ratification in both houses of Congress was overwhelming; passage by
two-thirds of the state legislatures, the requirement for a Constitutional
amendment, seemed assured. During the next year, thirty (of the necessary thirty-eight states) voted to ratify the amendment. But in 1974,
only three states ratified, only two in 1975. That left the amendment
three states short of ratification, where it remained until the time limit
on state ratification expired.[29]

In addition to working for passage of the ERA, feminists of the sixties
and seventies also worked for reproductive freedom, specifically through
the right to abortion. The right not to bear unwanted children was seen
by feminists as crucial for women's continued development. After several state legislatures passed abortion rights bills, the Supreme Court, in
January 1973, ruled that women had the legal right to abortion, without
restriction during the first trimester of pregnancy, and with increasingly
more limiting restrictions thereafter. In the summer of 1989, the Supreme
Court approved state-imposed limits to a woman's right to abortion, a rul-
ing that many think well decrease access to abortion, especially among
poor women. The reopening of the abortion debate, while welcomed
by some, may aggravate existing divisions among women and threaten
women's solidarity on other issues crucial to our future.

While reproductive freedom, and ultimately the right to abortion, have
been seen as necessary for women's full and independent participation in
adult life, some critics feel that the emphasis of modern feminists has too
frequently been on a woman's right not to bear children, to the exclusion

of guaranteeing her right to choose to bear children and to be supported during that process and afterward. As Hewlett points out rather strongly,

> The feminists of the modern women's movement made one gigan-tic mistake: They assumed that modern women wanted nothing to do with children. As a result, they have consistently failed to incorporate the bearing and rearing of children into their vision of a liberated life.... The modern women's movement has not only been anti-men; it has also been profoundly anti-children and anti-motherhood.... Motherhood is the problem that modern feminists cannot face.[30]

The fact that the modern feminists focused on a women's right not to bear children has had enormous consequences for the women's move-ment, most notably in the failure to gain ratification of the ERA. Hewlett continues,

> The great majority of women have children at some point during their lives, and few of these women ever cease to love their sons and daughters. For the majority of mothers their children consti-tute the most passionate attachment of their lives.... It is impossible to build a mass women's movement on an anti-child, anti-mother platform.[31]

Phyllis Schlafly, editor of the *Eagle Forum Newsletter*, was the most prominent leader of the anti-ERA, pro-family movement. The power of anti-ERA groups in defeating the ERA was due not only to their highly-efficient organization and creative leadership, but to the perceived rejection of motherhood by many feminist leaders. A survey of anti-ERA activists in Oklahoma showed that they were a rather homogeneous group, distinctly different from those who favored the ERA.

> The Antis were older than the Pros, had less formal education, were less likely to be in professional occupations, were more likely to be of rural origin and to live in rural or small towns at the time of the survey, and were more likely to be married and to have more chil-dren.... When combined with other facts about the political and religious affiliation and activities of the Antis [these demographic characteristics] suggest that the Antis belong to a particular culture tradition which plays an important role in their motivation to op-pose the feminist movement.[32]

Chief aspects of this cultural tradition were an unquestioning patriotism (my country right or wrong), strong anti-communist feelings, and reli-gious fundamentalism (especially belief in the inerrancy of the Bible).

There is almost no overlap in the churches to which the Antis and the Pros belonged. Almost half of the Antis belong to the fundamentalist Church of Christ, and another one-fourth were [southern] Baptists and Mormons. Over half of the Pros, on the other hand, were Methodist, Presbyterian, Episcopal, or Disciples of Christ, all liberal groups. Another twelve percent were Unitarians, the most liberal denomination of all.[33]

Members of anti-ERA church groups believe that the Scriptures are the literal word of God. Material contained in the Bible is as applicable to us as it was to those for whom it was originally written, who lived under very different political, economic, and social conditions. Antis feel they have an obligation to see that all people, even those who do not share their beliefs, live according to their interpretation of biblical injunctions concerning home and family life. By imposing their views on others, they believe themselves to be saving all of us from the wrath and punishment of God.

There is another approach to our biblical traditions that takes its work equally seriously. Mainline Christian churches and Reformed Jewish Congregations undertake the painstaking scholarly work necessary to interpret the 2000–3000-year-old texts into a message for *our* generation. In later chapters we will investigate a variety of ways in which biblical vision can be liberating and direction-giving for women today.

The Future of Feminism

As we have seen, the aim of the feminist movement in the United States, from its beginning in 1848 until the late 1970s, was to achieve for women legal and political rights that would enable them to be full participants in male culture. In order to shape culture, then, women would have to use traditional male methods and reject traditional feminine patterns of behavior. The ethic of care, long associated primarily with women, was largely repudiated by efforts to unburden women from domestic responsibilities. In her critique of feminism's approach to the family, Jean Elshtain puts it this way:

> Feminist protest that sought the elimination of this sphere of traditional femininity [that is, the family] was understandable when it was a response by women to conditions of their identities that had grown problematic.... But the end-point of this feminist argumentation... is ironically self-defeating, for it requires that women, in the name of feminism, embrace the terms of a public life that was created by men who had rejected or devalued the world of the

traditionally "feminine" with its "softer" virtues. Behold, the new woman as the old man![34]

Despite what many women experienced as rejection of family concerns and the virtues of care and nurturance by feminists, the basic human need for affiliation remained. Conflict between their realization of the importance of the ethic of care, and the feminist emphasis on self-development and rejection of old bonds of care, caused many women to become disenchanted. They were caught between two visions. Neither the family as oppressor described by Simone de Beauvoir and Betty Friedan in *The Feminine Mystique*, nor the individualism touted by feminists was satisfying. Many of these women recognized what humanistic psychoanalyst Erich Fromm calls our "need for relatedness."

At best, this need is satisfied in mature love, for Fromm, the embodiment of healthy, productive relatedness. Mature love involves "union under the conditions of preserving one's integrity, one's individuality"[35] and rests on the virtues of "care, responsibility, respect, and knowledge."[36] Mature love is not shared grudgingly, out of a sense of duty, but given voluntarily by one already assured of her or his own worth as a human being.[37]

In describing her family, Elshtain speaks a similar language:

> Our people . . . stressed responsibility to and for one's life as a social life lived among others, advocated going the "extra mile" (the Good Samaritan parable) and tempering justice with mercy (the Prodigal Son).[38]

So important is our need for family that humans will go to great lengths in their attempt to find fulfillment, including the formation of psychologically unhealthy relationships. In such families men frequently become dominant and women submit in order to maintain family cohesion. Unfortunately, this unhealthy way of relating is advocated by some authors of books on "Christian" marriage.

Isolated Scripture passages are quoted to set up a divine plan for marriage: the husband is the head, the wife is subject to him and must submit to his will. . . . Many advocates of this system believe that a wife may not go directly to Christ, but only through her husband.[39]

More recently feminist authors have begun to deal with the reintegration of family values into the feminist agenda. Today there is renewed interest in the family and in nurturing values, though certainly not as the sole purview of women. Recognizing that being cared for by a responsible person (and the act of caring for another) are prerequisites to authentic human existence, integrative feminists seek to redefine culture so that nurturing takes its rightful place in the priorities of life and work.

The right to choose is crucial to the personhood of woman. The right to choose has to mean not only the right to choose not to bring a child into the world against one's will, but also the right to have a child, joyously, responsibly, without paying a terrible price of isolation from the world and its rewarded occupations, its decisions, and actions.... The point is that *equality* — the rights for which women have been fighting for over a century — was, is, necessary, for women to be able to affirm their own personhood, and in the fullest sense of choice, motherhood. The point is, the movement to equality and the personhood of women isn't finished until motherhood is a fully free choice.[40]

One of the chief voices calling for a reintegration of nurturing values into the lives of women and men, in both the private and public spheres of life, is Angela Miles. She has used the term "integrative feminism" to describe this process. In contrast to the stress of early feminism on women's ability to work and relate "just like a man," integrative feminism stresses women's specificity and the infusion of feminine values into the public world:

Those reform, radical and socialist feminists who see the totality of their struggle in terms of women's equality tend to emphasize women's sameness with men. They respond to men's definition of women as different and unequal primarily by denying the difference. This denial of women's specificity allows them to refuse men's definition of women as less than human, but it does not provide a basis to go further to refuse men's definition of humanity as essentially male.[41]

The goal of feminism in the eighties, Miles believes, is the infusion of genuine alternative values associated with the feminine into the whole of human life. This perspective on feminist goals is important for creating a broader consensus throughout society, one that coincides at many points with the vision of religious communities. As she says,

More and more feminists are coming to recognize the importance of women's specificity, to see feminism as expressing an alternative vision and set of values rooted in that specificity and to use this alternative perspective in the articulation of a consciously universal politics.... Feminists must push for reforms which recognize the specificity and value of women's work and lives.[42]

Conclusions

It is our view that the vision and virtues found in Jewish and Christian faith form the foundation of an integrative feminism that would allow for a fuller and richer experience of life for all of us — a life that reflects better integration of family and work for both women and men, based on a more relational ethic. In the next chapter we will continue our discussion of how women and men got to the current point in their development.

We close this chapter with the words our foremother, Elizabeth Cady Stanton, spoke before the International Council of Women in 1888, when she was seventy-two:

> We who like the children of Israel have been wandering in the wilderness of prejudice and ridicule for forty years feel a peculiar tenderness for the young women on whose shoulders we are about to leave our burdens.... The younger women are starting with a great advantage over us. They have the results of our experience; they have superior opportunities for education; they will find a more enlightened public sentiment for discussion; they will have more courage to take the rights which belong to them.... Thus far women have been the mere echoes of men. Our laws and constitutions, our creed and codes, and the customs of social life are all of masculine origin. The true woman is as yet a dream of the future.[43]

Chapter 3

New Work Attitudes,
New Family Patterns:
Where We Find Ourselves Today

The structure of professional and managerial work currently calls for single-minded and continuous participation and commitment. . . . This career design disadvantages women, who are often faced with domestic, as well as occupational, demands.
　　　　　　　　　　　　— Mary Frank Fox and Sharlene Hesse-Biber

Just as the shape of the American family is changing, so too are the characteristics of the American worker. Forty-four percent of the time she is a woman.[1] But the practices and prevailing values of the workplace have changed scarcely at all. As Robert Bellah, a noted sociologist, suggests,

> If the ethos of work were less brutally competitive and more ecologically harmonious, it would be more consonant with the ethos of private life, and particularly of the family life. A less frantic concern for advancement and a reduction of working hours for both men and women would make it easier for women to be full participants in the workplace without abandoning family life. By the same token, men would be freed to a take an equal role at home and in child care. In this way, what seemed at first to be a change only in the nature of work would turn out to have major consequences for family life as well.[2]

The design of contemporary work life still assumes a male worker with a full- or at least part-time homemaker spouse. That only a small percentage (about 7 percent) of workers fit this description is only slowly dawning on employers, policy-makers, and women. Our characteristic virtues of adaptability and self-effacement have, to some extent, veiled the facts of the situation and allowed it to persist. As Bellah's words make clear, it is not primarily a matter of women seeking "special accommodations" in the workplace. It is a matter of public culture being shaped by women's experience and by nurturant values rather than solely by men's life-patterns and competitive values. Theologian Rosemary Ruether has said that whereas women are expected to embrace self-sacrificing love (*agape*) as the appropriate virtue for those in the domestic sphere,

> men are condemned to spend a major portion of their lives in a public world where . . . values such as *agape* seem to have no place.[3]

It is this situation that needs to be remedied — not by the rejection of feminine capacities for nurturance, self-giving love, relatedness, and mutuality — but by the infusion of these values into the public sphere and into the working lives of men as well as women. In order to bring these traditional strengths of women to the workplace, we will also need to develop virtues less familiar to us such as self-esteem, courage, assertiveness, independence, and clear-sightedness. Let us begin by looking further at how things presently stand, both in our work lives and in our home lives.

The Commitment

Despite enormous odds, there are growing numbers of women who want both to nurture a family and to contribute to the public world of work. As we noted previously, in order to investigate more closely the dilemmas women experience in their attempts to combine in meaningful ways their careers and family lives, we conducted our own survey and interview study of the lives of professional women and some of their husbands. Most of these women were in the fields of higher education, business, psychology, or nursing, but we also studied women working in social service, communications, law, medicine, and religion. Of the 153 women who responded to our initial survey, 86 percent worked full time, averaging 49.3 hours of work a week. Since the national average of working women who work full time is much lower (65–71 percent in 1985),[4] our sample can be described as strongly committed to a public vocation. Sixty-nine percent of our sample were married and 56 percent had dependent children, percentages roughly analogous to national averages for professional women.

Our results show not only the specific concerns of these women, but also the depth of their commitment to a balanced life. The women we studied felt a good deal of satisfaction with their professional lives and were optimistic regarding their professional futures, feeling that they would continue to progress in their careers. Overall, women who were satisfied with their work lives, in comparison to those who were not, tended to work a greater number of hours, experienced fewer demands from their spouse and children, felt it was likely that they could get the accommodations they needed in the workplace, and enjoyed a sense of being valued by their co-workers. At the same time, they expressed a significant level of commitment to their families, agreeing that if push came to shove, they would modify their career goals for the sake of the family.

The Stress

But our sample of women experienced great stress in attempting to combine career and family. One woman said,

> We have two small children and a ten-room house, and I have a job and he has a job. I can't do it all. It's driving me crazy. I sit down at 11:30 at night and I don't like it anymore.

The women we talked to said they were not satisfied with the amount of time they had for their children, for their spouses, for sleep, for housekeeping, for leisure activities, or for church and community involvement. Yet they very much wanted to achieve a life in which family and a public vocation could be satisfactorily integrated and mutually enriching.

While married women generally perceived their husbands to be supportive of them, they felt that they were the ones ultimately responsible for caring for the children, and their husbands agreed. Husbands felt more pressure than wives to spend a lot of time at work, but in general, they felt less stress from attempting to balance work and family concerns. In general, husbands reported that they got enough sleep, and were satisfied with the amount of time they had for their children, their church or community involvement, housekeeping, and solitude and private thought.

The Dual Burden

Other studies corroborate what the women and men in our study reported to us: Professional women in dual-career families have substantially greater responsibility than their husbands for the care and nurturance of the family.[5] Single working mothers bear these responsibilities almost entirely alone. With respect to the total number of hours women work, at home and at the place of employment, researchers conclude that

> ...women employed full time had total work weeks of 76 hours on the average....Employed women work longer hours than em-

ployed men and housewives.... For a seven-day work week employed women average from 10.5 to 12.6 hours per day ... [and] for
married women in full time jobs the work day is probably longer
than it was for their grandmothers.[6]

In addition to spending more time with their children, mothers, more
than fathers in dual-career families, are the ones who make the child-
care arrangements, compromise their careers for the sake of the children,[7]
and take time off from work when the children are sick.[8] Reflecting the
societal support for this unequal division of responsibility, we find that
employer-sponsored child-care centers are more common in companies
with a large percentage of women employees, and business managers
and executives feel a leave of absence to attend to child-care needs is
more appropriate for women employees than for men.[9] Sey Chassler
(1984), former editor of *Redbook*, describes the common expectation this
way,

> I had always thought I would get married and be somebody. What's
> more, I took it for granted that my wife would be responsible for
> the family in addition to her job. I would love and care for the
> children, but I wouldn't have to deal with their phone calls at the
> office. They'd call my wife at the office. That's what mommies
> are for, aren't they? No one had to tell the children that. No one
> had to tell me that. No one had to tell my wife that. We all knew
> it.[10]

Not surprisingly, in our study women who had young children experienced especially high levels of personal distress, feeling that they had
almost no time for solitude and private thought, and that they had less
time for themselves than did their spouses. As one women rather hu-
morously put it,

> I fix the supper; I feed the one-year-old; I cut the four-year-old's
> food up. In the meantime, [my husband's] done eating and in the
> living room watching television.

Other studies show that many mothers of preschoolers have a strong
orientation to a career but that they are not able to participate in their
professions as much as they would like.[11] These mothers of young children are willing to make significant career modifications for the sake of
their families, but they can also identify changes in workplace practice,
such as child-care facilities, flexible scheduling, and pro-rated, part-time
positions, which would make it easier for them to combine career and
family.

The problems of contemporary American women are not the result of some massive or inevitable conflict between work and family
life. Rather, they result because the United States does less than any
other advanced country to make life easier for working mothers. We
have less maternity leave, less subsidized child care, less job flexibility. And partly due to this deficit in our public policies, women in
America earn less, proportionately, than their counterparts in other
nations.[12]

Work policies that would be helpful to families have not been forthcom-
ing in our country. Some American women are beginning to wonder
why.

Solidarity among women is essential to a change in this situation.
But as we will see later, the ones most likely to recognize the limits
of individual family adaptation and to be willing to consider the need
for structural change in the workplace are the women who are themselves most heavily burdened by work-family stress. Of course having
a supportive spouse who shares one's concerns helps ease the strain.
Those who experience the fewest obstacles to career advancement are
the ones who have cooperative and supportive spouses, and thus, less
difficulty providing for the care of the children. Fully sharing child-
rearing duties is the single best predictor of happiness in a dual-career
family.[13] Our respondents with supportive husbands reported that they
had more time for themselves and less responsibility for the children.
Compared to their husbands, though, these women still expressed a
consistently greater desire for a part-time commitment to their career,
assuming equal opportunity for job security, status, promotion, and proportionate pay.

The tugs on one's mind and heart when one attempts to combine
family and profession are summed up for all of us by this woman:

> The difficulty is that part of me wants to excel at something I know
> I can do. And yet, when I look at my children...I want an intimate
> relationship with them and my husband. I can't do that if my career
> dominates my relationship. It's very difficult, and this is something
> I face every single day.

The Motivation

What is it that has brought so many women to this point? What is it that
keeps them going in the face of professional discrimination and personal
frustration? Research on this question led us to identify economic, psychological, and spiritual factors that lead women to continue to undertake
public careers despite the obstacles.

Economic Motivation

One important factor for many women, of course, is that they have to work. Adverse economic conditions for women in particular account for the dramatic increase in poverty rates among women and their children, the feminization of poverty. As we already know, 89 percent of single-parent families are headed by women. Over half of these families are living below the federal poverty line. Single-parent families headed by women are six times as likely to be living in poverty as are single-parent families headed by men.[14]

Following a divorce, only 15 percent of women are awarded alimony, and only 43 percent of those collect it regularly. Three-quarters of fathers pay no child support, even when required to do so by law! Personal income for divorced men drops, after they pay child support and alimony, 11 percent on the average. But their expenses drop as well, resulting in a net increase in disposable income of 30 percent. For women, income may increase slightly, but expenses increase greatly, resulting in an average income loss of 7 percent for her and her children.[15] "The typical outcome of a marital breakup in a family with children is that the man becomes single, while the woman becomes a single parent."[16] The increase in never-married mothers, most of whom receive no financial support from the fathers of their children, also contributes to the number of women and children living in poverty. Even when women work full time in year-round jobs, minimum wage pays them less than $7,000 a year. If women were paid wages equal to those that similarly qualified men earn, about half of the families now living in poverty would not be in poverty.[17]

For two-job and dual-career families, economic conditions coupled with rising lifestyle expectations also contribute to the number of women in the paid work force. One income, unless it comes from the very highest levels of professional or business life, can no longer support a family with typical middle-class expectations — home ownership, two cars, a good education for the children, interesting vacations. As one of the women in our study said,

> If you ask what has motivated us, has kept us going, it is the self-satisfaction that comes from the monetary reward. I love it. I feel good that I can contribute to the family.

Psychological Motivation

There are many women, though, for whom the economic motive, while still important, is not primary. A number of psychologists representing widely different theoretical perspectives have pointed to the importance of the human need to integrate love and work. Psychoanalyst Sigmund Freud said that the primary developmental task of an emotionally healthy, mature adult was to make satisfactory adjustment in two areas — love and work.[18] Abraham Maslow, coming out of the humanistic tradition, postulated a view similar to Freud's. Maslow saw the pinnacle of full human development to be realized through self-actualization. Self-actualization is not possible unless one has first experienced feelings of love, belongingness, and self-esteem. For most people a secure sense of love and belongingness is satisfied by family and friends. A healthy level of self-esteem results from one's achievements and the resulting recognition one receives from others.[19]

Erich Fromm, merging the psychoanalytic and humanistic traditions, emphasizes our human need for rootedness, a feeling of being loved not because of what we do, but just because we are. At the same time, we have a need for a separate identity, a sense of self, defined in terms of productive ability.[20] Erik Erikson, a neo-Freudian, adds his definition of healthy adult development: one's willingness "to regulate the cycles of work, procreation, [and] recreation so as to secure to the offspring, too, all the stages of a satisfactory development."[21]

Implicit in all these formulations is that women and men will both love and work. Maslow points out that when women only love and men only work, both women and men must settle for less than full human development.[22] In a society that limits women's work options, overtly or subtly, women cannot become self-actualized, just as in a society that discourages men from developing their ability to love, men cannot be fully human.

Increasing access to higher education has made professional life an expectation for many women. Although women undergraduates do not receive as much scholarship aid as men, perhaps because decisions are based on standardized tests that may be biased in favor of men's knowledge and characteristic way of thinking, for the past couple of years, women college students have outnumbered men. When it comes to graduate education — necessary for entry into most professions — men still outnumber women, but the numbers of women are growing, especially in the fields of psychology, accounting, law, medicine, and Protestant theology.

Improved contraceptive technology has contributed to lowering the birth rate in the United States as a whole and in individual families. A low birth rate combined with stricter immigration laws decreases the potential work force, making the participation of women workers even more critical. Reproductive freedom has also made convenient spacing of children possible. The more highly educated a women is, and/or the greater her income, the more likely she is to space her children close together, presumably so that her years with heavy child-care demands are compacted.[23]

In terms of psychological make-up, women who work for pay are more likely themselves to have had working mothers. As a group, daughters of working mothers have greater and more nontraditional educational and career aspirations than daughters of full-time homemakers. One of our friends, who always thought she was doing the best for her children by staying home with them, now worries that her daughter will not see all the options available to her.

Other studies show that women in dual-career families may be shaped by virtue of being an only or eldest child and having experienced some degree of tension in relationships with their fathers.[24] With respect to personality characteristics, dual-career women are more inner-directed, competitive, task-persistent, and have a greater need for achievement than their homemaker counterparts.[25]

Many of these women realize intuitively that work and family enrich each other. One is a better mother because she works, and a better worker because she mothers. She is thus willing to make the personal accommodations necessary for her to achieve some degree of work and family harmony.

The Spiritual Motivation

Some women participate in their professions and endure the hardship of the family/career juggling act not only for the sake of their family's economic well-being, nor solely for their own personal fulfillment, but because they feel the "call" to contribute their talents to reshaping our culture. This call does not come from a personal motivation, but from a communal or spiritual orientation.

Like Deborah in Hebrew Scripture and Phoebe in Christian Scripture, like Joan of Arc in the fifteenth century and Harriet Beecher Stowe in the nineteenth century, some women today feel called by God, or by their own deepest selves, to share their gifts in the public sphere of life. They feel an inescapable tie to what one person has termed the "community of strangers."[26] They realize that societies only become genuine communities when their members are able to act in ways that may not be in their own best interest, but are surely in the best interests of the larger group.

The experience of a call differs from a career in that it involves a sense of direction that affects one's lifestyle choices as well as one's work. Typically these choices emerge in the context of a growing understanding of one's personal talents and deeply held values. The outward expression of one's call may change over time, but one's inner motivation requires a lifetime commitment.

The Family

The motivation that women have for nurturing a family seems almost so obvious as to need no mention. Most women affirm the importance of family life and feel drawn to it themselves. Though our values are not reflected in governmental policy and laws that deal inadequately with the needs of women and children, many of us feel the opportunity to sustain and nurture defenseless young life to be of the highest order. The fact that 90 percent of women still choose to bear children in an age when pregnancy is optional, and that countless women have given up excellent salaries, prestigious positions, and a chance to offer their talents to the larger world, all for the sake of their children, attests to the value we place on mothering. Sylvia Hewlett, an economist, describes a day-long conversation she had with some of her former women students, all of whom had important careers and well-paying positions. About the day, she concluded,

> At the . . . reunion at my house, if there was one note that rang loudly and clearly through the room, it was that modern women — no matter how ambitious — yearn to have children. They tie themselves into knots, trying to figure out how to do this, but despite desperate effort, the odds are that a high proportion of them will fail.[27]

For women forced to choose between family life and a fully-committed career the choice is a difficult and reluctant one.

Women don't have a monopoly on tender feelings toward children. Increasingly, men too want the chance to express their nurturing selves. Ideally, one of the greatest values of the increased participation of women in the work force is that it frees men from some of their responsibility for the economic well-being of the family and allows them time and energy for their families. Many people have written about the resulting benefits that accrue to men and children. In chapters 10 and 11 we will discuss more fully the role of men in the private sphere of life.

The Marketplace

When women, either because of a spiritual, personal, or economic motivation, enter the public world of work, they find a system foreign to them in many ways. The whole structure of work life and of current career patterns reflects the normativeness of a male worker freed from domestic responsibility by a wife who supports his career pursuits while maintaining the family.[28] When she takes a job next to him without any modifications of work or domestic patterns she must compromise both career and family. Is it any wonder that so many professional women say that what they really need is a wife?

For the male with a spouse at home full or part time or for the single woman, a fifty-to-sixty hour work week, unexpected late meetings, and spur-of-the-moment travel have been considered manageable, or at least tolerable by the ambitious, as the price for success. But for professional women and their spouses in a dual-career family, and for single parents, such expectations are practically impossible to fulfill. Other social scientists put it this way:

> The structure of professional and managerial work currently calls for single-minded and continuous participation and commitment.... This career design disadvantages women, who are often faced with domestic, as well as occupational, demands.[29]

The Response

Despite these burdensome demands, women *are* participating in their professions and nurturing families. How do they do it? We believe that there is a relationship between a woman's attitudes about herself and her work life, her spiritual and ethical orientation, and her view of how to manage in the workplace. In our study, we found a strong consensus among women that integrating the private sphere of home and family with the public sphere of career is very difficult. But when we talked with women about how to change the situation, the consensus broke down. The women in our sample can be divided into two groups with respect to their attitudes toward the workplace.

These two attitudes are neatly summed up in their responses to two items on our survey: "It should be largely up to individuals and their families to make necessary adjustments to coping with a dual-career or single-parent family," and "Workplaces have an obligation to adjust to the personal and family needs of workers." Contrary to our initial expectations, the set of attitudes that clusters around each of these statements could not be described simply as traditionalist versus feminist, conservative versus liberal, or self-sacrificing versus self-assertive. For the sake of conciseness, we have called one the individualistic approach, since it emphasizes individual coping with the workplace as it stands today, and the other the relational approach, since it stresses societal solutions and workplace change in a context of our connections to one another.

The Individualistic Approach

Women in the individual responsibility group, those who believe it is up to the individual and her family to cope with the demands of the workplace, compared to those who felt the workplace should change to accommodate workers, can be characterized by the following descriptors. Most of this group:

1. thought career obstacles are due more to personal shortcomings than to external factors

2. did not feel the workplace would benefit from family-centered policies

3. opposed unionization

4. felt they have not benefitted from the women's movement

5. worked longer hours

6. were less highly educated

7. were less likely to have young children

8. were less likely to have made career sacrifices for their children

9. were basically satisfied with their career

The attitudes of this group are well expressed by a woman we interviewed, who said,

> We've tried some adjustments. I don't like them. We had one woman who wanted to nurse her baby at work. We had another woman who wanted to work at home. She was working on a terminal and it was possible just to dial it in, just like from the workplace, but I had problems with that. Even though we work on computers, we're interrupted by people. I thought it was a privilege to be able to do that [work at home]. We have a computer operator now who wants to do the work from another town, and maybe come in once a week, and they feel like they can do everything they can do in an office. But these kinds of accommodations I really have problems with.

When asked why she felt this way, she said,

> Probably it's just selfishness on my part. Accommodations were never made for me. Why should I go to all this trouble so someone else can stay at home for work?

Regarding the difficulties of arranging quality child care, one woman in this group was asked if she thought women were generally supportive of one another. She said,

I don't think we are. I guess she [pointing to another women] would say that what we really need is day care. Well, I don't care about day care. My kids are fourteen and fifteen.

Although this woman recognized the lack of support implicit in her response, she was unable to find a reason to identify with other women's needs. Another woman whose children were older said,

You know I've been through this [raising young children alone]. But I shared an office with a man who brought his child to work, and the child was in the office and directly interfered with my work. I felt tremendous resentment toward him and I didn't have any feeling that I needed to be flexible.

While it seems to us that occasional brief visits by children to worksites might be tolerated or even welcomed as we move toward a more integrated view of work and child-rearing, this woman's objection has some justification. Were more convenient, economical child care available, parents would be less likely to be faced with these awkward situations — unnecessarily difficult for both them and their co-workers.

Another woman put her views on individual responsibility more strongly:

But you know, I'll tell you another thing. Women are going to have to take the responsibility, not society. The women are going to have to stop using their kids as an excuse not to come to work.

Others in the group pointed out that while some women (and some men) use dishonest excuses for missing work, most women they know are very hesitant to miss work, even when children are genuinely ill. But this woman's comment is indicative of the predominant cultural attitude that sees women workers as somehow more troublesome than men. This attitude is that if women insist on working, then they had better learn to adjust to the realities of work. By deviating from traditional roles, women have brought these troubles on themselves.

None of the women in the individualistic group advocated policy changes that would enable women more fully to participate in a public vocation, such as on-site child care, longer paid maternity leaves with job guarantees, or shared rather than authoritarian management models. They felt that some careers/positions (such as college president) were closed and should continue to be closed to women with young children. In sum, these women have accepted, perhaps as the cost of their own career success, the separation of family concerns from the workplace, a traditional male pattern of work, and a sense that individual compromise rather than structural change is the appropriate response. This group of women do not question the normativeness of the male-derived patterns of the work world, and hence acquiesce in the definition of their own lives as "cumbersome" for the public world.

The Relational Approach

The second group of women, the one we call the relational group, felt strongly about the value of integrating career and family. They can be characterized by the following descriptors. Most of this group:

1. thought career obstacles are due more to external factors than personal shortcomings

2. felt the workplace was obligated to accommodate workers and would benefit from family-centered policies

3. somewhat favored unionization

4. felt they had benefitted from the women's movement

5. were younger

6. were more highly educated

7. were more likely to have young children

8. were likely to have made or be willing to make career sacrifices for children

9. were basically satisfied with their career (but slightly less so than the first group)

These women tended to question traditional workplace practices such as the fifty-to-sixty-hour work week, the necessity and desirability of working full time, and the expectation that family concerns would not interfere with or even be discussed in the workplace. One might be inclined to say that for many of these women, particularly those with young children, career is no longer, if it ever was, a top priority. Another possible interpretation, though, is that the presence of young children and the priority given to them, combined with a higher level of education, causes women to rethink the demands of the male-oriented workplace. Perhaps they are not so much rejecting their own call to a public vocation as they are rejecting the kinds of patterns it presently imposes and the schizophrenic division of public and private life that it requires.

As one of our participants, a research associate, so eloquently put it,

So far as I am concerned, the male-oriented values which govern behavioral expectation of professionals exclude family and health from their priorities. Workers and colleagues are not treated as resources, but rather as part of a mechanized process in which the company's market competitiveness is threatened by the accidents of human needs — even by the need to turn down that extra work which could lead to a promotion. The system of rewards and punishments which is reflected in these values works against a humane approach. Many companies could overcome some of these problems by instituting team management, shared positions, child-care facilities, and facilities to take care of sick children. But first, I think companies and professional institutions must place human needs at the top of their list of priorities.

Interestingly, the women in this second group felt highly valued by colleagues for their professional contributions. They also felt confident that if they asked for accommodations at work that would help them better maintain their family responsibilities, they would get them. But the responsibility for asking for accommodations was not seen as solely an individual matter, but as a communal obligation. In response to the woman who was frustrated by another's child in her shared office, a woman in the relational group said,

I feel the way she does when certain young children are brought to places, but I don't think the answer is to continue to bring them to places where they can't function in that room without destroying things or ruining people's work. What needs to be is places where the children of whatever age will be happy and will be constructive also. And we just don't do anything about that as a society. We're looking on it as a poor woman's path... when it's our entire society's problem.

Women who hold relational views strive to maintain nurturing values as they pursue a career, and are more likely to be aware of the need for structural change, to support cooperative efforts by workers and women's groups, and to question the traditional male-defined ethos of careerism. Neither group wholeheartedly supports nor wholeheartedly rejects a feminist agenda, perhaps because that agenda has in the past appeared confusing and contradictory to them.

The Goal

It is our view that our goal should be to work together for the structural changes necessary for both men and women fully to participate in professional life. That means that men and women will have equal access to high levels of achievement, recognition, and promotion, and that both women and men will have adequate time available for personal/family life. We are not interested in how women can become superwomen so as to fit into pre-existing male-dominated professional models, but in how professional work patterns can change to assimilate the vital contributions of women. The ambiguity some women feel in their willingness to work toward workplace changes is, we believe, due to several factors that we will discuss more fully in the next chapter.

If we appear to be assuming that family life is a "given" for most women, and that the difficulty lies in meshing a work life with the family, that is mostly correct. We also take as a "given" the importance to our society of maintaining strong family life. In the middle section of this book, we will be focusing on the spiritual challenges facing contemporary women and the resources we have to meet those challenges. With a different outlook on ourselves, and our lives as workers, it will become evident why workplaces must begin to accommodate the needs of families. But we also feel there are changes that need to come about in family life, especially with respect to men's participation in it. Men's role in reproductive labor will be discussed in chapter 4, and further specific changes in home life will be suggested in chapters 10 and 11.

Part II

New Virtues
for a New World

Chapter 4

Other Women's Daughters: Individualism and Relatedness among Working Women

What would lead...individuals to sacrifice their self interests to the public good and consciously link their destinies to those of their ancestors, contemporaries and descendants?   —Robert Bellah[1]

In chapter 2 we told the story of the woman supervisor who expressed her ambivalence about the Supreme Court Decision upholding a woman's right to job security after a maternity leave. This mixture of intergenerational care and pragmatic self-interest has puzzled us, particularly because this woman was so evidently a caring person. Yet she, like many other women we spoke to, had no way to connect the nurturing concern she felt for her own daughters with an equal concern for other women's daughters. As we have seen, it has been abundantly clear in the last two decades that not all American women support a feminist agenda. The crisis of feminism in this decade has arisen from the lack of consensus among women on what is needed. As feminist ethician Barbara Andolsen says,

> Women's lives are very different.... Some women are mothers, others are not. Some women come from upper class backgrounds, others...from the working class or from poverty.... Women have very different work experiences....If feminist ethics is to be based upon the experience of all women, then such differences in experience must be acknowledged and incorporated into feminist theory.[2]

Even women who profess to believe in women's progress express confusion about the goals and attitudes of the women's movement, and

55

many women continue to perceive feminism as excessively individualistic, anti-family, and unsupportive of nurturing values. The reasons for
this confusion and dividedness among women are complex. As we saw,
they derive partially from the historical relationship between feminism
and the family. In chapter 2 we also discussed how a clearer vision
is emerging from within integrative feminist scholarship that may bring
about a greater consensus between those who identify with feminism and
those who have, in the past, been highly ambivalent about it. Yet even
more fundamentally this dividedness seems to come from an inward contention between women's traditional spiritual and ethical formation and
the ethos of American public life. The values women are socialized to
display in family and neighborhood life are often in direct contradiction to
the values necessary for success in the work world. For instance, spending time talking with friends, neighbors, and children in order to maintain
our relationships with them conflicts with the efficient use of time needed
to compete well in our jobs. Putting the needs of others above our own
is lauded in our family circles and churches, but considered foolish by
our ambitious co-workers.

In chapter 3 we presented evidence of profound divisions in women's
perception of their disadvantaged position in the public realm, and in
their willingness to support structural change in their own behalf. Given
this situation we would like to explore how several traditional themes of
Jewish and Christian spirituality can help heal the rift between the public and private domains and their respective values, and concomitantly
contribute to greater solidarity among women. In this chapter we will
consider how a renewed understanding of *agape* love can transform both
productive and reproductive labor. We will also consider how an *agapeic*
or relational ethic might extend into the workplace and the public realm.
In chapter 5 we will reflect on how the individualistic ethic currently
shapes American life, and how it has negatively affected women's solidarity and our whole society's capacity to create structural change. Out
of these considerations will come the call for a public spirituality based
on a balanced care for self and others. In later chapters we will consider
the biblical sources for a spirituality that integrates self-esteem and social
communion. We will also delve further into the biblical notion of "calling" and discover models — both biblical and historical — for women's
experience of a "public vocation." In accomplishing this, it will become
evident that women's issues are not peripheral to a public spirituality, but
are central to the Christian project of renewing and redeeming public life.

The Ethics of Self-Abnegation and Its Critique

Much discussion in feminist ethics has centered on the debilitating effects on women of an ethic of self-abnegation associated with women's

confinement to the private sphere of home and family. No matter what religious tradition we came from, up until very recently "good women" were expected to be self-sacrificing. The notion of "self-sacrificing" love is associated with the Greek term *agape* in the Bible.[3] The term is prevalent in the New Testament in particular, where the alternative Greek word *eros* is used much less. Since *eros* is generally understood as "an appetite, a yearning desire, which is aroused by the attractive qualities of its object,"[4] it is often contrasted with the kind of love that is totally forgetful of one's own desires and that expects no satisfaction in return. It was this kind of love that women (much more often than men) were exhorted to exercise when their spouses and children were ungrateful and uncaring toward them, and when their own talents and hopes were submerged in the demands of domestic life and in their husbands' interests and careers. The translator of a classic study of *agape* describes it this way:

> Agape is by nature so utterly self-forgetful and self-sacrificial that it may well seem (from an egocentric point of view at any rate) to involve the supreme irrationality of the destruction of the self, as some critics have alleged it does. But in fact, *agape* means the death, not of the self, but of selfishness.[5]

There has been much debate on just how intrinsic the notion of "self-sacrifice" is to *agape*. In the rabbinic tradition of Judaism the command to love one's neighbor is considered a basic principle of the Torah, embracing all others, and in Christianity, *agape* has been considered to be *the* keynote virtue of Christian life.[6] In both testaments of the Bible, though, the main emphasis is on *God's* love for *us*. The response to that love made possible by God's grace includes both love of self and love of neighbor. God's love, creating the new realities among humankind, is itself the basis and motivation for love between people.[7] Love of our neighbor does mean solidarity with the stranger and the outcast as well as with our friends and co-workers. It *does* mean depending on God's love, accepting hardship and suffering, recognizing and taking responsibility for the workfare mother or AIDS-stricken child as warmly and completely as one cares for one's own family. However, *agape doesn't* imply self-abnegation for its own sake, and certainly not the loss of self-esteem. Rather it means the willingness to consider prudently some risks to the self in order to act boldly for the sake of a new community.

Any sufficient understanding of *agape* must include the paradoxical relationship of self-giving and self-esteem:

> Unselfishness is only a virtue if it is countered by self-respect. The two loves, therefore, so far from being opposites, appear to require the presence of each other.[8]

Self-love means regard for one's own integrity, trust in one's own insights and experience, and the nurturance of one's own gifts and abilities. "There are reasons for valuing the self which are identical with those for valuing others."[9] We have obligations to God arising out of our own selfhood, and we have obligations to ourselves arising out of the demands of justice. For instance, when demanding parents inhibit or interfere with our healthy independence and keep us psychologically tied to them, both justice and *agape* may require that our own development as mature persons be weighed significantly against a parent's desire. While there is clearly a place for self-giving love in any profound spirituality, the goal of our caring is the good of the other person or group, not our own martyrdom.

> Love intends the good of the other and not its own actual self-sacrifice or suffering. . . . It is the *neighbor* and not mutuality or heedlessness or sacrifice or suffering, who stands ever before the eyes of love.[10]

The biblical notion of *agape*, properly understood, includes an expansive and self-risking love, but it also implies the self-love and self-esteem that flow from God's love for us. It remains a uniquely important ideal, but one that has sometimes been distorted to women's disadvantage.

Insofar as *agape* has meant primarily women's self-denial for the sake of spouse and children and their containment in service roles, it has been criticized by feminists. Nineteenth-century feminist Elizabeth Cady Stanton is said to have remarked to reporters,

> Put it down in capital letters: SELF-DEVELOPMENT IS A HIGHER DUTY THAN SELF-SACRIFICE. The thing which most retards and militates against women's self-development is self-sacrifice.[11]

More recently Barbara Andolsen writes:

> It is no accident that women have been the ones to take the ethic of self-sacrifice most to heart, for women have been confined to the home — that arena where an ethic of self-giving seemed unambiguously appropriate. The contemporary overemphasis on self-sacrifice as the central Christian virtue is based upon an uncritical acceptance of the dichotomy between the private and public spheres of life. With industrialization the home and workplace have become separated. One set of values including service and self-sacrifice are said to govern action within the home; another set, including rationality and assertiveness, to govern the workplace.[12]

Rosemary Radford Ruether has suggested that "women attempting to live lives ruled by *agape* defined as total self-giving lose the ability to act as responsible, centered selves."[13] In another place Ruether continues,

> Religion and "femininity" came to be identified with each other [and with]...an ethical stance of altruism and self-sacrifice....But feminists generally do not simply want to...embrace the male model of humanity as self-centered and aggressive. They recognize that, however domesticated and marginated, those qualities assigned to the female, in fact, represent the better human qualities, those qualities more conducive to peace, love, and caring relationships.[14]

It is not so much that the world has no place for self-giving love, but rather that, as Bellah comments, "women today have begun to question whether altruism should be their exclusive domain."[15]

In some feminist thought, however, a considered critique of the notion of self-sacrifice has often degenerated into an uncritical acceptance of the predominant cultural ethos of individualism. Little attention has been paid to the socialization of women (especially those who actively pursue a career) into the ethical climate of the still male-oriented workplace — a climate in which healthy self-regard is not always balanced with other-regard, and in which nurturing values and familial demands are functionally ignored.

> "In business school, they teach you that it's always better to maintain good relationships with your colleagues in the long run," says one MBA student at a well-known Massachusetts business school. "But in the short run, it pays to screw the other guy — even if that guy happens to be a woman. When I first got into school, I felt very uncomfortable with that idea. But if you try to do it differently in class, you soon find that you're not doing very well. And so, eventually, you catch on." Women in power also catch on to other facts of corporate life — for example, that executives are supposed to distance themselves from, not identify with, female subordinates.[16]

This fusion of popular feminism and American individualism has presented as an ideal an image of the "new woman" that is morally ambivalent. Linda Gordon states,

> In thinking about the family, contemporary feminism...contains an ambivalence between individualism and its critique....The rejection of gender is an ultimate commitment to the right of all individuals

to develop to their highest potential. Unfortunately, the most visible heroines of such struggles immediately suggest some of the problems with this uncritical individualism; for example, a new image of the liberated woman, complete with brief-case, career, sex partners, and silk blouse, but absolutely without nurturing responsibilities.... Parts of the feminist movement identify with this ideal.[17]

Gordon suggests that such an image is not really the product of feminism but of the American economic ethos. The 1987 movie *Baby Boom* reminded us of the ephemeral attraction of such a life. We may have had it ourselves once — but then Baby came along. We settled for "quality time" with our child instead of the singles bar scene (and probably came to like it better), and washable clothes that would survive baby's burps instead of silk and wool. We swiftly adjusted our job priorities from a hardwood desk and rapid promotion to flextime and child-care benefits. It is vital that we re-think just how much of American individualism should be part of the feminist ideal and how much should be subjected to a feminist critique.

Although self-abnegation and women's consequent loss of self-esteem have clearly contributed to the victimization of some women by their fathers, their husbands, and their employers, the place of a genuine self-sacrificing altruism in society is being re-evaluated by feminists. Feminist theologians are attempting to restore to women a sense that *agape* may require a healthy self-assertion in relationships and a commitment to a public career, and that both of these can be compatible with the gift of self for others. Barbara Andolsen writes:

> While feminists have rejected an ethic which demands total self-giving of women as a means of promoting family stability within industrial society, some would concede that sacrificial acts can be legitimate. Anna Howard Shaw (Methodist minister turned suffragist orator)... could accept the idea that self-determining women would make sacrifices for the sake of great moral causes, including but not limited to, the cause of women's rights.... Shaw advocated that self-sacrifice be balanced by self-assertion, and that sacrifice be made manifest by women in the public realm as well as in the domestic sphere.[18]

The difficulty does not lie with the validity of the notion of self-sacrificing love *per se*, as much as it does with its inappropriateness for an already disadvantaged social group, and its confinement to the feminine and private realm:

Women have demonstrated that excessive self-regard is not the sole root of human evil. Frequently for women the problem is too little self-assertion rather than too much. Neither self-sacrifice nor other regard captures the total meaning of *agape*.[19]

It is our contention that women and men in our society need to reclaim the *agape* ethic. We need to learn to *act for others* out of a deep care for our life as a community. This, however, precludes the kind of self-effacement that inhibits women from *acting* at all, particularly in the public realm. Sara Ruddick in writing about "maternal thinking" warns against the kind of feminine powerlessness that makes mothers unquestioningly pass on the values of the dominant culture — even when those values include violence and oppressive relationships. She says,

> Inauthenticity constructs and then assumes a world in which one's own values do not count.... It gives rise to the values of obedience and "being good," that is, it is taken as an achievement to fulfill the values of the dominant culture.... A "good" mother may well be praised for colluding in her own subordination, with destructive consequence for herself and her children, ... training her daughters for powerlessness, her sons for war, and both for crippling work in dehumanizing factories, businesses, and professions. It may mean training both daughters and sons for defensive or arrogant power over others in sexual, economic, or political life.[20]

There is a good illustration of this in the book *The Color Purple* by Alice Walker. Celie, oppressed and beaten by her own husband, Mr. _____, tells her grown stepson that the only way to manage his independent-minded wife, Sofia, is to beat her:

> Harpo want to know what to do to make Sofia mind.... He say, I tell her one thing, she do another. Never do what I say. Always backtalk.
> You ever hit her? Mr. _____ ast. Harpo looked down at his hands. Naw suh, he say low, embarrass.
> Well how you spect to make her mind? Wives is like children. You have to let 'em know who got the upper hand. Nothing can do that better than a good sound beating....
> I like Sofia, but she don't act like me at all. If she talking when Harpo and Mr. _____ come into the room, she keep right on. If they ast her where something at, she say she don't know. Keep talking. I think bout this when Harpo ast me what he ought to do to her to make her mind. I don't mention how happy he is now. How three years pass and he still whistle and sing. I think

bout how every time I jump when Mr. _____ call me, she look
surprise. And like she pity me.
     Beat her. I say...[21]

But Celie soon regrets her words. When Sofia calls her to account for her
disloyalty, the way opens for their reconciliation:

Dear God,
     For over a month I have trouble sleeping.... A little voice say,
Something you done wrong. Somebody spirit you sin against.
Maybe.
     Way late one night it come to me. Sofia. I sin against Sofia spirit.
     I pray she don't find out, but she do.
     Harpo told.
     The minute she hear it she come marching up the path, toting a
sack. Little cut all blue and red under her eye....
     You told Harpo to beat me, she said....
     I didn't mean it, I said.
     Then what you say it for? she ast.
     She standing there looking me straight in the eye. She look tired
and her jaws full of air.
     I say it cause I'm a fool, I say. I say it cause I'm jealous of you.
I say it cause you do what I can't.
     What that? she say.
     Fight. I say.
     She stand there a long time, like what I said took the wind out
her jaws. She mad before, sad now....
     I stop the little trembling that started when I saw her coming.
I'm so shame of myself, I say. And the Lord he done whip me little
bit too.
     The Lord don't like ugly, she say.
     And he ain't stuck on pretty.
     This open the way for our talk to turn another way.[22]

Only later in the story, when Celie has gained self-esteem and some
personal freedom, can she act in authentic solidarity with other women,
making amends for her wrong to Sofia.
     As we saw above *agape* does imply the willingness to forego one's
own immediate comfort and convenience and to accept suffering and
possibly even death in order to bring fuller life to others. However, most
recent interpretations of the biblical notion of *agape* stress the complementarity of self-love and other-regard. Even when their compatibility
is not immediately evident, women need to think twice before assuming
that the best thing they can do for another is to suppress their own needs,

insights, or desires. Often the best thing we can do for other persons, whether it be our spouses or children, or our society as a whole, is to challenge them to accept us as responsible, gifted, independent, and intelligent adults. A new appropriation of *agape* would see it as embracing the virtues of self-esteem, self-assertiveness, courage, and independence. *Agape* clearly implies the importance of relationality, solidarity, and social communion, as well — themes that have been important to the women's movement from the beginning, even as self-abnegation was being called into question.

Traditionally nurturing and relational values have been connected to the realm of home and family. At least since the late eighteenth century this has been considered a "private" realm separate from the "public" world ruled by an individualistic ethos. Both scholars of religion, such as Robert Bellah and Parker Palmer, and feminist scholars have focused on the disastrous effects, from an ethical standpoint, of this dichotomization. They point us to the reintegration of the ethos of home and work. We will focus on the work of Bellah and Parker in the next chapter. One approach taken by feminist scholars has been to recognize the interplay of work and love in both reproductive and productive labor.

The Labors of Love: Productive and Reproductive Work

The most basic understanding of *agape* implies a love that gives life. We give life to others in many ways — through the "labors" of childbirth, through the "world-building" that is the production of life-supporting goods and services, through child-rearing, through artistic creativity, and through intimacy. Reproductive labor encompasses not only pregnancy and birth, but the long years of nurturing and rearing a child into adulthood — everything from caring for the physical and mental health of our families, to helping our children with their schoolwork, to attending their soccer games. Productive labor involves the making and distributing of various goods and services. Although we can distinguish these two areas of labor, there is a great deal of overlap between them. Cooking a meal, conducting a community symphony, and building a house could all be said to have both reproductive and productive dimensions. One cares for those who come after us, not only by feeding and clothing children or by befriending teen-agers, but also by being faithful to environmental gifts, by advancing medical technology, and by criticizing popular mores. When Erik Erikson discusses the primary developmental task of middle adulthood he names it "generativity" — a term that encompasses both the productive and reproductive work of our prime years — the task of caring for the next generation.

Both productive and reproductive labors seek to create value. Although it has traditionally been productive labor that has been "paid" and valued as work, reproductive labor creates value of a uniquely precious kind.[23] In the traditional division of labor, Hilary Rose states,

> Women's labor is of a particular kind.... Perhaps to make the na-
> ture of this caring, intimate, emotionally demanding labor clear,
> we should use the ideologically loaded term "love." For without
> love, without close interpersonal relationships, human beings, and
> it would seem especially small human beings, cannot survive. This
> emotionally demanding labor requires that women give something
> of themselves to the child, to the man. The production of people is
> thus qualitatively different from the production of things. It requires
> caring labor — the labor of love.[24]

As we noted in the discussion of "integrative feminism" in chapter 2, part of the new consciousness arising in the women's movement — a consciousness that was only subliminally apparent in the earlier stages — is a recognition of the importance of that which has been associated with the feminine and domestic. While the full integration of women into public culture remains a primary goal, women insist that it should not and need not be at the cost of neglecting nurturing labor. But it is often difficult to see how this reproductive labor "fits in" to the male production-oriented economy. As Miles says,

> Equal access to rights and privileges... which remain male-
> production oriented is a partial programme. Women's and human
> liberation requires a far more radical change in the structures and
> values of social and personal life to accord primacy to the reproduc-
> tion of self-actualising people as ends in themselves.[25]

While certain aspects of the reproductive process are specifically women's experience, in its broader implications reproductive labor — that is, the long years of nurturing and rearing a child into adulthood — is not gender-specific any more than productive labor is. Mary O'Brien reminds us that

> the integration of women on equal terms into the productive process
> is a necessary but not sufficient condition of liberation. Liberation
> also depends on the reintegration of men on equal terms into the
> reproductive process.[26]

Despite its traditional association with the domestic sphere, there is a public as well as a private dimension to reproductive labor. How we raise our children determines the character of the next generation of our society. It is commonly said that if we wish to transform our society we need to begin with the upcoming generation, but many of us have discovered how difficult that is. We may want our sons to be gentler, our daughters to be more sure of themselves, and our world to be free of violence and brutal competitiveness, but everywhere we turn — T.V., advertisements, neighborhood kids — current cultural values and practices are reinforced, and our meager efforts seem fruitless:

> My daughter Anne's babysitter once asked her if she'd like to bake some gingerbread men. Anne said, "Only if we can make some gingerbread women, too." Remembering that now makes me sad. Oh, I'm glad she thought of the gingerbread women then, but now I see my careful nurturing stamped out by school and peers. These days Anne has to jump rope while the boys play basketball in gym class. I wonder if she still remembers that there are gingerbread women.

We do see some changes occurring — more role models for an integrated life, textbooks that feature women mathematicians and doctors, and T.V. shows such as "Sesame Street" that stress cooperation and the gentle arts of social intercourse. But more fundamental changes are needed, changes such as a truly equal sharing of child-rearing and domestic duties by fathers, and equal sharing of a public vocation by mothers. Such changes would benefit the psychological development of our children, as well as give them a broader sense of opportunity. In chapter 10 we will discuss further the suggestion that daughters who are able to identify with their fathers as well as their mothers are less likely to fear competitive situations or develop dependent relationships with men. Likewise, sons who are able to maintain closeness to their mothers as well as their fathers may be less likely to fear intimacy or need to dominate women. These transformations arising from our parental practices and assumptions are difficult to achieve. They require "prophetic" activity, in its original biblical sense. The prophets of Hebrew Scripture were not so much "foretellers" of the future as they were insightful and active opponents of the moral, social, and political evils of their day. Because they were sensitive to the shortcomings of their own society they were considered odd at best, and dangerous at worst. They not only spoke, but also acted, in a way that helped to create a better future. We, too, can be "prophets" when we act as though we already live in a society free of stereotypes. We can dignify reproductive work by consciously socializing our children into a gender-equal culture, and we can strive to anticipate and create that culture by our familial and personal decisions.

There is another aspect to child-rearing that is public as well. The incorporation of men into reproductive work will change them and make them more attuned and responsive to the importance of this kind of labor. Sara Ruddick, in her study of maternal thinking, claims:

> The most revolutionary change we can make in the institution of motherhood is to include men equally in every aspect of child care. When men and women are living together with children, it seems not only fair but deeply moral that they share in every aspect of child care. To prevent or excuse men from maternal practice is to encourage them to separate public action from private affection, the privilege of parenthood from its cares.... Assimilating men into child care both inside and outside the home would also be conducive to serious social reform. Responsible, equal child caring would require men to relinquish power and their own favorable position in the division between intellectual/professional and service labor as that division expresses itself domestically.[27]

Ruddick goes on to point out the benefits this would have for the public world of work:

> If men were emotionally and practically committed to child care, they would reform the work world in parents' interests. Once no one "else" was minding the child, there would be good day-care centers, with flexible hours, day-care centers to which parents could trust their children from infancy on. These day-care centers, like the workweek itself, would be managed "flexibly," in response to human needs as well as "productivity," with an eye to growth rather than measurable "profit." Such moral reforms of economic life would probably begin with professions and managers servicing themselves.... However, their benefits would be unpredictably extensive.[28]

If reproductive labor is ordinarily considered to be a "labor of love" requiring forgetfulness of self in order to bring forth and nurture young life, it is perhaps less obvious that productive work can also be a labor of love, with a private as well as a public dimension to it. We do productive work in order to provide for ourselves and our families, and to satisfy our own creative energies. In this sense, it is "private" and even individualistic, although it may be done in the "public sphere." Women need to do productive work for those reasons, as well as men. But both women and men may also see their productive work as a "public vocation." We need to work *for* the community, and because we have unique gifts to bring to that community.

Often women's productive work has simply been ignored by men — not because it makes an insignificant contribution, but because its goods and services are consumed immediately. Food preparation, cleaning, and laundry, as most women know (and many men are learning!) are no sooner "completed" than they must be begun all over again. Clare Fischer writes:

> Women's repetitious labors in the production of goods and services that are consumed immediately and therefore unenduring are perceived in [Hannah] Arendt's terms as lacking the vitality of world-building.[29]

Yet "world-building" need not refer only to the production of enduring products or institutions. As we have pointed out the nurturing and formation of children, family, and home is a cultural task par excellence, and hence one best achieved through the unique contributions of both men and women. Fischer also notes that in making international estimates of food production no account was taken of the 50 percent of Third World food that is produced by three million of its women.[30] Thus "women's work," whether reproductive or productive, has tended to be undervalued. As long as status and higher wages accrue to the male worker's productive work, it will take great courage and discipline for families to choose to model a new way of doing things. For men, the call to love means an enthusiastic acceptance of their role in reproductive labor, while for women the call to self-esteem and responsibility means taking up their growing role in the public sphere, as well as insisting on the great value of their reproductive work.

Agape in the Workplace

If it is vital to bring reproductive labor into public consciousness, it is equally important that the public sphere be transformed by the sensibilities of generative care. Let us consider, then, how women might bring their traditional ethos of care for others into the workplace.

Sheila is a chemist with an M.B.A. She chose to teach at a university, for considerably less than she would make in industry, because she felt the flexible hours would make it easier to manage job responsibilities as she began her family. One of her colleagues, Brenda, related this story to us:

> When Sheila had her first child in August of her second year at the university there was no question about her having a six-week paid maternity leave that extended into the first quarter of the academic year. Our school's one-sentence maternity policy indicated maternity leave would be treated like a disability, and that meant paid leave for six weeks after a normal delivery, and whatever other

time off a doctor indicated was necessary. For the next two years Sheila was a hard-working and valued member of the faculty, even as she balanced her new motherhood with full-time teaching. There was no question that her contract would continue to be renewed.

In the spring of her third year when she became pregnant again, she approached her department head and ultimately the dean with what she thought was her good news. Her child was due in October, a relatively awkward time for the academic calendar, so she thought it would be helpful to the school to discuss how her leave might be handled in the fall. The next thing she knew, she had received a letter saying that she would be given an unpaid leave of absence for the entire fall semester, and her contract would be issued beginning in January. When she initially appealed to the administration she was told that since she was on a nine-month contract she wasn't really covered by the disability clause through the summer, and she wasn't being fired — just not re-hired.

The rest of us women on the faculty only learned about this slowly, as Sheila's way was not to make a big scene about it. I didn't know Sheila that well — she wasn't in my department — but I knew enough to figure that she needed some support from other women in dealing with this — in any case, all women were ultimately threatened by this kind of administrative behavior. After a few phone calls to verify what we were pretty sure was the case — that the administration's action was simply illegal under the terms of federal law[31] — several of us called a meeting of any interested women on the faculty. Quite a few came, some with helpful information, and others just with support.

Sheila told us that she had gone from initial disbelief and rage to a kind of defeated resignation — I think she just felt it wasn't worth fighting this alone — potential legal fees, etc. — even though she knew it was wrong. We came up with a couple of strategies, and fortunately, the very first one worked. Armed with the specific legal information she needed, Sheila simply wrote a letter to the administrators stating the illegality of what they had suggested. She was given a contract for the full year. But it was stipulated that if her actual disability occurred before her contract began at the end of August (i.e., if she became sick or had a premature delivery in mid-August) she would not be covered under the terms of the school's current policy.

This whole episode was incredible and scary to many of us women on the faculty — we thought a reasonable policy was firmly in place. Since this episode several of us have tried to get the maternity policy spelled out more clearly, but the most we've really achieved is to get a re-write of the disability policy, so it would include summer disabilities — since that affects men as well! We're all already overwrought trying to work full time and take care of our families — we don't have time for this kind of nonsense. We know this is a crucial issue for women at our university in the future, but it's hard to keep fighting these battles when we are already stretched to our limits.

This incident provides good material for reflection on the concrete meaning of *agape* love in our lives. In this situation would self-sacrificing love have best been exemplified by Sheila's resignation to the loss of her position and income for a semester? As her own reaction indicated, something in our socialization — in our traditional understanding of feminine virtue — makes us reluctant to make waves, particularly on our own account. Even when we suspect a genuine injustice, we are easily convinced that we are "just being selfish." Indeed, Sheila, married to a lawyer, could have survived without the extra semester's income — could have convinced herself that "good mothers stay home with their infants." But it would not have been her choice. And more importantly, had this incident passed with no one objecting, there would have been even less choice for the next woman, who may indeed have needed the income to survive.

It was not easy for Sheila to stand up and insist on her rights, and she probably would not have done so without other women's support. Ultimately she must have understood that authentic virtue — justice motivated by love for the women who would come after her — meant engaging in a distasteful struggle. The effort on the part of the other women on the faculty was small, but it was significant. They squeezed a little more time and energy out of their crowded days; they gave up those fifteen precious minutes of leisure time — just for one or two days — to make a difference for the future. Although their action might be understood as "enlightened self-interest," for many of them maternity leave was no longer a personal issue. But they sensed a connectedness to this woman, their colleague, and to younger women for whom they could smooth the way. While it may seem like a modest, unheroic kind of example, we feel this story is one illustration of the new kinds of virtue to which women are called as they take their place in the public realm alongside men. Self-giving love has a place in the marketplace as well as in the home.

Another instance of a feminine, relational ethos operating in the workplace is exemplified by Peggy, an agency director who had a small child herself:

My staff is all females, and all but one of them have children. I let them arrange their own schedules as long as they get their work done and get in their forty hours or twenty hours or however many hours they're supposed to be working.... And two of my staff people have to work in the evenings, so that does include some times when there might be a school function for one of their children. But then they just switch their time about. We're really flexible that way. And in their employee evaluations they have said that they really find that a big help,... to know that if there is something that their child needs, they know they can do that. It's really helpful to them. It eases their minds.

There is nothing particularly extraordinary about this woman's willingness to adjust to the family needs of her staff, except that it doesn't always happen that way. What is encouraging in her account is that the relational, caring ethos that undoubtedly characterizes her private life has not been submerged by the competitive pressures of the workplace. She is typical of the women we studied who saw that with a little creativity and a little giving on everyone's part structures could be adjusted to human needs, rather than human needs being subordinated to existing structures.

A common concern for a new integration of public and private lives can provide the basis for developing a broader consensus on family and work issues, especially among those who share a religious vision of social communion and of other-centered commitment. It is this sense of social interdependence and responsibility — of loyalty to "other women's daughters" — that is the foundation of a public spirituality, and also the point of coincidence between biblical ethics and feminist goals.

Chapter 5

Rediscovering a Public Spirituality

Generosity of spirit is thus the ability to acknowledge an interconnect-edness. . . . It is a virtue that leads one into community work and politics and is sustained by such involvements. — Robert Bellah

The conflict women experience between caring for the needs of others and caring for their own growth has its roots in our dual socialization — in the mixed messages we receive as we grow to adulthood. We are taught first to be self-sacrificing nurturers, and then, in the work world, we are taught to develop our selves and our careers with little regard to the cost to others. Thus, this conflict derives to a great extent from the tendency of modern culture to relegate ethical and spiritual concerns to the private sphere. We have seen how some women are bridging the chasm between public and private domains by bringing a relational ethic into the workplace. But to do so goes against the expectations of current workplace practices. For every woman we spoke with who saw the need for structural solutions and who espoused a relational ethic, another woman acquiesced in the male-derived patterns of the work world and envisioned only individual strategies for coping with it. Thus, we must continue to examine the obstacles that inhibit so many American women and men from believing that an integrated life is possible, or from committing themselves to work for it. Part of the answer may lie in the conflict between altruism and individualism that continues to cause tension in our spiritual lives — a tension that is still reflected in the underlying attitudes of different segments of the women's movement.

The issues affecting work and family that we have discussed above are fundamentally issues of justice, love, and human liberation — ethical and religious issues. This has long been recognized by feminist ethicians and theologians, of course. In describing the work of feminist ethicists, Andolsen says,

Our personal experience and social analysis lead us beyond the confines of what is called "secular" life — forcing us to ask religious questions and to affirm religious insights.[1]

But as Robert Bellah has pointed out, we have no language within secular society today in which to speak of ethical responsibility to others — to the community of "strangers" as Parker Palmer calls it.

American Individualism and Its Critique

One of the greatest obstacles to women's solidarity on work and family issues is the individualistic ethic that pervades American society and that has divided the women's movement as well. The two beliefs that characterize an individualist ethos as described by Bellah are: (1) that the primary obligation in life is to the self, and in the public sphere that is, for all practical purposes, the only obligation; and (2) that any further obligation that is admitted is in the private sphere and has been freely chosen by the individual, not "imposed" by the inherent rights of the other. These views are exemplified by a woman therapist interviewed by Bellah's associates:

> Margaret's image of the world sharply limits the demands she feels people can make upon one another, even in the closest, most committed relationships. Even bonds of marriage and parenthood don't overcome the isolation that is ultimately the lot of each individual: "I'm responsible for my acts and what I do." Asked whether she was responsible for others, she replied, "No." Asked whether she was responsible for her husband, she replied, "I'm not. He makes his own decisions." What about children? "I...I would say I have a legal responsibility for them, but in a sense I think they are responsible for their acts."[2]

According to Bellah the problem is not so much that Americans are unwilling to care for those close to them, but that they "had difficulty when they sought a language in which to articulate their reasons for commitments that went beyond the self."[3]

From the division in our survey population it seems evident that some women *are* comfortable with a notion of obligation in both personal and societal relationships and do not see these as conflicting with their sense of worth and rights as individuals, while others find such obligation highly problematic. Traditionally women have thought more in terms of relationships than in terms of isolated individuals, yet the ideology of American individualism has taught us all "to be conscious primarily of our assertive selves."[4] We need very much to create a language in which dependence and independence, obligation and freedom are not seen as antithetical.

It is in the public sphere — as it has been shaped by the dominant male culture — that an individualistic ethos is most evident in practice. An article in the *Boston Globe* compared the 1989 film *Working Girls* with the film *9 to 5* made ten years earlier. While the earlier film showed women working together to change the rules of the workplace, *Working Girls*

> only serves up tired old myths about how women can survive in the workplace. . . . In both the film and real life, women professionals face enormous institutional pressures that often turn even the most well-intentioned of them into the stereotypical competitive male workaholic. . . . Upwardly mobile woman are taught that competition, not cooperation, is the name of the game in the world of work today.[5]

The person who is expected to "manipulate, cajole, and intimidate those [she or] he manages," as Bellah describes it, and to place personal achievement, security, and satisfaction above any obligation to others, may live by a completely different kind of ethic in the private sphere.[6] But the world of work and the private domain "have become radically discontinuous in the kinds of traits emphasized and the moral understandings that guide individuals within them."[7] Moreover, there is also a danger that the calculating individualism of the workplace may be extended into the realm of intimacy, home, and community.[8]

For many women it does not seem to be the attitude of altruism toward children and family that is most obstructive to their solidarity in seeking societal and institutional changes. As we have seen, those who manifest a relational ethos in family matters are more likely to affirm the value of common social movements and to feel that economic institutions do have some "obligations" to the common good of society. In the article on *Working Girls* quoted above, the author emphasizes that many real-life working women *are* recognizing that "going it alone won't get you very far." She quotes Kristine Rondeau, the lead organizer of a newly-recognized union of clerical and technical workers at Harvard University — a union made up mostly of women. According to Rondeau,

> In our union, we, personally, have spent a lot of time thinking about values. And what we decided was that we don't want any part of the "me" generation. . . . We don't equate a big salary with personal success. Life is a lot richer and more complicated than that.[9]

The language of moral responsibility seems to come more naturally to these women, although it gets little support from the predominant ethos described by Bellah.

On the other hand, the group of women who acknowledge no modification of their career goals by family concerns and who exhibit more thoroughly career-oriented behavior are more likely to speak and understand the language of individual choice and responsibility with little sense of their own or others' obligations beyond the self. We can surmise that, at least for some, it is their more complete immersion in the public sphere and perhaps their determination to succeed in it that makes them more susceptible to the prevailing "managerial/therapeutic" ethos of individualism.

Thus Bellah concludes that American individualism has brought about the loss of a language for interpersonal obligation, the predominance of manipulative self-interest, and the exclusion of moral relationships from the public sphere. In the centuries of transition from the medieval synthesis in which a common religious ethic dominated daily life, to the tolerance of modern secular culture for a wide variety of religious and ethical views, we have lost any touchstones for a moral consensus. The philosophical justification of private property by Locke coincided to some extent with the privatization of religion and with a growing individualism in ethics. Because of the "frontier" situation of America, the trend toward "rugged individualism" was accentuated in this country — much more so than in Europe. There is very little foundation in the modern American worldview for engaging in cooperative action for the public good.

All of these trends should be of concern to the women's movement. The solution for women is not to eliminate "generosity of spirit" from their lives but rather for them and for their male counterparts to recognize altruism as an appropriate virtue for the public sphere, and one essential to common democratic action. In Bellah's words,

> Generosity of spirit is thus the ability to acknowledge an interconnectedness — one's "debts to society" — that binds one to others whether one wants to accept it or not. It is also the ability to engage in the caring that nurtures that inter-connectedness. . . . It is a virtue that leads one into community work and politics and is sustained by such involvements. . . . It is a virtue that goes against the grain of much of the American cultural tradition.[10]

Bellah does not, by any means, wish to deny the values of individual choice, individual fulfillment, and individual responsibility. Yet their separation from any grounding in mutual connectedness or any moral vision of a public good that transcends and obliges the self poses great difficulties for any kind of social change. On what grounds should women care about issues that concern other women and families but are not of direct concern to themselves? Moreover, why should they direct time and energy to those concerns and risk their own hard-earned credibility in the man's world in the process? And further, why should men or employers or society at large have any obligation to make changes that are not immediately or obviously in *their* self-interest? This takes us full circle to the question with which we began chapter 4:

> What would lead . . . individuals to sacrifice their self-interests to the public good and consciously link their destinies to those of their ancestors, contemporaries, and descendants?[11]

Why should we care for "other women's daughters"?

Regaining the Perspective of Social Interdependence

It is in order to answer this question that we take up a stance as religious persons committed to particular visions and values. We have used the term "social communion" or "human communion." With these phrases we bring to mind the biblical call to Israel to be a just community mutually responsible for its individual members. In the biblical book of Deuteronomy, as well as in many prophetic texts, Israel's fidelity to the covenant with God is judged according to its success in creating a new kind of community. For instance in Deuteronomy 14–16 we read the following:

> At the end of every three years you must take all of the tithes of your harvests for that year and deposit them at your doors. Then the Levite (since he has no share or inheritance with you), the stranger, the orphan and the widow who live in your towns may come and eat and have all they want. (Deut. 14:28–29)[12]

> You are not to exploit the hired servant who is poor and destitute, whether he is one of your brothers or a stranger who lives in your towns. You must pay him his wage each day, not allowing the sun to set before you do, for he is poor and is anxious for it; otherwise he may appeal to the Lord your God against you, and it would be a sin for you. . . . You must not pervert justice in dealing with a stranger or an orphan, nor take a widow's garment in pledge. Remember that you were a slave in Egypt and that the Lord your God redeemed you from there. That is why I lay this charge on you. (Deut. 24:14–15; 17–18)

> You must rejoice in the presence of the Lord your God in the place where the Lord your God chooses to give his name a home, you and

your son and daughter, your serving men and women, the Levite who lives in your towns, the stranger, the orphan and the widow who live among you. Remember that you were a slave in Egypt and carefully observe these laws. (Deut. 16:11–12)

Because the community of Israel remembers its shared history as an oppressed group in Egypt, it in particular must be sensitive to the stranger, the oppressed, and the needy among its people. All members of the community are responsible for the less fortunate, and all should be assured of justice and compassion in business dealings. As all have suffered together in famine and war, so should all rejoice together in abundance.

Another powerful image of interdependent community is expressed in New Testament descriptions of the Body of Christ. Paul writes:

Just as a human body, though it is made up of many parts, is a single unit because all these parts, though many, make one body, so it is with Christ. . . . Nor is the body to be identified with any one of its many parts. If the foot were to say, "I am not a hand and so I do not belong to the body," would that mean that it stopped being part of the body? . . . If your whole body was just one eye, how would you hear anything? If it was just one ear, how would you smell anything? . . . As it is, the parts are many, but the body is one. The eye cannot say to the hand, "I do not need you," nor can the head say to the feet, "I do not need you." What is more, it is precisely the parts of the body that seem to be the weakest which are the indispensable ones. . . . If one part is hurt, all parts are hurt with it. If one part is given special honour, all parts enjoy it.

(1 Cor. 12:12, 14–15, 17, 20–22, 26)

In many passages of Hebrew Scripture, as well as in New Testament stories such as the Good Samaritan, the "stranger" is our neighbor for whom we are responsible. After Jesus has quoted the words of Hebrew Scripture (Lev. 19:18) that we must love our neighbor as ourselves, a young man challenges him with the words, "And who is my neighbor?" (Luke 10:29). Jesus then tells the story of the man who has been beaten up by brigands and left in the road half dead. First a priest passes him by, then a Levite does the same. Only the Samaritan traveller, considered to be an alien and a heretic by orthodox Jews of Jesus' day, responds to the man, takes him to an inn, and pays for his care. Jesus asks:

"Which of these three, do you think, proved himself a neighbor to the man who fell into the brigands' hands?" "The one who took pity on him," he replied. Jesus said to him, "Go, and do the same yourself." (Luke 10:36–37)

Our neighbor, then, is the stranger, the alien, the heretic. It is not simply that we must be neighbors to them, but that they have already acted as neighbors to us by sharing life with us. Loving our "neighbor" as ourselves implies involvement with people we do not know — that is, with the public sphere.

This biblical vision of interdependent community is part of our common Jewish and Christian heritage. In fact every great religion of the world seems to incorporate some kind of vision of human and cosmic unity and interdependence. It is a fact of nature, it is the content of much religious experience, and it is the foundation of every ethical system worthy of the name. Re-creating a sense of mutual interdependence and solidarity in both the public and the private sphere is clearly among the ultimate aims of feminist theology and ethics. Woman's propensity for a relational ethic rests on her profound intuition of human communion.

Among the women we studied, the sense of relatedness and responsibility to others is often allied with traditional desires for nurturing. Rather than seeing this as an abandonment of the feminist vision we believe it should be seen as women's self-affirmation of their own relational/maternal experiences and of their right to a fully integrated life. The values of interdependence and connectedness that they express do not conflict with their serious desire for a public vocation, but only with their willingness to accept it on present male-oriented terms. As we have pointed out, *agape* has its place in this ethos, not as a tool of women's subjugation, but as a condition of common vision and action. A relational ethic is essential to humanizing the workplace *and* to stretching our loyalties beyond the domestic sphere to the sphere of public action on behalf of a wider good. A religious vision is relevant and necessary as the foundation for such an ethic and for a judicious critique of individualism:

> The habits and practices of religion and democratic participation educate the citizen to a larger view than his purely private world would allow. These habits and practices rely to some extent on self-interest in their educational work, but it is only when self-interest has to some degree been transcended that they succeed.[13]

In his book *The Company of Strangers*, theologian Parker Palmer develops this theme beyond Bellah's sociological analysis. Palmer's basic focus is our need for a spirituality of care for the public realm based on the biblical insight of our relatedness to the "stranger" and our mutual interdependence:

> Public life is — simply and centrally our life among strangers, strangers with whom our lot is cast, with whom we are interdependent whether we like it or not.... The word public as I understand

it contains a vision of our oneness, our unity, our interdependence
upon one another.... To acknowledge that one is a member of the
public is to recognize that we are members of one another.[14]

The mission of religious communities and the pursuit of public life both
have to do with the overcoming of fragmentation and brokenness, with
the forging of "one Body" with a common vision and a common life. Both
the "Kingdom" and the "public" represent a hope for human unity.[15]
Genuine community is rooted in the fundamental belief that, despite
our differences, we are all children of the same creator God — a truth
that we come to know through "contemplation and vulnerability and
self-giving."[16] In this sense a profound Jewish or Christian spirituality is
necessarily a "public spirituality":

> The spiritual life, the inward life, the life of prayer faithfully pur-
> sued, will bring us back and back again to the public realm.[17]

The churches in recent centuries, and particularly in the United States,
have for a variety of reasons withdrawn considerably from the public realm. Although there have always been ways in which Christian
churches and Jewish congregations showed some concern for the public
realm, their preoccupation has been with the private sphere — the family, domestic relations, and personal (hence, to a great extent, private)
morality. Given the strong American tradition of separation of church
and state, this tendency is understandable. Yet real respect for our religious and ethical convictions means that they *will* have an effect on our
views of public policy. Thus no one's good is served by shielding these
convictions from the light of public debate.

We recall Palmer's words:

> The God who cares about our private lives is concerned about our
> public lives as well. This is a God who calls us into relationship
> not only with family and friends but with strangers scattered across
> the face of the earth.... We need to see that in a healthy society the
> private and the public are not mutually exclusive, not in competi-
> tion with each other.... They work together dialectically, helping to
> create and nurture one another.[18]

It is interesting that the efforts throughout the twentieth century to re-
examine the churches' responsibilities toward the public realm coincide
with the efforts of women to re-integrate the private and the public
spheres in their own lives. Although we cannot explore this in depth
here, there would seem to be some evidence of a reciprocal relationship.

As we noted earlier, it has often been women's spiritual and moral sensitivities that propelled them out of privacy into the public realm. One
thinks of women such as Harriet Beecher Stowe, Angelina and Sarah
Grimke, Jane Addams, Lillian Wald, and Eleanor Roosevelt. Moreover,
once involved, whether by choice or necessity, in the world of work and
public discourse, it has often been women who have brought their "private" moral sensibilities to bear on oppressive situations and raised these
concerns within their church communities. This kind of motivation is
hinted at in Hewlett when she speaks about the late nineteenth-century
rationale for women's suffrage:

> Instead of presenting the vote as an assault upon the family and tra-
> ditional ideas of "women's place," feminists increasingly portrayed
> it as a means of bringing women's natural moral and spiritual con-
> cerns to bear upon government.... In the words of Jane Addams, it
> was a way for women to become the housekeepers of the nation.[19]

The point however is not that women have some sort of innate moral
superiority over men. Rather, the point is that they were not socialized
(up until recently) to avoid moral questions or repress nurturing values
when they left the private domain.

We have described the need for a correctly understood *agape* within
the public domain — the kind of care for the other, "the stranger," that
is finally the means to realizing the biblical vision of community. But it
is also the case that a healthy public life fosters our interest in the good
of others. The dominant mood of self-interest that pervades our times is
not necessarily an indictment of human nature. Rather, without a healthy
public life, other-concern has not been evoked or nurtured.[20]

It is scarcely a new message to say to people of faith that self-giving
love belongs in every part of their lives. But it *is* one that has been
misinterpreted and overshadowed by the dominant ethos of individualism and the privatization of morality. Thus for Palmer, for Bellah, and
for integrative feminism, the overcoming of the dichotomy between the
public and the private domains is key to the redemption of social life.
For both women and men this means not repressing nurturing and self-
giving sensibilities and values when they enter the workplace. But the
call to *agape* and to human communion also means that our spirituality includes a commitment to concrete and courageous action for "other
women's daughters" and sons, in the public sphere.

Conclusion

The visible problem that faces women today is whether or not they can
fully participate in a public vocation and significantly influence the public

realm while remaining committed to the actual nurturing of a family and to relational values. The obstacles to that, given the dual burden of responsibility women presently carry, and the discriminatory effects of the male-oriented workplace, are enormous. But the deeper question is why so many women and men continue to envision and espouse solutions based only on individual accommodation, and why they have failed to act together to achieve liberating institutional change. At least *some* concrete solutions are there for the taking, but there has been no consensus that could elicit solidarity in seeking them, even among women.

The reasons for this appear to be complex. On one hand, many women continue to acquiesce in the normativeness of a male-oriented public culture, even though it has meant dismissing their own life experience as unworthy of consideration. In doing so they have been increasingly socialized into its individualistic ethic. Another reason, however, is that there was no clear alternative vision that fully accounted for women's experience. For all that women undoubtedly owe to the early stages of feminism, the low priority it placed on family concerns and its uncomfortableness with women's specificity, meant that it failed to achieve a broad consensus. It may also have alienated some women precisely because of its ambivalence about a self-giving relational ethic and its preference for the language of individual self-actualization.

But we are at a new moment. Both earlier feminist agenda and the predominant individualist orientation of our culture have been subjected to extensive criticism. Perhaps it should not surprise us that the results of these critiques lead in a similar direction. Fundamental social change cannot occur without some ethical consensus in the public realm — some compelling vision of our interdependence with others who do not necessarily belong to our private world. The integration of love and work, of reproductive and productive labor, of public and private vocations proposed by recent feminist scholarship coincides at many points with the call to transform private religious commitment into a public spirituality. In the next few chapters we will investigate more fully how the biblical tradition offers us images and models for the virtues that are essential to us today.

Chapter 6

Biblical Roots for a New Spirituality for Women

Our collaboration, then, extends back in time as we draw wisdom from our sisters who have gone before us. Hence these are our authorities: women whose names may be barely known to us, much less to the male authorities, but nevertheless, who sustain our vision of a "different heaven and earth." We must locate ourselves in this historical stream — the long revolution — which is rooted in a past and is moving towards a future which we are striving collectively to realize.[1]

— Shelly Finson

There can be little question that what we find in the Bible about women's roles and women's call is very mixed. We are well aware that both in the last century and among fundamentalist Christians today, the Bible has been the main source of arguments for women's subordination in society and their confinement to the domestic sphere. That is why we are not attempting here to raise up "proof texts" to show that the Bible teaches women's equality. It is evident that without proper interpretation of passages within their literary and cultural context, any number of "proof texts" can be found to support any view one wishes. Certainly we can find passages that view women as inferior, as well as those that support women's full and equal status before God and in society. Does that mean we should forget about the Bible and go about our twentieth-century business bereft of our spiritual heritage? Is there any way, amid these conflicting uses and misuses of Scripture, that we can reclaim our biblical roots and find in them a meaningful authority and energizing vision for today? This was the question that motivated Elizabeth Cady Stanton to begin her work on *The Woman's Bible*. It was not just the fact that the Bible had been used against the women's movement that concerned her, but her fear that without the effort of women's biblical scholarship, women "would abandon religious faith altogether."[2]

Perhaps there is no oppression greater than being deprived of our own history and our own spiritual legacy. And, in fact, *there is* a legacy to be reclaimed, and *there are* "foremothers" whose lives can, in various ways, become models for our own. As Robert Bellah points out, our whole society needs to rediscover common spiritual foundations from which we can redress some of the excesses of individualism and on which we can build a just and caring society. For women to come together and to find creative solutions to the spiritual and ethical dilemmas posed by our new roles, reappropriating our heritage is essential. Biblical scholar Katharine Doob Sakenfeld has written:

> ... feminists who intend and hope, like the biblical prophets, to work within their religious heritage must address themselves to the authority of the Bible in the life of their community of faith. They must seek faithful ways of recovering, reinterpreting, and discerning God's ways in the tradition handed on in the Bible.[3]

Even though we recognize the massive effects of the prevailing patriarchy of Jewish and Greco-Roman culture on the male biblical writers, we *can* reclaim the experience of women in the biblical tradition who despite, and even *because of*, that patriarchal oppression emerge as models of full human personality and as leaders in nearly every aspect of the public cultural life of their community. This task of recovery, remembrance, and reconstruction of women's experience is not an easy one. In the imagery of biblical scholar Elisabeth Schüssler Fiorenza, it is a matter of figuring out what the submerged part of an iceberg would look like, when all we can see is its tip. The Bible presents us with plenty of "horror stories" of patriarchalism — men handing concubines and daughters over to rapists, at least one sacrifice of a young girl, women treated as property, deprived of most legal rights, subject to stoning for adultery because their word is unacceptable testimony, reduced to degrading dependence on distant relations or to miserable poverty if they are widowed or divorced, humiliated because they bear no children, or required to marry a male relative ten or fifteen years their junior in order to bear a son. What is less obvious are the subtle ways in which some male writers, even with the "best" intentions and with an ear to God's Word, will inevitably misunderstand and misrepresent women's actions, words, and role in God's community. Yet, with a blend of careful scholarship and trust in our own intuitions and worth as women, we will discover a number of women whose self-esteem, boldness, quick wit, and determination enabled them to survive and even gain sufficient admiration (or at least astonishment) to become remarkable and memorable to male scribes. These women are our foremothers and sisters, particularly important to us women of the twentieth century and mothers of the twenty-first, who desperately need such models to complete the task of liberation. Like them, we risk a great deal when, out of love and faithfulness, we depart from our submissive, self-deprecatory roles and sing a new and glorious song to Yahweh.

But is it really useful or necessary to undertake this complex effort to reclaim a two- to three-thousand-year-old heritage? Besides the obvious fact that we still belong to Jewish and Christian communities, and that, in spite of their patriarchalism, they are *our* communities as well as our husbands' and fathers', there are some other good reasons to look to the Bible. As Mary Ann Tolbert has said:

> The Bible...is not only a book that has justified slavery, economic exploitation, and sexual oppression; it is also a book that has informed liberation, the infinite worth of the individual, and the call to fight against evil.[4]

From a historical standpoint, the Bible evidences brief periods of relative egalitarianism in its communities, inspired by a Spirit that was too quickly suppressed. Historically, the Bible can also show the dependence of current gender roles on twentieth-century cultural patterns. For instance, just as we have discovered in the history of women's work in America, we also find that in pre-industrial biblical times, there was little question of women's active participation in the economic life of the community. Further, biblical women who are remembered and esteemed as contributing to their faith communities are characterized more by the boldness, cleverness, and even the irreverence of their activity (e.g., in Gen. 18:12–15 Sarah is greatly amused at God's suggestion that she will soon become pregnant!) than by their submissiveness. This seems to indicate that these remarkable biblical women do not follow stereotypical twentieth-century gender patterns for women.

Overall, the Bible is a story of human liberation — the liberation of both individuals and communities from every evil and oppressive situation — from the enemies that dwell within and among us as well as without. The fact that ancient biblical communities did not fully grasp the implications of God's liberating work for the reality of women's lives does not mean those implications are not there, nor does it mean that we can be faithful to God's liberating Word and work *today* without making women's cause the cause of our religious communities.

Before we proceed with our task of redefining women's virtue with the help of our foremothers, we need to figure out a way that is both honest and hopeful to read this very paradoxical document. That means recognizing the need for careful interpretation, assessing the patriarchal context of its writers, and understanding some of the different approaches that feminist scholars are taking to the Bible today.

Women Interpreting the Bible

The Need for Interpretation

For many of us women, particularly those raised in the evangelical traditions of home Bible study and literal readings of Scripture, the efforts
of today's women scholars to recover "the real story" of women in
the Bible may sometimes seem strained and overly technical. Virginia
Ramey Mollenkott has addressed this question very powerfully, and we
would encourage readers who have this concern to read her explanation
themselves.[5] As Mollenkott points out,

> If secular literature requires self-discipline and training, how much
> more does the Bible require and deserve well-trained, carefully dis-
> ciplined readers! The more one believes that the Bible is divinely
> inspired, the more eager one should be to read with precision and
> alert attention to detail.... The experience of many serious students
> of the Bible has taught us that the Bible sometimes records the hu-
> man limitations of the human beings who were the channels of
> God's Word to us. How then will we be able to sift out which pas-
> sages reflect human limitations and which passages reflect the will
> of God for all times and places? There is no easy formula. We can
> do it only by careful study of the text, paying attention to all the
> methods of precise scholarly interpretation. And we must immedi-
> ately suspect any reading which contradicts the thrust of the whole
> Bible toward human justice and oneness....[6]

In this chapter and the next two chapters, we will be building on the
insights of such scholarship, without reproducing all of its technical ap-
paratus. We invite the reader to consult some of the basic sources listed
in the bibliography or particular sources cited in the notes for fuller explanations.

Biblical Authors and Patriarchal Culture

There is a simple dictum that many of us who have taught Scripture used
to use with our students. "The Bible is the Word of God in the words
of men." Ten or twenty years ago we thought that the last word of that
dictum was a generic term for humanity. The phrase remains a good
way of expressing the fact that God could only speak to humanity in
the words (and concepts) that ordinary humans, like ourselves, could use
and understand in the particular time and place in which they lived. But
now we are aware of how *literally* we must understand that "the words
of men" are also "the words of males."

We have already alluded at some length to the predominance of a highly patriarchal culture in the biblical world. As in our own day, a patriarchal culture can be defined as one in which maleness is seen as normative humanity. Generally speaking, women in such a culture simply acquiesce in its definition of themselves as different (and deficient) humans. As Ruether reminds us, because the Bible was written by, and mainly for, males,

> Women have not been able to bring their own experience into the public formulation of the tradition. Not only have women been excluded from shaping and interpreting the tradition from their own experience, but the tradition has been shaped and interpreted against them.... The androcentric bias of the male interpreters of the tradition, who regard maleness as normative humanity, not only erase women's presence in the past history of the community but silence even the questions about their absence, since women's silence and absence is the norm.[7]

Thus we can't expect to recover very much of "herstory" — of the many common women who lived, prayed, made friends, worked, and trusted in God without overtly challenging the status quo. We more easily know of the women who asserted themselves and acted upon their experience of God's call in spite of cultural constraints. Our generation of women is hardly the first to question patriarchal authority — biblical women did it too. And there have also been men, who without escaping the influence of patriarchalism, have at least been attentive, with the help of the Spirit, to the real women they knew. So when we look we actually find more than we might expect. Schüssler Fiorenza tells us that it might be well to place a warning label on biblical texts:

> "Caution! Could be dangerous to your health and survival...." Without question, the Bible is a male book. Yet women in all walks of life testify to a different, inspiring, challenging, and liberating experience with the Bible.... We have to acknowledge that not all biblical stories, traditions, and texts reflect the experience of men in power or were written in order to legitimate the patriarchal status quo.[8]

This is the paradoxical character of the Bible of which Mary Ann Tolbert speaks.[9] Because its texts range from those which are liberating to those which are oppressive to women, it can't all be read or interpreted in exactly the same way. Some of the New Testament passages most troublesome to contemporary women (e.g., those stressing the headship of the male and the submission of women) can best be understood as the efforts of male church leaders to suppress the radical egalitarianism of the first wave of Christians so that this new religious community would not appear ridiculous or effeminate to its potential converts — whether they were Jews, Greeks, or Romans.[10] These kinds of passages require one kind of approach. Passages that are more illustrative of women's dignity can be read in a different way. It is important to recall here that it is not only the biblical writers, but also its official interpreters, from the early church fathers down to the leaders of our own day, who have been almost exclusively male. When, as women, we re-read with fresh eyes passages that we have only known through male preaching and teaching, we are often surprised at what we find in the text. Those of us who have heard women pray or preach are often startled by the new closeness we feel to God, how much more personally we experience the presence of the divine Spirit. Leading others in worship and study is another fruit of women's biblical scholarship.

Different Approaches to Feminist Interpretation

Elisabeth Schüssler Fiorenza has outlined a four-dimensional interpretive or "hermeneutical" model that she feels is appropriate to women's biblical scholarship.[11] Some texts lend themselves to one or the other; many texts may require the application of all four hermeneutics. The *hermeneutics of suspicion* recognizes the pervasiveness of patriarchalism on all biblical texts, even those about women or generally supposed to be "flattering" to them. The *hermeneutics of remembrance* aims to recover the memory and experiences of women through a historical reconstruction of all the texts in the Bible. Such a hermeneutics recognizes that it can only do biblical women justice by keeping "alive the memory of patriarchal oppression" as well as the memory of their victories and struggles.[12] Schüssler Fiorenza suggests that we have to read the "women passages" as indicators and clues of the larger picture and understand that women were at the center of biblical life. We read these passages "not as descriptive and comprehensive information but as the visible tip of an iceberg which for the most part is submerged."[13] It is through this hermeneutics that we can discern the existence of original "communities of equals" that are only barely perceptible in the biblical texts. The third dimension is that of *a hermeneutics of proclamation*, which critically judges between texts, determining which are genuinely "Good News" for our communities today and which simply perpetuate patriarchal misogyny. The last dimension, *the hermeneutics of actualization*, "employs all our creative powers to celebrate and make present the suffering, struggles, and resurrection of our biblical foresisters and foremothers."[14]

Rosemary Ruether has taken a somewhat different approach to recovering women's story in Scripture, but her conclusions are not too different from Schüssler Fiorenza's. She reminds us of how often religion and sacred texts have been used to "sacralize the existing social order," and she notes that this function of religion is also found in the Bible. But, she goes on to say,

> this function of religion ... is in contradiction to an alternative perspective which seems to this author to constitute the distinctive expression of biblical faith. In the prophetic perspective, God speaks through the prophet or prophetess as critic, rather than sanctifier of the status quo. ... This critique of society includes a critique of religion. ... In the words of Amos 5:21, 24, "I hate, I despise your feasts, and I take no delight in your solemn assemblies. ... But let justice roll down like waters, and righteousness like an everflowing stream."[15]

Thus Ruether's approach is to focus on the *prophetic tradition* within the larger canon of the Bible and to see it as a key to the rest of the Bible. The content of this tradition is not a fixed agenda, but in each epoch it seeks to discover the way that God's liberating Word needs to be spoken to the community. This focus on the prophetic tradition in Scripture has some affinities to Schüssler Fiorenza's hermeneutics of proclamation. As we mentioned above, this prophetic tradition has been recognized and appropriated by women throughout Jewish and Christian history, but this appropriation has not always survived the writing of the texts.

> Is this the first time that prophetic critique has been appropriated by women? ... Our affirmation of the full humanity of women includes the assumption that women themselves have not just begun to affirm their humanity in modern times but have always affirmed their humanity. Patriarchal indoctrination of women to accept their own inferiority and triviality has never been complete. ... Thus the question is not whether women have ever applied the good news to themselves as women, but how and to what extent the records of this feminist hermeneutic have survived the effects of patriarchal erasure of women's self-affirmation from the collective cultural memory.[16]

After summarizing some of the different ways women scholars are approaching the biblical texts, Katharine Sakenfeld writes:

> One may move from one approach to the other in the order described here, but one may also enter into feminist dialogue with the Bible beginning with any one of these approaches. Feminist interpretation moves back and forth among these options.[17]

In these chapters our emphasis will be less on the historical reconstruction of particularly difficult texts than on a literary examination of texts that are chosen because they immediately suggest some application to our lives today — that is, texts where women exhibit atypical and creative behavior in face of the pressures of patriarchy, or (as in chapter 8) texts where women are fulfilling a public role in response to God's call.

Remnants of an Egalitarian Tradition

Many biblical scholars today, both men and women, are convinced that they can discern the existence of communities in both early Israel and early Christianity that took seriously the full equality of women and men before God and in which women had roles of major religious, intellectual, and political leadership. Understanding some of the texts that reveal such prophetically egalitarian communities will lay the groundwork for what follows.

Genesis 2–3: "A Helper Equal to Him"?

We know from historical/critical scholarship that the first five books of the Bible (the Torah, or Pentateuch) and the Deuteronomic History (Joshua, Judges, Ruth, Samuel, and Kings) did not receive their final form until about 550 B.C.E., although a few passages within these books may have been written down as early as the tenth or twelfth century B.C.E. Most scholars accept the hypothesis of several authors or editors for these books, commonly known as the Jahwist, Elohist, Priestly, and Deuteronomic editors, or J, E, P, and D. For our purposes sorting out the oldest traditions from the more recent is probably useful only insofar as it helps us recover the remnants of egalitarian insights and practices that survived later editing. We all know that while the description of the creation of the human in Genesis 1:27 lends itself to an egalitarian reading — both male and female are created in the image of God — the more familiar description in Genesis 2:18–23 has been used to lend credibility to the notion of an order of creation in which the male is "the head" of the woman.

Recent scholarship shows that this interpretation has no basis in the text and is, in fact, a mistranslation of the original Hebrew. One author who has contributed to this discovery is Michael Rosenzweig, who argues that the phrase *ezer k'neged* in Genesis 2:18 (sometimes rendered *ezer neged*) has been misunderstood and mistranslated.[18] He points out that in the King James Bible and in the Jewish Publication Society's 1917 version this phrase is translated as "a help meet [i.e., suitable] for him." Popularly, "a help meet for him" became a "helpmeet" for him, thought to be an archaism for "help-mate." Recent translations attempt to correct this misunderstanding by using a phrase such as "a fitting helper for him" or "a helper fit for him." But this translation of k'negdo is still unclear, confusing, and potentially demeaning to women. By looking at parallel uses of k'negdo in other Hebrew writing such as the Mishnah and the Talmud, Rosenzweig finds that in similar contexts it is most often translated as "equal to" or even "greater than." Thus, in Genesis 2:18, Yahweh announces the creation of "a helper equal to" the first human. There is no inferiority implied in the term ezer or helper either, since it is a word often used for God (cf. Ps. 33:20, 115:9–11, Exod. 18:4, and Deut. 33).[19] If we accept Rosenzweig's conclusions and those of other scholars such as Phyllis Trible,[20] it would seem that both the earlier Jahwist writers of Genesis 2–3 and the later Priestly editors (authors of Gen. 1) recognized an equality between women and men at the very heart of God's creative act.

Elizabeth Clark tells us that, to the credit of its Hebrew interpreters, Genesis 2–3 was not used as a justification for a negative attitude toward women in other parts of the Bible. Eve, for instance, is not used as a symbol of female sensuality, stupidity, and treacherousness in the Hebrew Scriptures; it was the early Christian fathers who used her in that way. She goes on to say,

> in fact, recent attempts have been made, with some success, to show that the myth of Eve in Gen. 2–3 is in no way insulting to woman, but rather depicts her as an equal to Adam, the completion of creation. Such myths, read with fresh eyes, have led at least one Old Testament scholar to remark that "depatriarchalizing" is not something we have to bring to the Old Testament text; "it is a hermeneutic operating within Scripture itself. We expose it; we do not impose it."[21]

This last point is a crucial one. There is no escaping the patriarchalism of much of the Bible. But misinterpretation and mistranslation have often made us miss the egalitarianism that is just as truly present within it. Our task as women of faith is to make sure that we don't miss it, and that our communities don't either.

Early Israel

Are there any indications that an egalitarian understanding of creation ever made a difference to Israel's society? The evidence seems to show that it was the young communities in the first flush of their love relationship with God that were most likely to have fuller and more equal roles for women. Leonard Swidler concludes that the earlier traditions in Hebrew Scripture show more evidence of treating women favorably than the later ones do.[22] Likewise, in reflecting on the prophet Huldah, who was consulted by the priesthood during the reign of King Josiah (2 Kings 22:14), Duane Christensen asks how we are to explain the fact that in the Deuteronomic tradition of early Israel women are singled out to occupy major roles in both the royal and prophetic offices. The writers of this Deuteronomic tradition probably came from the priestly establishment at Anathoth, a suburb of modern Jerusalem. They preserved the so-called Northern tradition in ancient Israel, which was more archaic, and thus more rooted in the agrarian values of a time before the kingship was established. In that agrarian society the sexes were treated with relative equality. There was a high regard for the place of women in both political and religious leadership. Both Huldah and Jeremiah came from this locale, and both apparently belonged to this group.[23]

Jesus' Ministry

Glimpses of better days for women do appear in the ministry of Jesus as well, although not all gospel passages make that evident. Schüssler Fiorenza, through a hermeneutics of remembrance, is able to affirm that the group that arose around Jesus did not accept things just the way their Jewish society had always done them. Rather, Jesus called into fellowship a community inclusive of both rich and poor, pious and sinners, influential and powerless, women and men.[24] Another scholar writes,

> It is probable that Jesus' teachings.... attracted women because of the new roles and equal status they were granted in the Christian community.... Jesus broke with both biblical and rabbinic traditions that restricted women's roles in religious practices, and...he rejected attempts to devalue the worth of a woman, or her word of witness.... [25]

Mollenkott focuses on Jesus' sayings about divorce in Mark 9:4–12 and Matt. 19:3–9 as evidence of his desire to inaugurate a community of equals. Whereas in Deuteronomic law women could be divorced by their husbands (in some interpretations for very trivial causes, such as burning their husband's dinner!), they could not themselves obtain a divorce. One way, then, to read Jesus' teaching on divorce is to see it as requiring an equal moral standard for men and women rather than a "double standard."

> Jesus himself harks back to God's original intention, when the Creator "made them male and female," as the basis for a single moral standard for men and women. By playing off Deuteronomy against Genesis, Jesus is not questioning the inspiration of the Old Testament but is showing that certain passages were inspired to meet

specific needs in response to human hardness, while other passages (recognizable by context) convey God's ultimate intentions for the human race.... It is high time to follow Christ's example in the interpretation of Scripture.[26]

It appears, then, that Jesus does consciously intend to reverse much of the patriarchalism of his culture in the new community that he is announcing. For a brief time women did exercise a genuine "discipleship of equals" within the Christian community. Further evidence for that exists both in Acts and in Paul's Letters (see chapter 8 for a description of the active apostolic roles of women such as Prisca, Lydia, Junia, and Phoebe), despite efforts of second-century Christians to suppress it.[27]

Galatians 3:28 and Paul

> For as many of you as were baptized into Christ have put on Christ. There is neither Jew nor Greek, there is neither slave nor free, there is neither male nor female; for you are all one in Christ Jesus.
> (Gal. 3:27–28)[28]

Certainly this wonderful passage in Paul's Letter to the Galatians is the key to the "secret garden" of the early Christian community of equals. Schüssler Fiorenza claims that this passage is best understood as part of a baptismal liturgy for the first Christians, which Paul quotes approvingly, although it would not have been original to him:

> The new self-understanding of the early Christian movement is expressed in Galatians 3:28. In the new, Spirit-filled community of equals all distinctions of race, religion, class, and gender, are abolished.... Exegetes more and more agree that Galatians 3:28 represents a pre-pauline baptismal confession.... By reciting this baptismal formula, the newly initiated Christians expressed their Christian self-understanding over against the societal-religious creeds of their surrounding Greco-Roman culture.... The Christians affirmed at their baptism that all religious-patriarchal distinctions were abolished in Jesus Christ.[29]

She goes on to mention how this new self-understanding of the early Christians allowed women to have major leadership roles as prophets, apostles, and teachers. If this passage does indeed pre-date Paul, it is nevertheless he who quotes it as the quintessence of our new life and freedom in Christ. In the mainstream of biblical scholarship two views seem to prevail as to Paul's attitude toward women. One view is that

Paul was a radical egalitarian, as evidenced in passages such as Galatians 3:28, quoted above, and 1 Corinthians 11:11–12, where Paul says,

> In the Lord woman is not independent of man nor man of woman; for as woman was made from man, so man is now born of woman. And all things are from God.

The arguments about Paul's real views are to some extent dependent on the question of which letters of the thirteen attributed to Paul were actually written by him, and which were written by later authors who used Paul's name as their authority. Most scholars agree that at least Ephesians, 1 and 2 Timothy, and Titus were written after Paul's death.[30] Many scholars believe that there are also certain passages in the authentic Pauline letters that were added later rather than written by Paul himself. Thus, for those who hold that Paul was an uncompromising egalitarian, the passages that subordinate women to men (including those in the authentically Pauline letter 1 Corinthians) are all considered to be later additions to the authentic Pauline corpus. For instance, William Walker claims:

> That Paul's own teaching and practice were, in fact, radically egalitarian, particularly as regards the status and role of women, has been made increasingly clear by recent studies of Gal. 3:27–28, which asserts the absolute equality of the sexes in Christ, 1 Corinthians 7, which insists that the two sexes have precisely the same freedom and the same responsibility in the marriage relationship, and the various New Testament references to women as Paul's honored and esteemed co-workers in the church. The authentically "Pauline" materials are consistently and radically egalitarian in their outlook; the later "Paulinist" materials are equally consistently "patriarchal." ... "Paulinist" teachers and writers found it necessary to "tame" or "domesticate" the now deceased Apostle.[31]

There is some good evidence for this position, but a more moderate position, less dependent on the question of the authorship of particular passages, is that Paul did recognize that the new life in Christ meant a radical overturning of present societal relationships, but he was ambivalent about just how much of this new ethic could be realistically implemented in the present situation of the church. According to this interpretation, Paul was concerned that order and credibility be maintained in the existing patriarchal society, at the same time that he personally affirmed and implemented radically new roles for women. Most scholars agree that the "headship of the male" and subordination of women passages in Colossians, Ephesians, 1 Timothy, Titus, and Peter reflect the situation of the second-century church and are not authentically Pauline, although they would have come from teachers claiming continuity with Paul. Constance Parvey describes this later situation:

> Near the end of the first century A.D. and the turn of the second, the intertime ethics of Paul has disappeared. The eschaton, the fulfillment of the end times, had not come.... It is in this context that 1 Timothy is written. Here the position of women is very restricted. Prayers must be said only by men. Women must dress modestly and act soberly. They must listen quietly and always be learners, and they must fill all of their hours with good deeds. Specifically, women must be quiet and must not domineer over their husbands. As if this were not enough, women were no longer mentioned as being saved by incorporation in Christ and by life in the new creation, but women are mentioned only as "saved through motherhood." (1 Tim. 2:15) The reasons for this hardening of attitudes toward women remain unknown. It certainly was in part related to the realization that the end times were not soon to come. This probably took the edge off the ethical imperative and led to a kind of spiritual slowdown.[32]

While the passages in the pastoral epistles clearly reflect the situation of a time after Paul, the passages such as 1 Corinthians 14:34–35, where women are told to keep silence in church meetings, are harder to dismiss as non-Pauline. However, they do show some internal incoherence. For instance, could the same person who in 1 Corinthians 11:5–6 assumes that women do pray and prophesy in public worship (although they are to cover their heads with a veil!), then insist in 1 Corinthians 14:34–35 that women can't speak at all in public worship?

Krister Stendahl resolves the dilemma about Paul by arguing that Galatians 3:28 represents the Christian ideal that Paul wholeheartedly embraced, but that could only be gradually implemented in the actual life of the communities he was founding. It is not the case that Paul understood these radically new forms of equality to apply only to the human in relationship to God, but rather Paul saw their social implications. Stendahl says,

> Thus we have seen how the first of three pairs — Jews/Greeks — is clearly implemented in the actual life and structure of the New Testament church. When it comes to the second pair — slave/free — there are slight and indecisive signs of the implications involved. What about the third pair, the one with which we are particularly concerned in this study, "Not male and female"? It is our contention that all three of these pairs have the same potential for implemen-

tation in the life and structure of the church, and that we cannot dispose of the third by confining it to the realm *coram deo* [merely in relationship to God].[33]

In Stendahl's view, even if some of the authentically Pauline passages represent a compromise with the prevailing ethic of his time (as Paul's Letter to Philemon does in the matter of slavery), that is no excuse for Christian communities today:

It should not be such a strange idea for us that the full consequences of the new life in Christ are not immediately drawn and applied. If we are right in describing the statements of 1 Cor. 11:11–12 and Gal. 3:28 as pointing beyond what is actually implemented in the New Testament church, then they must be allowed their freedom; and the tension which they constitute must not be absorbed or neutralized.... The correct description of first-century Christianity is not automatically the authoritative and intended standard for the church through the ages.[34]

Perhaps the most telling argument, though, is Paul's own behavior. Repeatedly, he greets and affirms the women who are co-workers and missionaries in the young Christian community and who are leaders of the local "house" churches that held their meetings in the leaders' homes. Paul does not condescend to them, but rather in several cases he recognizes that they preceded him in working for the gospel, and that he is indebted to their leadership. His use of the baptismal confession of Galatians 3:27–28 indicates his recognition that an egalitarian community is part of the tradition of Jesus himself, and thus not something that he, Paul, can trifle with!

Images of God and Women's Self-Understanding

In considering the resources we have for women's spirituality today, we have looked first to the egalitarian traditions contained within the Bible. Surely, another resource for us must be a renewed understanding of the Divine Mystery. Our understanding of God necessarily affects our understanding of ourselves as women. And there is little question that false images of God as solely masculine have contributed to women's oppression and poor self-esteem. On the other hand, the reclamation by women of feminine images of God contributes to our sense of self-worth. Canadian feminist Monique Dumais cites a recent study that establishes this connection:

The research work of Kathleen C. Zang has attempted to show the psychological relationship between symbols of God and self-esteem. By means of a study of a group of Christian feminists, she has demonstrated that the use of feminine symbols for God manifests and stimulates an acceptance of their life as a woman and a positive affirmation of their experiences. In this manner, she shows clearly the ethical implications of feminine symbolization of God on the life of women, as well as on the creative quality of relations among women which would follow suit.[35]

Mollenkott's book *The Divine Feminine* deals in depth with this question, and we can scarcely do better than to draw on her work here.[36] She begins by pointing out that when God is perceived only as husband-like or father-like, then husbands and fathers are perceived as god-like, and the result is the disastrous exploitation of wives and daughters.[37]

> The type of relationship that suggests itself when only one partner is godlike is a dominance-submission relationship. The type of relationship that suggests itself when both partners are godlike is mutuality.[38]

But where would we get the audacity to suggest that the God of biblical faith could be imaged in feminine terms as well as in masculine ones? We get the audacity from the Bible itself! And from holy people throughout our Jewish and Christian traditions. The most basic point we need to keep in mind is that God is Mystery, and that all our images for God, both personal and impersonal, are our feeble attempts to understand and relate to this Source of Love, Power, and Goodness that by its very nature exceeds our capacity to capture in a single image. To confine the Divine Mystery to something we have created is the very meaning of idolatry. On the other hand, a variety of images for God enriches our appreciation of who God is for us.

Earlier in this chapter we looked at the passages in Genesis 1 and 2 that deal with the creation of the human. Women and men, we saw, come from God's creative "hand" as equals. And more importantly, *both* male and female are created "in the image of God." The implication of that is clear. If woman, too, is in the image of God — if woman is "god-like" — then God must include what is woman-like in the Divine Self. While the preponderance of images of God in the Bible are masculine, biblical writers were also inspired to use images of God that were clearly feminine and maternal. "If God can be compared to a woman as well as to a man, then no real-flesh human being should be categorically subordinated to another on the basis of her sex."[39] Let us look at a sampling of these biblical images of God.

Maternal Images of God and the Status of Nurturance and Child Care in Our Culture

Mollenkott tells us that the image of God as a maternal deity is the most pervasive of the biblical images of God as female.[40] In Isaiah 42:14, God is in travail to bring forth justice in Israel:

> From the beginning I have been silent,
> I have kept quiet, held myself in check.
> I groan like a woman in labor,
> I suffocate, I stifle. (JB)

In Deuteronomy 32:18 we find the balancing of male and female images of God's reproductive activity:

> You were unmindful of the Rock that begot you, and you forgot the God who gave you birth. (RSV)

Isaiah 49:15 reveals God as having the total devotion of a nursing mother:

> Does a woman forget her baby at the breast, or fail to cherish the son of her womb? Yet even if these forget, I will never forget you.
> (JB)

God is also depicted as a mother bear, a mother eagle, and most familiarly, as a mother hen. In Hosea 13:8 we read,

> Very well, I will be a lion to them,
> a leopard lurking by the way;
> like a bear robbed of her cubs I will pounce on them
> and tear the flesh around their hearts. (JB)

God's fierce love for us is like the protectiveness of a mother bear, ready to fight for her children. In Deuteronomy 32:11, God is a mother eagle teaching her eaglets to fly, hovering just beneath them and catching them if they fall:

> Like an eagle that stirs up its nest,
> that flutters over its young,
> spreading out its wings, catching them,
> bearing them on its pinions. (RSV)

The same image occurs in Exodus 19:4:

> You have seen what I did to the Egyptians
> and how I bore you on eagles' wings
> and brought you to myself. (RSV)

Because of the timidity of our translators who tend to avoid feminine pronouns, or perhaps because of our own conditioning, we often miss the fact that images such as these are necessarily feminine. Jesus, of course, uses the mother hen image explicitly in Matthew 23:38 and Luke 13:34:

> Jerusalem, Jerusalem. . . . How often have I longed to gather your children, as a hen gathers her chicks under her wings, and you refused! (Matt. 23:37–38, JB)

In addition to the references to the activities of God that are biologically maternal, such as giving birth and suckling, there are a number of other images that show God as a caring, nurturing parent. Hosea 11:3–4 and Isaiah 46:3–4 depict God as teaching, disciplining, hugging, carrying, and cleansing the child Israel, or wiping the tears from our eyes. Isaiah 66:13–14 says,

> Like a son comforted by his mother
> Will I comfort you. (JB)

All these texts bring to mind activities typically those of a mother.

In another verse of Isaiah 66 God is depicted as a midwife assisting at the birth of Jerusalem's children:

> Am I to open the womb and not bring to birth?
> says Yahweh.
> Or I, who bring to birth, am I to close it? (Isa. 66:9, JB)

Perhaps these passages are enough to convince us that the work of maternity and of child-rearing is truly the work of God. The fourteenth-century English mystic Julian of Norwich did not hesitate to claim this:

> To the property of motherhood belong nature, love, wisdom and knowledge, and this is God. This kind, loving mother who knows and sees the need of her child guards it very tenderly as the nature and condition of motherhood will have. . . . This work, with everything which is lovely and good, our Lord performs.[41]

And in another place, she writes,

> As truly as God is our father, so truly is God our mother.[42]

It should give us pause to reflect on the low status and privatized character that we have accorded to parenting and child-rearing when we read
these passages. God's work is maternal work, and thus our nurturing
activities, whether we are men or women, are primary ways in which
we image and imitate God.

Other Feminine Works of God

It often goes unnoticed that one of the earliest activities of God recorded
in Genesis is God sewing clothes for Adam and Eve (Gen. 3:21). We are
familiar with the many references to God's "handiwork" (e.g., Ps. 8:3),
yet we rarely think of it as the delicate result of a woman's fingers at work
embroidering or making lace. In Psalm 123, God is the mistress of the
household to whose hands we her handmaids should look with devotion:

> Like the eyes of a slave-girl
> Fixed on the hand of her mistress
> So our eyes are fixed on Yahweh our God. (JB)

Another passage that reveals God as nurse or midwife, a role always
played by women in biblical times, is found in Psalm 22:9:

> Yet you drew me out of the womb,
> you entrusted me to my mother's breasts;
> placed on your lap from my birth,
> from my mother's womb you have been my God. (JB)

The feminine side of God is also evident in the personification of Wisdom — the creative, ordering Spirit of God — as feminine.[43] Mollenkott
also points out that the term "Shekinah," which referred to the glory of
God dwelling among the Israelites, was feminine in gender.[44] According to Hebrew scholar Raphael Patai, "To say that God is either male
or female is . . . completely impossible from the viewpoint of traditional
Judaism."[45]

One may be tempted to ask, at this point, how we could have missed
so much. Fortunately, we are not the very first to notice these feminine
images of God. Not only Julian of Norwich, but male saints and mystics
such as St. John Chrysostom, St. Bernard of Clairvaux, Meister Eckhart,
and John Donne, to name just a few from the Christian past, recognized
that imagery for God could be feminine as well as masculine. Unfortunately, the prevalence of masculine interpreters, teachers, and translators
of the Bible have effectively made the feminine aspect of the biblical
God a well-kept secret.

What this means for our spirituality as women may only gradually dawn on us. We have spent some time on it here, because it is so crucial to our growth as women of God-like virtue that we see our own unique experience as embodied women as also part of the experience of God. God is like us women, and we are like God! With this perspective, however, it is not necessary to see ourselves as limited to stereotypically feminine activities, any more than God is. As men and women we each image God who is at once feminine and masculine, mother and father, architect, engineer, seamstress, and midwife. Like God, God-like, we women are called to productive work and generative care.

Chapter 7

A Spirituality of Self-Esteem and Social Communion

God's Divine Intervention did not prepare us to be victims. When we adopt a victim's stance, instead of a sacred reverence stance toward ourselves and each other, we are subverting God's creative act....Victims do not make good lovers. — Fran Ferder

One of the remarkable things about the Bible is that it is not just pious writings about holy people. Rather it is a record of a real community of wounded, warted people like ourselves, struggling to survive and to become a better community — more faithful and more just. Those who are remembered include a few people of outstanding virtue or vice, but many more who realistically combine good and evil, strengths and weakness, in various proportions. People like Abraham and Sarah, Moses and Miriam, Ruth and David come off very humanly when we read the Bible with care. Yet they, and many others less illustrious than they, are remembered for their unique contributions to the building of God's community on earth. Our goal in this chapter is to find realistic models for women's spirituality today.

> Today our search for our spirituality has its roots in the history of other women who, in the past, made an effort to survive and be creative in a society that both distorted and manipulated their lives. In their stories can be seen our attempts to break into new consciousness and thus to claim our spirituality.[1]

Self-Esteem: Women as Survivors

As we have seen, the foundation of spirituality must be a healthy self-esteem. In particular, the freedom to use feminine as well as masculine images for God may help us to esteem our womanhood as a unique

100

reflection of God's image. With low self-esteem we may gain a reputation as "nice" or "sweet" because we fulfill others' expectations of women as naturally selfless and accommodating. But underneath the "niceness" is often a deep-seated emotional dependency on the approval of others. In writing of women's spirituality Joann Wolski Conn reminds us of the dark side of women's "virtuous" behavior:

> Women spending themselves on their family, their students, their patients...often have low self-esteem....Their inability to be assertive and their lack of self-worth can result in covert manipulation, pretended helplessness, evasion of conflict situations. Their desire for peace at any price has a high cost: repression of anger can result in bouts of depression.[2]

While the intellectual conviction of our equal status as images of God is a good beginning, its consequences have not always been fully understood, nor has it completely penetrated and transformed our hearts and lives. Sometimes it seems as though we achieve a certain kind of self-esteem, often based on our productive work, *in spite* of the fact that we are women, rather than *because* of the unique ways in which we women reflect God. Let us look at three women in the Book of Genesis whose self-esteem had every reason to be threatened, and yet whose stories reveal that they had a remarkable resilience under painful and oppressive conditions. In interpreting these passages we will be keeping in mind that they have come down to us through male writers. Thus we are looking below the surface to discover the feelings, struggles, and insights that these women must have experienced, and the transformations they must have undergone. The actual biblical record gives us only hints through the outward behavior of these women.

Sarah and Hagar

Almost as soon as we are told Sarah's name in Gen. 11:29, we are told that she is barren (Gen. 11:30).[3] She is beautiful (her name means "princess"), yet from the very beginning she is portrayed as something of a liability to Abraham. Abraham's fears about Sarah's beauty causes them to be thrown out of Egypt (Gen. 12:10–20). Another grave difficulty arises when Sarah is not able to have a child. Women's status in a patriarchal society depended almost solely on their ability to bear a healthy male child. Thus Sarah's self-worth is going to be constantly challenged by the pity or disdain of her household. Sarah thinks she finds a way out when she arranges for her Egyptian slave girl Hagar to sleep with Abraham, hoping that she (Sarah) will have a child "through her" (Gen. 16:1–3). But she hasn't counted on Hagar's own independence and pride. Both of the women are caught up in achieving self-esteem through meeting the demands of patriarchy. The bad feeling that soon surfaces between them has little or nothing to do with competition for personal intimacy with Abraham. It has everything to do with "looking good" through giving him a boy-child. As soon as Hagar conceives she scorns her mistress:

> And once she knew she had conceived, her mistress counted for nothing in her eyes. Then Sarai said to Abram, "May this insult to me come home to you! It was I who put my slave-girl into your arms but now she knows that she has conceived, I count for nothing in her eyes." (Gen. 16:5, JB)

Sarah retaliates by getting Abraham's permission to mistreat her, and Hagar tries to run away. She returns only because God understands her plight and promises her a son who will father many generations. In this direct experience of the Divine, Hagar's self-esteem is restored and she finds the courage to return to her very awkward situation.

So far this story seems to have little to recommend it to women today! And it doesn't get much better. When Sarah finally conceives Isaac she is, of course, delighted. But no sooner does she see Hagar's son, Ishmael, playing with Isaac than her insecurity returns and she demands that both mother and son be sent away. Does it seem strange that God takes the side of both women? It is a measure of their oppression, perhaps obvious even to the male biblical writer, that God sees fit to vindicate them both. In accordance with Sarah's wish, God allows Abraham to send Hagar and Ishmael away, even though Abraham is "greatly distressed" to lose his son. But God also protects Hagar and Ishmael and renews the promise to "make him into a great nation" (Gen. 21:8–21, JB).

The question that may occur to us in reading this story is, "But why is this in the Bible?" The standard answer, of course, is that Sarah is the mother of Isaac and the ancestress of the people of Israel. But why all the sordid details? A more likely answer is that the story was re-membered and retold because the heat of the conflict between these two women was truly legendary! And because it made for a good story. If both the matriarch and her slave girl exhibited insecurity and a need to be affirmed through successful childbearing, they also exhibited an un-willingness simply to submit quietly to their oppressive situations. These were two strong women who ultimately insisted on their own rights in the ways open to them. It is interesting that neither of them is portrayed as particularly pious, nor do they accept their womanly lot with tradi-tional passive virtue. Sarah is so determined not to accept the fate God has apparently given to her (16:2) that she tries a rather innovative way of having children! When it backfires, she is not contrite, but calls on

God to justify her action! Hagar finds that by conceiving a child she is not only equal to her mistress, but has surpassed her. When she is treated badly, she does not accept it as fair punishment for her pride, nor does she retreat into quiet resentment; she runs away. While such an action may at first glance seem like an act of desperation (after all, she was pregnant at the time, and without a protector), it may also be interpreted as an affirmation of her own dignity. She knew that she deserved to be treated better. Sarah and Hagar were remembered for their indomitableness as much as for their maternity.

It is, of course, one of the great evils of a patriarchal system that by undermining women's self-esteem women are forced to compete for men's favor and are easily tempted to resentment and hostility toward other women. Sarah and Hagar are clearly cases in point. So are Rachel, the beautiful, favored, but initially barren wife of Jacob, and Leah, her less-favored but more-fruitful older sister. Although there are obvious parallels to Sarah and Hagar, the two sisters ultimately seem to work things out a little better (see Gen. 29:1–31:16). Below we will recount the story of two early Christian martyrs, Perpetua and her slave-girl Felicitas. Although they too were mothers and they too felt the divisions imposed by class and patriarchy, the story of their solidarity in facing death presents an interesting contrast, and perhaps counterbalances the story of Sarah and Hagar.

Tamar

The Tamar with whom we are concerned is the Canaanite daughter-in-law of Judah in Genesis 38.[4] Her story is a classic example of a woman using her boldness and ingenuity to make the most of a miserable, no-win, male-defined situation. Like women in so many other biblical stories, this woman is remembered for very unconventional and daring behavior. It would seem that while ancient Israelite society made all sorts of laws to keep their women literally "under wraps," they couldn't restrain their admiration, or at least amazement, at the occasional woman whose self-esteem, intelligence, and courage enabled her to make male ascendancy look a little ridiculous.[5] Tamar's husband, Er, offends God, and dies. According to the obligation of levirate marriage (Deut. 25:5–10), a man was required to marry his brother's widow if she was childless and to raise up any children to be his brother's heir. Thus, after Er's death, Tamar is given to Onan, best known for his method of birth control. For whatever reason, Onan is unwilling to provide children to Tamar, and as a result, he also dies (Gen. 38:11). There is a third brother, Shelah, who is still a child. Judah promises to give Shelah to Tamar when he comes of age. In the meantime Tamar is sent home to her father. But the text tells us what Judah was really thinking: Shelah "must not die like his brothers" — the implication, of course, being that Er and Onan's deaths were somehow Tamar's fault.

We can imagine what life was like for a very young widow like Tamar with no children. Unless her father were wealthy, she would have been considered an economic burden on the household. She would be unable to share fully in the experiences of nearly all the other young women who would be married and bearing children. She had no future. Sooner or later Tamar became unhappy about it. We are told that "a long time passed" (Gen. 38:12). It becomes evident that Judah is not going to fulfill his duty toward Tamar by giving her to Shelah. Judah's wife dies, and Tamar learns that he will be traveling through her area on his way to a sheep-shearing. She takes off her widows weeds, wraps herself in a heavy veil, and sits at the crossroads. Judah comes by, takes her for a prostitute, and propositions her. She agrees but not without cleverly requiring a pledge of the seal, cord, and stick he is carrying as surety for future payment. While her intention seems to be only to get an heir for herself and Er (in Gen. 38:26 Judah approves Tamar's conduct) rather than to make Judah ridiculous, she succeeds in doing both. She conceives a child, is accused of playing the harlot, and when her situation is reported to Judah he commands that she be taken out and burned! Tamar must have known the possible consequences of her behavior. It confirms our intuitions about her desperation that she was willing to take such a risk in order to have a life worth living. But "as she was being led off " she produces the pledges and sends them to her father-in-law, who confesses that she is in the right and he is in the wrong (Gen. 38:24–26). Throughout the story there is no hint of Tamar's behavior being disapproved, although it is unconventional to say the least! Whatever judgments our culture might make about the strangeness of ancient Israelite marriage law, the essential point is that she understood that fulfilling her duty to God, and to herself, required bold and intelligent action, not meekness, self-effacement, or passivity.

Intelligence and Authority

The Wise Women of David's Reign

Not all women in Israel were in a plight such as Tamar's, where the most noteworthy use of their intelligence was to find clever ways to survive in a man's world. In the period of Judges and the early monarchy a number of women are remembered as authoritative sources of wisdom to the community. Among them are the two wise women of 2 Samuel 14 and 20. In 2 Samuel 14 the wise woman of Tekoa is called upon to play a role much like Nathan in 2 Samuel 12. In this story David's daughter Tamar is raped by her half-brother, Amnon. Amnon, who is David's first-born son, is then killed by her brother Absalom. David is furious about Amnon's murder, and Absalom flees from his father's wrath. Three years later, David longs to see Absalom again, but is reluctant to call him home. Joab, David's general and right-hand man, summons the wise (or "quick-witted") woman of Tekoa to tell David a story that will mirror his own situation. Claiming to be a widow with two sons, she recounts how one son killed the other, and how her relatives want to kill her remaining son as punishment. She asks David to decide the case in favor of her son so that she will not be left childless. He agrees. She then, in the most tactful way possible, points out the parallel between her own (fictional) situation and David's situation with his son Absalom. David agrees to allow Absalom to return home. Although the woman admits to David that Joab has put her up to this clever ruse, she is clearly the one responsible for its success. In discussing this woman Claudia Camp argues for the independent intelligence, ability, and authority of this woman:

> There are . . . at least three bases on which to argue for the authorita-
> tive role of the Tekoite woman in this situation. First, the authority
> that comes from wisdom is not simply a matter of knowing what
> to say, but also of knowing when and how to say it; execution
> is not separable from insight for the wise person. . . . The sequence
> of David's responses to the woman's tale was unpredictable; thus,
> quick-wittedness on her part was indispensable. The delivery of
> her accusation had to be carefully timed and forcefully executed,
> but also accurately modulated so as to effect the desired response.
> It is improbable that any but a person practiced in the art of con-
> frontation . . . could have managed this situation effectively.[6]

In 2 Samuel 20, a second wise woman appears. There has been an up-rising against David led by a certain Sheba. Sheba and his men are in the city of Abel, and Joab and David's men are besieging it. As they are battering the walls of the city, the wise woman appears on the outer wall. Appealing to Abel's reputation as a city of justice and peace and to its status as "a mother city in Israel," she negotiates a settlement with Joab — Sheba's head in return for raising the siege. Her intelligence and authority are evident not only in her ability to convince Joab, but also in her capacity to lead her own townspeople to deliver what she has prom-ised. We are told that "the woman went back into the town and spoke to all the people as her intelligence dictated" (2 Sam. 20:22). Camp tells us,

> As for the wise woman of Abel, her authority is without question,
> both in her commanding stance before Joab and in her obvious influ-
> ence among her people. Her advice is apparently taken, moreover

with the same seriousness that a respected royal advisor expected his to be heard. The people act with unquestioning alacrity.[7]

We often think of intelligence and the ability to speak cleverly and well as the outcome of natural talents, rather than as "virtues" in the sense of moral qualities. Yet many women in our society today suppress their natural intelligence and leadership out of a variety of social motivations. We don't want to threaten or alienate men, we are afraid of the responsibilities that intelligence implies, we have been repeatedly made to feel that we are stupid or incompetent, or just not quite capable of doing the kind of things required for "success" in professional or academic fields. Our lack of self-esteem sometimes hinders our ability to speak and write with confidence and authority, and we are not, by and large, trained from childhood in the arts of public speaking and debate. Women such as the wise women of Tekoa and Abel can encourage us to foster and use our gifts of intelligence, diplomacy, and articulate speech in the service of our communities, as they did.

The Gentile Woman of Matthew 15 and Mark 7

In the New Testament we find another story in which a woman's quick wit, courage, and tenacity make her an excellent match for Jesus in a rabbinic-type argument. Her assertiveness, born of her desperate concern for her daughter, is a model to those of us who find it difficult to break out of stereotypically acceptable behavior. She is commended by Jesus for doing so.

   In Matthew's account, this anonymous woman follows Jesus shouting for help for her daughter. He ignores her. She is such a nuisance that his disciples plead with Jesus to give her something in order to get rid of her. She kneels at his feet, asking for his help, and Jesus utters what is probably his most offensive saying in the Gospels: "It is not fair to take the children's bread and throw it to the dogs" (Matt. 15:26, RSV). Undoubtedly swallowing some anger and what little pride she has left, she immediately responds "Yes, Lord; yet even the dogs eat the crumbs that fall from their masters' table" (Matt. 15:28, RSV). As Sharon Ringe has commented, this is apparently one incident in the life of Jesus when he is "caught with his compassion down."[8] Ringe reminds us that this woman apparently did not accept the low esteem in which society held herself and her daughter. For the sake of this daughter, the woman stepped out of the bounds of traditional, submissive behavior and stood up to Jesus. The quick verbal interchange, typical of rabbinical methods of argument, reveals her intelligence and ability to cut to the heart of the matter. Ultimately, she bests Jesus in the argument, gains what she has sought — the healing of her daughter — and is commended by Jesus for her faith and (in Mark) for the insight she has shared.[9] As Ringe points out, she becomes, in a very real sense, a "teacher" to Jesus. The woman's faith

> has the effect...of enabling Jesus to see the situation in a different way. That new perspective appears to free Jesus to respond...to become again the channel of God's redeeming presence in that situation. Whatever provoked the initial response attributed to Jesus (whether we should conclude that he was tired, or in a bad mood, or even that he appears to have participated in the racism and sexism that characterized his society), it is the Gentile woman who is said to have called his bluff. In so doing, she seems to have enabled him to act in a way apparently blocked to him before. Her wit, her sharp retort, was indeed her gift to Jesus — a gift that enabled his gift of healing in turn. Her ministry opened up the possibility of his.[10]

Her gift, we are reminded, was not the gift of submissive obedience, but rather the gift of the realistic insight that comes with being poor and marginal to society. Her gift was also that of courage, the courage of one who has little, other than her daughter, to lose. But she esteems herself and her daughter's life enough to risk her "respectability" in the eyes of others.[11]

Women, Anger, and Assertiveness: Jesus in the Temple

The familiar New Testament story of Jesus angrily cleansing the Temple is often used to remind us of the legitimate role of anger in a healthy life of response to God. It is especially appropriate to us as women, however, and thus bears some reflection. Fran Ferder, psychologist and spiritual writer, stresses that anger is God's gift to help mobilize us toward the ends of God's reign. As an emotion it is neutral in itself, but used with reflection and prudence it can be a powerful energizer in struggling against evil situations.[12] For instance, in the story of Jesus in John's Gospel,

> It is not the commercialism or dishonest business transactions that disturb Jesus. Rather, he feels that the temple is being destroyed.... What Jesus is attacking is the religious system: a system requiring buying and bartering for something tangible in order to be worthy of offering sacrifice. Jesus attacks the oppressive structure which denies the reality that pilgrimage people are good enough without goats, pigeons, or lambs. Their inherent goodness stands on its own merits.[13]

What Jesus did out there in the courtyard of the Temple "was not very pretty."[14] Sometimes such a strong reaction is called for, but it cannot be haphazard or without reflection. Just as Jesus was a reflector, who acted out of his anger only when he saw it as a necessary alternative, so we are called to the responsible and thoughtful use of anger:

> People who are filled with a tremendous amount of energy to bring about the . . . reign of God, . . . people who are really filled with zeal for God's house, have two things. They have sustained anger out of which their energy comes and they also have at least one eye on the Gospel, and it is from the Gospel that they draw a sense of direction. They are very careful that the methods and tactics that they use to break down barriers have threads of connection with the Gospel they are fighting for. When that connection is not there, we are not filled with zeal for God's house.[15]

It may be worthwhile to recall here the distinction between anger and assertiveness. Jesus was more than assertive — he was angry! And, as Ferder has pointed out, that is a natural biological occurrence that we can, with care, channel into energy for correcting oppressive situations that obstruct the coming of God's reign. Anger, however, carries with it an element of aggression (one of the few things men seem to have more of than women). Habitual aggression is not particularly good for our own bodies, nor for interpersonal relationships. Aggressive people frequently get what they want in the short run, but trample on other people in the process. Through assertive behavior we stand up for our own rights, dignity, and self-worth while preserving those of other people. Assertion is sustained out of a deep conviction of the rightness of our need or our goal and our own sense of ourselves as worthy human beings. It enables us to make our goal known, with clarity and tenaciousness, like the Gentile woman we discussed above. The quality of assertiveness is a virtue for us women today because it allows us not to become victims:

> God's Divine Intention did not prepare us to be victims. When we adopt a victim's stance, instead of a sacred reverence stance toward ourselves and each other, we are subverting God's creative act. . . . Christianity is about making lovers, not victims. Victims do not make good lovers.[16]

As we have already discussed, our care for others must be balanced by esteem and care for ourselves. At the same time, genuine self-giving love of others — agape — requires that we develop a strong self to give. The virtues of assertiveness and courage will make us neither victims nor aggressors, but "good lovers."

Positive Action and Courage

Nearly all the women we have described so far have acted with a certain kind of courage. Without it they could not have exceeded the bounds of conventional expectations of women, sometimes risking their lives as readily as their reputations. Two stories from the later period of ancient Israel were written precisely to commend the courage of women in delivering the Jewish people from their enemies. While both stories are considered to be works of fiction, there is every reason to suppose that real women in Jewish history acted with similar courage, although perhaps under less spectacular circumstances. In any case, these women were intended as models and heroines for Israel.

Judith

The book of Judith is not a part of the Hebrew or Protestant canon, but it can be found in Catholic Bibles or among the apocryphal books in Protestant Bibles. This book tells the story of the siege of the town of Bethulia in Israel by one of King Nebuchadnezzar's generals, Holofernes. The city is desperate. Without water, men, women, and children are dying from thirst. The crowd implores the city's defenders to capitulate to Holofernes' army although it will mean becoming slaves and breaking some of the Mosaic laws. Judith is described as a wealthy, beautiful, and pious widow who, with the help of another "woman of affairs" (Jth. 8:10 JB), manages her late husband's estate. Uzziah, leader of the town's forces, says of her, "Today is not the first time your wisdom has been shown, but from the beginning of your life all the people have recognized your understanding, for your heart's disposition is right" (Jth. 8:29–30, RSV). However, Uzziah's flattery is followed by his condescending advice to Judith to go and pray for rain! Judith is clearly too smart to follow that advice. She replies, "Listen to me. I intend to *do* something . . . " (Jth. 8:32, JB, emphasis added). She does, however, go and pray in sackcloth and ashes. In contemplating an act of violence she recalls her father Simeon's use of the sword to vindicate the violation of a virgin. She asks the Lord, "the shatterer of war," to break the violence of the Assyrians "by your might" and to "give the needful courage to this widow's hand" (9:2–19).

Although we can see in this story the masculine assumption that one final act of violence will be able to bring violence to an end, the author also portrays a certain healthy horror and fear of entering into this cycle of violence on Judith's part. Judith takes off her widow's clothes, grooms and dresses herself in her finest, and with her woman servant goes off to the camp of Holofernes. She claims to have come because of her distress at her compatriots' breaking of God's law, which she feels will lead to their imminent defeat. Holofernes, charmed and desirous of her, treats her with apparent respect, invites her to a meal in his tent a few days later, and then tries to seduce her. However, he falls asleep from drunkenness before getting too far, and Judith is able to decapitate him as he sleeps. She returns to Bethulia with his head, the Jews attack, and the army of Holofernes flees (Jth. 10–15).[17]

One could read this story as one of a woman co-opted into imitating male violence. There may be some truth to such a criticism, but we can also read it as a story of a woman, inevitably part of a violent society, who felt called upon to take an active role to relieve her city's suffering rather than to sit by and let its leaders abandon both hope and faith. Today women are proposing creative alternatives to all forms of violence, including those perceived as "patriotic duty." But Judith is still a reminder that women are called to take an active role in our political communities. Like Judith, we "intend to do something" to transform our situations. We do it, with prayerful reflection, and with a prudent understanding that action and decision carry heavy responsibilities and sometimes ambiguous consequences.

Esther

Of all the stories about women in Hebrew Scripture Esther's story may be the one best known to us. Unlike Judith she does not seem to have been naturally endowed with self-confidence and independence. One commentator notes that the evidence of the story indicates just the opposite. She was apparently an orphan raised by her cousin Mordecai under a very strict regime. She belonged to the Jewish community in Persia, descendants of the Babylonian exiles. She was taught to be a traditional woman in every way — submissive, obedient, charming in her quiet self-effacement. Selected in a sort of beauty contest to become part of King Ahasuerus' harem, she ultimately is chosen to be his queen:

> [Esther] was a very timid young lady. Her passivity is emphasized.... She was put in the charge of Hegai, overseer of the harem, where she immediately found favor in Hegai's eyes.... Hegai was a eunuch. Womanly wiles could not have made an impression upon him.... The only answer is that Esther had to be likeable. As Midrash avers, she must, truly, have had charm. More, she was submissive, demanding nothing, accepting her lot, making no waves. Who wouldn't like such a charge?[18]

Mordecai appears as an unbending, undiplomatic man who refuses to bow down to the newly-promoted Haman, a sort of chancellor to the king. Angered by this, and discovering that Mordecai was a Jew, Haman convinces the king to carry out a massive pogrom against all the Jews in

the empire. Mordecai dresses in sackcloth and ashes and makes quite a
scene at the palace gates. Esther's timidity is evident again. Embarrassed
and confused by Mordecai's action, she sends down some clothes for him
to wear, and only later inquires as to what is wrong. Thus, "it was upon
this obedient and careful young woman that a tidal wave descended."[19]
Mordecai tells Esther to go to the king and ask for the withdrawal of
the terrible edict against the Jews. Esther, undoubtedly terrified, reminds
Mordecai that anyone, including herself, who approaches the king unbid-
den risks being slain immediately, unless the king reaches out his sceptre
toward the person. And, after all, she hadn't been called to the king for
thirty days, so she has no reason to believe she will find special favor
with him. Mordecai replies with several arguments:

> Do not suppose that, because you are in the king's palace, you are
> going to be the one Jew to escape. No; if you persist in remaining
> silent at such a time, relief and deliverance will come to the Jews
> from another place, but both you and the House of your father will
> perish. Who knows perhaps you have come to the throne for just
> such a time as this? (Esther 4:12–14)

Is it the carrot or the stick that convinces Esther? There was imminent
danger of her death no matter what Esther chose, but the appeal to the
responsibility incumbent upon her now that she had the outward status
of royalty seems to have awakened a sense in Esther that God's hand
had indeed led her to this moment:

> For there can be little doubt she must often have wondered how it
> was possible that she, who was so unequipped, could have been
> chosen queen.... Her fate, then, was no longer a mystery or an
> astonishment; it has been ordained. At the same time, it evoked
> that conduct inherent in majesty, for if she was, indeed, royal, being
> appointed by Providence Itself, she dared not be servile. How else
> explain her instant metamorphosis? How else explain this timid
> mouse of an Esther suddenly speaking with imperial accents?... "If
> I perish, I perish" (4:16).[20]

The story ends, as we know, with Esther rising to her new sense of calling and approaching the king. In the apocryphal Greek additions, she
is described as nearly fainting from fear as she enters the king's hall.
She initially finds favor with the king, but must still act with great diplomacy and circumspection over a number of days, before the triumph
over Haman and the reversal of the edict is complete. Frieda Hyman
summarizes her story in the following way:

Rarely has so poorly equipped a woman grappled so heroically with
so dangerous a challenge. As lacking as her cousin-father was in
judgment and diplomacy, so was she endowed with hitherto hidden
or smothered intelligence, intuition, and courage.[21]

Many of us, with a little imagination, can identify with Esther. We are
not often called upon to confront kings in order to save our communities, but we are often in positions where we are fearful to approach
figures of authority — both male and female — even though justice and
love are in danger of being violated. Sometimes we, like Esther, are
surprised to find ourselves suddenly in positions of some power and authority ourselves. It might even be the case that our traditional feminine
qualities of charm, accommodation, and "niceness" got us there. When
the group from which we come (ordinary workers, other working parents,
or women in the "lower ranks") is experiencing injustice or oppression,
even in small ways, are we ready like Esther to say, "Perhaps I have
come to this position for just such a time as this?" We will probably not
need to say, "If I perish, I perish," but we may need to say, "If I lose my
job, I lose my job." While the risk is very real, we may find, like Esther,
that in acting decisively and with courage, we not only retain credibility
and admiration among our colleagues and superiors, we fulfill a calling
of love that our communities will long remember.

Perpetua and Felicitas

In our search for womanly "profiles in courage" it seems worthwhile
to leave the Bible briefly in order to recount the story of two exceptional
women of early Christianity. Although the stories of Christian martyrs are
often excessively "pious" and unrealistically glowing in their accounts,
there can be little doubt that underneath these legendary accounts were
real people whose courage and faith were witnessed by their communities
and attested to by secular sources. In introducing the description of these
two women's martyrdom, Rosemary Ruether writes,

Becoming a martyr might not seem like a liberating leadership role
for women. Martyrdom has come to be associated with a long-
suffering endurance of women's suppression by patriarchy. But
in early Christianity the woman martyr was seen quite differently.
Martyrdom among the more radical groups of early Christians was
seen as both the highest act of resistance against the evil power of
the state that represented the Kingdom of Evil, and also the clos-
est possible identification with Christil. . . . Resistance to the state also
sanctioned the right of Christian women to reject the claims of the
patriarchal family. The high-born Roman woman Perpetua spurns

the claims of her father, as well as the appeal to her recent motherhood, to brave the conflict.[22]

In the existing account, several young catechumens — those preparing for
baptism — are arrested together. Perpetua is a young matron of about
twenty-two with an infant son who is still nursing. Felicitas, her slave-
girl, was eight months pregnant. The first part of the story is told by
Perpetua herself. Her father comes to convince her to change her mind:

"Have regard to your brothers, have regard to your mother and
your aunt, have regard to your son, who will not be able to live
after you. Lay aside your courage and do not bring us all to de-
struction; for none of us will speak in freedom if you should suffer
anything." ... And I grieved over the grey hairs of my father, that he
alone of all my family would not rejoice over my passion.... Then,
because my child had been used to receive suck from me, and to
stay with me in prison, I sent Pomponius the deacon to my father
to ask for the infant, but my father would not give it to him. And
even as God willed it, the child no longer desired the breast, nor
did my breast cause me uneasiness, lest I should be tormented by
care for my babe and by the pain of my breasts at once.[23]

The story continues with the account of Felicitas's delivery of her child
while she is in prison awaiting martyrdom:

As the day of the exhibition was drawing near, she [Felicitas] was
in great grief lest on account of her pregnancy she should be delayed — because pregnant women are not allowed to be publicly
punished — they poured forth their prayer to the Lord three days
before the exhibition. Immediately after their prayer her pains came
upon her, and when with the difficulty natural to an eight month's
delivery, in the labour of bringing forth she was sorrowing, some
one of the servants of the Cataractarii said to her, "You who are in
such suffering now, what will you do when you are thrown to the
beasts...." Thus she brought forth a little girl, which a certain sister
brought up as her daughter.[24]

The story continues,

And so stripped and clothed with nets, they were led forth. The
populace shuddered as they saw one young woman of delicate
frame, and another with breasts still drooping from her recent
childbirth.[25]

The constant reminders of the maternity of these two women, associated in a patriarchal culture with weakness and dependency of character, present a vivid contrast to the steely courage with which they ultimately meet their fate. These are not ethereal virgin martyrs, but flesh-and-blood women who despite their single-minded faith knew and felt fully the joys of ordinary home life that they were surrendering. They suffered and cried out in childbirth just like other women, they feared the pain of overfull breasts when a child is weaning. They were not impervious to the natural pains of women, nor would they be merely stoic in what was to follow. Briefly we catch a glimpse of the love that had grown up between them, despite the differences in their station, and the strength they lent to each other. After their first confrontation with the wild beasts,

> She [Perpetua] rose up; and when she saw Felicitas crushed, she approached and gave her hand, and lifted her up. And both of them stood together; and the brutality of the populace being [momentarily] appeased, they were recalled to the Sanavivarian gate.[26]

In the final scene of this drama, the martyrs exchange the kiss of peace, and Perpetua's last act of courage is described:

> The rest indeed, immovable and in silence, received the sword-thrust.... But Perpetua, that she might taste some pain, being pierced between the ribs, cried out loudly, and she herself placed the wavering right hand of the youthful gladiator to her throat. Possibly such a woman could not have been slain unless she herself had willed it, because she was feared by the impure spirit.[27]

The physical bravery of Perpetua fills us with a mixture of dread and awe. But the moral courage and solidarity of these women is of even greater interest to us today. Not only did they face the fear of physical pain and death, but they faced grief and anger from members of their family. (Perpetua's father, we recall, wouldn't let her see her child while she was in prison.) We can surmise that, especially without the support they drew from each other, they could have been plagued with self-doubt and self-reproach for apparently abandoning their infant children. They must certainly have been reproached as "unnatural" mothers by most of their society. It is interesting that the Christian church, which has always revered the vocation of motherhood, nevertheless has also affirmed that there are vocations which take precedence over it, or in which maternity and a call to radical Christian witness are combined. These mother-martyrs had a public and historical vocation that transcended, but did not negate, their vocation to motherhood. Like so many women today in South Africa, in Latin America, and in our own country, the call of the reign of God may mean challenging the powers of an oppressive state or institution. Painful choices must be made between the demands of family life and the need for visible witness and leadership from women. Perpetua and Felicitas knew that their son and daughter would be cared for, and they believed that their children's future would be a better one because of the witness of their mothers.

Independence, Interdependence, and Solidarity

Ruth and Naomi

Returning to Hebrew Scripture, there is one pair of women who cannot escape our notice. Like Perpetua and Felicitas, these two women stand together in history as companions who brought out the best in each other. Where the arrangements of patriarchal society drove a wedge between Sarah and Hagar, the absence of patriarchal patronage lead Ruth and Naomi to depend on each other for strength. The overt theme of the book of Ruth is the filial piety of Ruth, the Moabitess great-grandmother of King David. Yet the theme of feminine interdependence is not far from the surface. Was the biblical author unconscious of the significance of the blessing the elders utter when Boaz agrees to marry Ruth? The elders say, "May the Lord make the woman who is coming into your house, like Rachel and Leah who *together* built up the House of Israel" (Ruth 4:11, RSV, emphasis added). The obvious intent of the blessing is to ask that Ruth be as fertile as Rachel and Leah were together. (They were helped in bearing children to Jacob, we might recall, by two servant girls as well!) But for us, perhaps this phrase can remind us of how *fruitful* we can be when we work together. Ruth would never have become David's ancestress without her devotion to Naomi, or without Naomi's help. We will sketch the outlines of the story as briefly as possible.

Naomi and Elimelech and their two sons moved to Moab during a famine. The sons married the local girls Ruth and Orpah, but soon Elimelech and his two sons all die. The three women, left without any male protector or relatives in the area, were in a fairly desperate situation. Naomi is decisive. She will simply have to return to her people in Bethlehem as a poor widow, but her daughters-in-law should return to their parents' houses. They are young and might be able to marry again. Orpah eventually agrees, but Ruth "clings" to Naomi, with the moving phrases, "Wherever you go, I will go.... Your people shall be my people, and your God my God..." (Ruth 1:16, JB). Naomi must have been well-worn from her suffering, for when she returns to Bethlehem, the townspeople murmur, "Can this be Naomi?" Ruth then takes the initiative to go out and glean from the fields so that the two women will have something to eat. More or less by chance, she comes to the field of her father-in-law's relative Boaz, who has heard of her piety toward her mother-in-law, and treats her with kindness and respect (Ruth 2:1–23). The next move is Naomi's. Understanding the situation and recognizing the need to make the most of the levirate law in order to give Ruth a better life, she urges her daughter-in-law to bold and, again, unconventional action! Ruth is to sleep at the feet of Boaz and, when he wakes, to offer herself in marriage to him (Ruth 3:1–9). The dialogue between them makes it evident that Boaz is an older man, and that he thinks Ruth might be able to do better! (Ruth 3:10). He is delighted to accommodate her, however, and after clearing things up at the city gate, he marries her. Naomi becomes the nurse of their son Obed (Ruth 4:1–16).

One commentator on this story has noted how the women gradually "take charge" of the situation when they are no longer "protected" by a male "proprietor." Upon the death of their husbands, Ruth and Naomi have to be independent — they have no other choice. Although they ultimately come under the patronage of a man again, it is the man of their own choosing and the result of their combined ingenuity and mutual devotion:

> The women are the catalysts for divine intervention. Reacting to the limitations of patriarchal society, they shock, provoke, and intimidate. In 2:2 Ruth announces her intention to go gleaning in a field belonging to a person in whose eyes she can find favor.... Her ingenuity triggers Boaz's recognition of her qualities; i.e., her devotion to her mother-in-law.[28]

As many women can attest, the hard-won discovery that one *can* make it alone, without a mate or a father — or perhaps just without the *approbation* of a mate or a father — is a source of strength that changes our lives forever. Ruth and Naomi may live in Boaz's house, but one can be sure that they were in charge of their own lives. Such independence, though, is only the outcome of a healthy interdependence. For one thing, there was no pretension on Naomi's part that she and Ruth could live fulfilling lives completely outside the institutions of their own society. But most of all, both women recognized that the strength of their friendship was an invaluable resource for life in a difficult world. When Obed is born, the women say to Naomi:

> The child will be a comfort to you and the prop of your old age, for your daughter-in-law who loves you and is more to you than seven sons has given him birth. (Ruth 4:15)

The Latin root of the word "virtue," we might recall, means power, potency, or strength. All of the women we have remembered here were women of power. Their power did not lie primarily in psychological or physical violence nor in sexual seductiveness. Holofernes and Judah are the victims of their own runaway desires, and Ahasuerus and Boaz seem to respond to the genuine goodness and courage in Esther and in Ruth rather than merely to their physical attractiveness. Their power lay in their self-esteem, and in their intelligence; it lay in their courage, their assertiveness, and their independence; and it lay in their care for, and solidarity with, one another. Women's spirituality, then,

> can be characterized as socio-relational, for it is grounded in our awareness of the relationship between ourselves as individual women and our social reality. . . . We need to be in solidarity with other women as we travel our path.[29]

Our solidarity with other women today might begin with a sense of solidarity with these women who have gone before us — with Sarah and Hagar, with Tamar and Judith, with Ruth and Naomi, with Perpetua and Felicitas. It might also begin with remembering the many nameless women, like the Gentile woman of Matthew 15, whose stories we know, or even those whose stories we don't know, but in whose arms and hearts our future has been carried.

Chapter 8

Daughters of Deborah:
Rediscovering Women's Public Vocation

In order to enthuse the souls of women, a woman judged, a woman decided, a woman prophesied, a woman triumphed.
—St. Ambrose on Deborah[1]

Throughout Jewish and Christian history women have worked near the home, in the home, and far from home in a variety of economic, intellectual, and political roles. Sometimes those roles were taken for granted; at other times the women who filled them were ridiculed, fiercely opposed, or even burned as witches. It is no wonder then that despite the fact that the overwhelming majority of women have been in the public workplace in the United States in recent years, women remain ambivalent about their rights and obligations to such work. As we saw earlier, they are particularly apologetic about their right to cultural and social support when they deviate from their "traditional" role. In the United States, the Catholic bishops have been working for several years on a "Pastoral Response to Women's Concerns." In its first draft they state:

> Single and married women, with or without children, still experience the pressure to choose between upholding the values associated with women's traditional roles and contributions they want to make to society at large. They report a two-fold dilemma: guilt if they stay at home and guilt if they leave for paid work.[2]

A number of the women we interviewed spoke of their guilt at leaving their children, even when they were convinced of their need or call to work in the public sphere. One woman told us,

> The hardest part for me in my job was [when the children were] around five, six, . . . when they really realize you're gone . . . and it

118

matters to them, and they say, "Gee, Mom, I wish you didn't have to go to work...." They do that really pathetically every time.

Yet the Catholic bishops' Pastoral Response goes on to say,

Our heritage teaches that women should be free to choose to work or not to work outside the home.[3]

If, as women of faith, we can understand the authentic basis of that choice, perhaps we can alleviate some of the guilt and some of the ambivalence women are feeling as they struggle to live a life that integrates the public and private dimensions of their vocation. There is, of course, a hidden irony in the statement above, for while many of us have long felt called to work outside the home, a choice to "not work at home" has never been part of the equation, nor is it likely to be in the immediate future!

Although, as we have seen, women work in the public sphere for a variety of reasons, not the least of which is *necessity*, from a standpoint of faith it is appropriate to ask whether we are *intended* by God to do so. One way to approach this is to ask whether women have, historically, experienced and responded to a call from God — a vocation — to work in the sphere of public culture. To answer this in the affirmative, as we intend to do, is not to say that all women experience exactly the same call nor that all women will live out their call in exactly the same way.

In this chapter we will first look at the notion of "vocation" and "public vocation" more closely. Then, in this chapter and the next we will try to discover precedents and models for our affirmation of women's experience of a public calling. Our "models" come from Hebrew Scripture, from the New Testament, from the High Middle Ages, and from the nineteenth century. Despite the fact that they come from four different millennia, there are some themes that recur in these women's stories. One theme is the conviction these women have that they are stewards of the talents that have been given to them. Consequently they express a strong need to "be useful." Another is the sense of obligation or impulsion that comes both from the concrete experience that has shaped their identity and from an explicit sense of divine command. A third theme that emerges is that when women respond to a call that involves them in the public sphere, their experiences in it often lead them to look at their gender in a new way. The biblical stories reviewed in this chapter leave us only hints of this latter theme, but the women we studied from the medieval period on are often led from their primary vocation into a secondary vocation that has to do with removing the obstacles and misunderstandings they have experienced as women.

Since most of us today work in occupations in the "secular" world, and since women's call to ministry has already been defended in many quarters, we have chosen to emphasize particularly, though not exclusively, women whose call was in some sense to "secular life" rather than to religious ministry.

Vocation

The notion of "calling" from God or "vocation" is a biblical notion that pervades both the Hebrew and Christian Scriptures. Yet for many centuries it lost its general character and came to be associated only with a "vocation" to an explicitly religious form of life and work. With the Reformation, secular labor — our part in the creative work of God in the world — was again understood to be a vocation of great dignity:

> Laity who had not thought that what they did in home, field or shop had any religious significance were told that their everyday work was as much a calling of God as was the praying of the monk in a cloister. "What you do in your house," said Luther, "is worth as much as if you did it up in heaven for our Lord God. For what we do in our calling here on earth in accordance with His word and command He counts as if it were done in heaven for Him."[4]

Vocation as Divine Invitation and Authentic Self-Discovery

In a study of a group of people whom its author called "resistance professionals," the notion of vocation as a source of human meaning was clearly evident, although the term was not explicitly used.

> Participants in this study spoke consistently of a link between professional work and human meaning. They described their work as closely linked to their self-understanding, a reflection of their most deeply held convictions. They spoke of their professional role in relation to ideas of direct love, direct service, and simple charity.[5]

Vocation is a key to human meaning because it implies an immediate connection between who we are as unique human persons and who we are in relation to a Divine or Transcendent Purpose for the world. It answers our questions, "Who am I?" and "What am I to do?" Of course, those answers, and hence our vocations, are not always immediately obvious. That is why the notion of vocation seems to unite a sense of divine command or "invitation" with the struggle for authentic self-discovery.

A vocation "will be a command of God addressed to a specific individual — a command that does not follow from more general ethical principles."[6] That is, what I am called to be is not just a "good person" in general, but a very specific, limited, precise kind of person. Some obligations are mine because I am a rational, moral human being; others are mine because of the particular person I am. The great Danish philosopher Kierkegaard apparently felt he had to renounce marriage to his beloved Regina in order to be the kind of person/philosopher he needed to be. Robert M. Adams discusses Kierkegaard's sense of vocation:

> Kierkegaard sees the vocation first and foremost as a vocation to be a certain kind of person — and, in the closest connection with that, to pursue certain projects which, in his view, are partially constitutive of selfhood. . . . His vocation is part of what gives him existence, his life, a unity that is humanly and morally significant. It is part of what matters about his being himself.[7]

Sometimes we wonder if there is an opposition between our own deepest desires and needs and the call of God in our lives. Often the perception of such an opposition leads us, on the one hand, away from companionship with God or, on the other hand, away from genuine self-discovery. It can be the source of much confusion and distress, particularly for us women who face many obstacles to achieving a strong personal identity and moral autonomy. But writers on vocation, as well as the women whose stories we will recount, attest to a fundamental unity between the process of self-discovery and the realization of the shape that God's call is taking in our lives. For instance, a woman might remain in a nursing career out of a sense of obligation that this is a "good thing to do" even though she is miserable and resentful doing it. What she really longs to do, and knows she can do with some success, is to play and teach violin. With serious reflection, prayer, and guidance, she may ultimately discern that to be her true calling. For some people who have difficulty discovering or responding to their calling, psychological and spiritual healing may help to liberate them from the limitations of their upbringing or the oppression of their current situation. Adams tells us that there is a mistaken conception that vocation

> . . . has nothing much to do with my own desires and feelings. But I think it would be more typical to perceive my vocation as rooted in a divine purpose for my life in particular, which precedes and conditions my desires and feelings, but which is manifested and perceived (in large part) through them and not in complete independence of them. This is an important reason for connecting vocation with selfhood. . . . It is difficult to think of God's relation to us on the model of a supervisor who distributes various tasks to subordinates with-

out its mattering very much to the selfhood of the employees which one gets which job.[8]

To claim a particular vocation for ourselves is a serious matter, since it implies a certain gift and authority from God. Thus such a belief requires reflection and testing over time. Traditional tests of a vocation include its ability to bring peace and integrity to our lives, its conformity to what our community generally believes about ethical obligations and God's purposes in the world, its foundation in a life of prayer and love, and its fruitfulness. The value of actual results as a test is a tricky one. For instance, if I turn out to be a terrible salesperson, it may be a good sign that sales are not my vocation. But if in fund-raising for the arts in a particularly difficult community I meet daily apathy and discouragement, I may still feel a deep conviction that I must go ahead and do it.[9]

Vocation, Work, and Relationships

A recent and very legitimate objection to the use of the term "vocation" arises from the dehumanizing character of work in some modern industrial contexts. When I put the same small part into an electronics board hour after hour, or when I must clean offices at night for people I never see, it is difficult to think of one's labor as a vocation, or even as part of God's call to me. It is no wonder that many of us women (and men) who must work in jobs such as these to survive see our "real" vocation in our parenting and in our family relationships. We may agree with Dorothy Sayers's vision of what work should be for us, but find it a far cry from our own lives:

> Work is not, primarily, a thing one does to live, but the thing one lives to do. It is, or should be, the full expression of the workers' faculties, the thing in which he finds spiritual, mental, and bodily satisfaction, and the medium in which he offers himself to God. . . . We should no longer think of work as something that we hastened to get through in order to enjoy our leisure; we should look on our leisure as the period of changed rhythm that refreshed us for the delightful purpose of getting on with our work.[10]

There is clearly a need to address the conditions of modern labor. When there is no possibility of a creative contribution of my uniqueness to a job, when there is no opportunity to feel its connectedness to an overall project that is worth doing, or to the community it serves, it is difficult and perhaps even harmful to conceive our labor as part of God's call to us. But when necessity involves us in such labor it is particularly important to conceive of our vocation more broadly. Our personal vocation may involve us in particular jobs, projects, or tasks, but it is not limited to these. These tasks or particular labors we may undertake may be part of our vocation, but they do not necessarily exhaust it. For instance, quite apart from our job, we may feel called to speak out on a particular issue on a regular basis throughout our life. It might be a call to humanize our workplaces, or it might be the need for stimulating local activities for our children. It is a personal, not a universal obligation, and thus, "you see it as a task that has your name on it, and religiously as a vocation or part of your vocation."[11]

Part of our vocation may also be the particular relationships in which we are involved, and to which we are uniquely responsible — relationships to our family, to our co-workers, and to our community:

> Vocation, as Reformation thought conceived it, was the calling of a life — the whole being of the person offered in the service of God.... In our time, especially in middle-class Protestantism, work has been exalted to such an extent that [the notion of] vocation is confined almost entirely to the sphere of work.... The work ethic, if it is not balanced by other emphases, can become demonic. A more balanced view of the place of daily work would be wholesome and liberating...a doctrine of vocation that claims all of existence will summon workers to attend to the concerns of the common life. This means, specifically, strengthening home and family life, taking a responsible role in politics and participating in the union movement as it strives to recover its role as an ethical force in modern society.[12]

For most of us, work in the public sphere is first of all an economic necessity. Yet, even when we work for economic survival we may come to perceive our work as an integral part of our overall vocation as persons. For "participation in the work of creation...is part of the...[biblical] ideal of life."[13] For other women and men, the need and desire to work stems more explicitly from a profound sense of being called to use their gifts and talents to contribute to their communities and to shape public culture. Desire and necessity may both be instrumental in determining the exact contours of our vocation. But, as Robert Bellah has pointed out, the communal dimension of work is essential to the notion of vocation or "calling":

> In the strongest sense of a "calling," work constitutes a practical ideal of activity and character that makes a person's work morally inseparable from his or her life.... The calling not only links a person to his or her fellow-workers. A calling links a person to the larger community, a whole in which the calling of each is a contribution to the good of all.... *The calling is a crucial link between the*

individual and the public world. Work in the sense of the calling can never be merely private.[14]

Whatever the determinant of our work life is, the desire to pursue the vocations of spouse and parent may mean that for some period of our lives we would prefer to give less than full time and energy to our vocation outside the home. As another one of our participants said,

> I'm an industrial engineer by training. I'm teaching [college] right now, but eventually I would probably want to get back in industry. I would like to be a plant manager, middle management, corporate level, that type of thing. But right now, with young children, and in that stage of my life, flexibility or...job-sharing or something is crucial so that I can keep my feet wet, and keep in touch without completely separating for awhile. Then maybe eventually I will get back into more hours.

This rhythm of energy put alternately into our private and our public labor could shape men's working lives as well as women's. Current patterns of work life make it very difficult for either parent to moderate their work commitments for a few of the prime child-rearing years.

In a 1988 report on National Public Radio, male law partners insisted that women (or men) lawyers who wanted to practice law part-time for a few years after having children, just "couldn't compete" with the lawyers who were available from "8 a.m. to 8 p.m." every day.[15] Aside from the fact that twelve-hour days are dehumanizing for anyone, such a stance indicates an incredible unwillingness to change the status quo in a creative manner. A personal physician isn't available to her clients twelve hours a day. Why should lawyers have to be? We used to expect that our personal physicians would be available to us twenty-four hours a day, until a few doctors thought better of it. Now we're satisfied that a colleague will be on call in an emergency. Lawyers are intelligent people. With a little determination and a little imagination they could change their work lives so as to include the valuable services of part-time professionals.

The Public Dimension in Every Vocation

It is our conviction, however, that the notion of a "public vocation" is broader than just paid work outside the home. It should also include any form of contribution to public culture to which we genuinely feel called by God, whether it be community theater, care of other parents' children, or environmental activism. As we saw earlier, there is clearly a public dimension to our reproductive labor. In this sense, we believe that all of us are called to a "public vocation." As one writer has expressed it, "good work, or vocation, also exemplifies a sense of social relatedness, and thereby creates community."[16] If as biblical people we recognize that a just and caring community is part of God's purpose for the world, then our focus cannot be narrowly on our own or our own family's good. But this is not a view that has wide currency in our society today. Speaking of the vocation of professionals, Robert Bellah says,

> The professional is certainly concerned . . . with service — with ends that transcend self-interest, with public good. Yet the ethic of service is subtly starved by the thin sustenance provided by civil society.[17]

Our discussion of *agape* in chapter 4 was intended to restore an understanding of self-giving love as a virtue and an obligation in the public sphere as well as in the domain of personal relationships. It is at the heart of any true vocation.

Women and Public Vocation

A New View in Our Churches

Historically, the vocation to motherhood has *not necessarily* excluded women from being called to public activity and a public vocation, nor should it today. Women, as well as men, are called by God to take responsible and influential roles in the political, intellectual, economic, spiritual, and artistic spheres of their world. And men, as well as women, are called to take responsible and influential roles in the sphere of parenting and homemaking. Increasingly this conviction is renewing even some of the more conservative of our religious communities, as they reflect seriously on our biblical heritage. A recent article in the evangelically-oriented national magazine *Christianity Today* indicates that a new understanding of our traditional roles is finding wide acceptance. In that article Ruth Tucker writes,

> Only women can give birth, and only women can nurse babies. These biological functions generally influence their attitudes toward the nurturing of young children. At the same time, women are equally suited to conduct matters outside the home. . . . Certainly no serious scholar today would argue that women are any less capable of being history teachers, medical doctors, or Supreme Court Justices. The Bible would seem to support both these contentions. The natural desire for women to have children is seen in the lives of such women as Sarah, Hannah, and Elizabeth. . . . However, Scripture also speaks of women who were involved in careers. Lydia was a seller of purple dye; Priscilla was a tentmaker with her husband;

and the woman in Proverbs 31 was involved in a variety of money-making activities outside the home. And, though arguments from omission should be considered cautiously, it is interesting to note that Jesus did not define a woman's place as in the home or say that the family and domestic duties were her primary responsibilities.[18]

The U.S. Catholic bishops' Pastoral Response to Women's Concerns, which we quoted above, also refers to Scripture in support of women's public vocation:

> Women ministered and served with Jesus throughout his life.... Women were discoverers of the empty tomb and first witnesses of the resurrection (Mt. 28:7). They, too, received the Holy Spirit at Pentecost (Acts 1:14); ...and provided homes for the breaking of the bread (Rom. 16:3; 1 Cor. 16:19). Women prophesied (Acts 21:9) and taught others about Jesus (Acts 18:26). Likewise they were persecuted and jailed with the men (Acts 8:3).[19]

Although in this passage the document focuses more on women's public ministry, in the following selection of passages, there is an unequivocal affirmation of women's secular vocations as well. The Pastoral first quotes Pope Paul VI, who in an address in 1964 called for:

> 1. The recognition of the civil rights of women as the full equals of men, whenever these rights have not yet been acknowledged;
> 2. Laws that will make it really possible for women to fill the same professional, social, and political roles as men, according to the individual capacities of the person....[20]

The document then quotes a 1987 address of Pope John Paul II in a similar vein:

> Precisely because of their equal dignity and responsibility, the access of women to public functions must be assured.[21]

Finally, the bishops state that,

> We further commit ourselves to support legislation that fosters the efforts of women to achieve professional roles and to have access to public functions on a basis equal to that of men.[22]

The tenor of these statements is matched by that of Ruth Tucker in her article in *Christianity Today:*

Clearly, women have been involved in domestic duties as well as careers and activities outside the home since biblical times. These two spheres of life are both legitimate for women and should not be viewed as necessarily incongruous.[23]

We have quoted from these two sources at some length to make it evident that in both evangelical Christianity and Roman Catholic Christianity, the tide has turned. Women's public vocation is no longer being denied. Yet such affirmations mean little if women's traditional domestic responsibilities remain exactly the same — that is, if some of those responsibilities are not assumed by men and by society at large. Fortunately, Tucker recognizes this, as do the Catholic bishops:

Churches have a unique challenge to issue to husbands, as well. . . . Past expectations of the mother being the sole keeper of the home must be revised. Christian husbands of working wives should take the lead in modeling joint parenting and housekeeping.[24]

Contemporary church teaching underlines, moreover, that both parents ought to be encouraged to view their involvement in raising children and contributing to personality formation as a participation in the most critical vocation in the church. The husband has an obligation to share in the domestic chores and in care of the children. Children benefit from the guidance and involvement of both parents. Masculine and feminine qualities are harmonized and balanced more perfectly when the child learns from both mother and father.[25]

The document of the Catholic bishops goes on to stress the church's concern that legal and social supports be in place to allow women the freedom of choice that they say is "our heritage":

While . . . women are increasingly entering decision-making positions, the rules and regulations affecting their lives are still made primarily by men. . . . To condone unjust employment practices, to refuse to abide by affirmative action required by law, to discriminate in hiring and in benefits for women who are mothers — such policies are always wrong. . . . Attentive to the special needs of women who work outside the home, we will therefore endorse laws and actions that allow for parental leaves without loss of job continuity, opportunity for advancement or diminished health and pension benefits; that seek to establish safe and affordable day-care centers near the workplace of parents; that hold fathers responsible for child support.[26]

Vocation and Our Relational Obligations

No matter how much support we have from spouses and from our societies there will be times when we feel torn. In the 1988 film *A World
Apart*, the story is told of a woman journalist in South Africa in the
early 1960s who feels called to participate actively in the struggle against
apartheid. The story centers less on the political struggle than on the
relationship between this woman (in real life, Ruth First) and her young
adolescent daughter, who suffers ridicule, loss of friendship, loneliness,
and a sense of abandonment because of her mother's arrest and impris-
onment. The mother, of course, suffers even more knowing what she is
asking of her daughter. Can a vocation that sometimes compromises our
family and relational obligations be a genuine one? Distinguishing between a true sense of vocation and merely a "strong desire" on our part
to do something, Adams reasons that a well-tested vocation can indeed
take precedence over other normal ethical obligations:

> An issue about vocation that arises quite clearly ... is whether it can
> be right to pursue a vocation when it impinges painfully on the
> interest, or even the rights, of other people.... It seems to me that a
> divine vocation, or even a subjective but plausible sense of vocation,
> or of something like vocation, does have more force than a mere
> strong desire has to override a *prima facie* obligation.... No doubt
> more than one account might be offered of what gives a sense of
> vocation more justifying force than mere desires, however intense,
> can have.... But it is hard to see why theists would not think that
> having a vocation ... from God to do something would indeed be a
> strong justification for doing it.[27]

The story of Perpetua and Felicitas recounted in chapter 7 is a precedent
for this kind of situation. Like them, the woman in *A World Apart* was
a good mother in every sense of the word, but a mother whose public
vocation could not be denied. The film ends with a note on her assas-
sination nineteen years later, but in the meantime she and her daughter
came to understand each other. Her daughter, Shawn Slovo, with great
pride, has told her story in the screenplay for the film. Our selfhood is at
stake in our response to the divine call. If we are less than our best selves,
less than committed to communities that transcend our own families, we
will have little legacy to leave to our children.

Women in Public Vocations in Hebrew Scripture

We do not know much about Deborah's natural children, but we do know
she was "a mother in Israel" (Judg. 5:7) and that she has left us, her

daughters, a great inheritance. Before reflecting on her story, though, let us take a more general look at women's participation in Israelite society.

Women's Economic Role

It seems evident from many texts that, despite their low legal and social status, women's active participation in economic life was taken for granted during much of Israel's history. As Tucker noted, the woman of Proverbs 31 undertakes a great deal of independent business:

> She gets up while it is still dark,
>   giving her household their food,
>   giving orders to her servant girls.
> She sets her mind on a field, then she buys it;
>   with what her hands have earned she plants a vineyard.
> She puts her back into her work
>   and shows how strong her arms can be....
> She holds out her hand to the poor,
>   she opens her arms to the needy....
> She makes her own quilts,
>   she is dressed in fine linen and purple....
> She weaves linen sheets and sells them,
>   she supplies the merchant with sashes.
>   (Prov. 31:15–17, 20, 22, 24, JB)

This "superwoman's" economic prowess even reflects positively on her husband, for

> Her husband is respected at the city gates,
>   taking his seat among the elders of the land.
>   (Prov. 31:23, JB)

Though we do not know exactly what period of Israel's history this writing comes from, as an ideal it apparently had a long-standing appeal. Much agricultural work falls to women in peasant societies. Israel was undoubtedly no exception. The woman above "plants a vineyard" on land she has bought herself. A woman like Ruth, with no land of her own, would have to resort to "gleaning" what she could from the fields of others. Judith, with the help of her "woman of affairs," was the manager of her late husband's estate (Jth. 8:10).

In the latter period of ancient Israel there appears to have been a Jewish version of "putting hubby through college." We are told,

Women were entrusted with maintaining their husband's shops or being guardians or even creditors. The practice which became common among the rabbis was for their wives to maintain the family *and business* while the husband and possibly the older son studied the Law. Rabbi Akiba credited his wife for his wisdom because she supported him for years while he studied. This was long seen as an ideal of Jewish social practice.[28]

Women's economic role in ancient Israel was not necessarily any measure of her liberation, unless, like Judith, she were independently wealthy. But it does testify to a longstanding and more or less universal tradition that women's contributions are as essential to the economic sphere as to the domain of child-rearing. Only a very foreshortened view of history and anthropology could argue otherwise.

Women as Prophets, Social Critics, and Political Advisors

The role of the prophet in Israel lies somewhere between that of a religious revivalist and that of a social critic. Among the few but prominent women who are called prophets are Miriam, Deborah, and Huldah. Caught between God's call and the people's expectations, the role of prophet was never an easy one. As a woman prophet, Miriam had the added trouble of being a threat to her brother Moses' authority. Miriam is called a prophet when she leads the women of Israel in singing and dancing to celebrate the victory over the Egyptians (Exod. 15:20ff.). But when she and her other brother, Aaron, challenge Moses' authority, God comes down on Moses' side. Still, in affirming Moses' particular call, there is no suggestion that Miriam is not just as authentically a prophet. In Micah 6:4, Miriam, Aaron, and Moses are all venerated as leaders of the Exodus.[29]

We saw in chapter 5 how the two wise women of the book of Samuel fulfilled roles that can best be described as those of social critic and political advisor. One admonished a king for his self-pity; another brought about the end of a siege by her diplomacy.[30]

Much later, toward the end of the Deuteronomic History, we find the prophetess Huldah delivering the word of the Lord to King Josiah (640–609 B.C.E.). She is apparently from the town of Anathoth, the center of the "northern" or "Moses" tradition that retained the egalitarian leanings of early Israel. King Josiah's men have discovered the "Book of the Torah," which the previous leaders of Judah had abandoned. Josiah is distressed when he hears the Torah read and asks Hilkiah the high priest to find out what he is to do. Hilkiah consults Huldah, who does not mince words in denouncing Judah's unfaithfulness to the Lord. But she also announces God's recognition of Josiah's repentance and his deliverance from the disasters to come. There is nothing to distinguish Huldah from her male counterparts. Like them she delivers God's word for Israel, and like them she is revered as a prophet.[31]

Deborah

As the only woman among the judges who led Israel between the time of Moses and of Saul, Deborah is perhaps unique in holding an official position of political leadership. The judges came to their positions as a result of personal charisma, and Deborah must have had a great deal of it. She is called judge *and* prophet (Judg. 4:4). That means she rendered legal and personal decisions, she was a military leader, and she spoke God's word to her community. When she calls for the military man Barak to tell him how he is to defeat the opposing army, he refuses to go into battle unless she accompanies him. She marches to battle with him (Judg. 4:10), but reproves him for his reluctance. In fact, the battle is won because another bold woman, Jael, pounds a tent peg through the head of the enemy's commander, Sisera. Deborah had told Barak it would be that way:

> "I will go with you then," she said, "but the way you are going about it, the glory will not be yours; for Yahweh will deliver Sisera into the hands of a woman." (Judg. 4:9, JB)

When the battle is over the triumph is celebrated in a song praising God's deliverance through the hands of Deborah, "a mother in Israel," and Jael, "blessed among women" (Judg. 5:7, 24). Given Deborah's importance in the primitive history of Israel, it is obvious that a woman's call from God may take her far from the domestic sphere. Yet hopefully, it will not take her far from the nurturing concern for her community that makes her also "a mother *of* Israel." Pam Scalise reminds us that,

> Extraordinary women like Miriam, Deborah, and Huldah are the exceptions that shatter the rule of male dominance in Israelite society. Their ministries are evidence that women are not disqualified by their gender from positions of leadership and they are not exempt from God's call to serve.[32]

Women in Public Vocations in New Testament Christianity

In chapter 5 we dealt with some aspects of the status of women as reflected in the New Testament. In particular, we noted that underneath

the obvious evidences of patriarchalism, we can clearly detect an egalitarian tradition, undoubtedly originating with Jesus and continuing, perhaps
with some practical modifications, through Paul's lifetime. In this section
we will concentrate on evidence of the public roles women filled, both
in the early church and in the secular world to which they belonged.

Women Apostles

The term "disciple" (*mathetes*, "student") ordinarily refers to any of Jesus'
followers, but the term "apostle" (*apostolos*, "envoy" or "messenger") is
usually reserved to those of the inner Christian circle who witnessed Jesus' resurrection and had a special mission in the early community. A
common objection to women's public leadership in Christian communities is that "if Jesus had wanted women to do such things, why did he
choose only men as apostles?" One traditional response to such an objection is simply to point out the overwhelming patriarchy of Jesus' and
the New Testament writers' culture, which would have made women in
"official" positions of teaching and leadership an impossibility. But, in
fact, we now have excellent evidence that the earliest church *did* recognize some women as "apostles," as well as in a variety of other public
roles. The Gospels indicate that women met the criteria of apostleship
and were recognized as the first witnesses of the resurrection, despite
efforts to play down their role by the men who wrote these Gospels and
by the later church. Schüssler Fiorenza writes,

> According to Paul all those Christians were apostles who fulfilled
> two conditions: they had to be (1) eyewitnesses to the resurrection
> and (2) commissioned by the resurrected Lord to missionary work
> (cf. 1 Cor. 9:4). Luke...maintains that only those Christians were
> eligible to replace Judas who had accompanied Jesus in his min-
> istry and had also witnessed the resurrection. According to all four
> Gospels, women fulfilled these criteria of apostleship that Paul and
> Luke have spelled out.... According to all criteria of historical au-
> thenticity women were the first witnesses of the resurrection. This
> fact could not have been imagined in Judaism or invented by the
> primitive Church.[33]

Schüssler Fiorenza goes on to point out that these first witnesses to the
resurrection are identified by name, and thus must have been well-known
and have played important roles in the beginnings of the Christian movement in Palestine. Mary of Magdala was probably foremost among them,
since all four Gospels record her name. The names of those who accompanied her vary.[34] Much confusion has surrounded the identity of Mary
Magdalene; she is popularly thought of as the prostitute who repented

of her life, wiping Jesus' feet with her tears. There is no clear evidence in the Gospels that this is the case. The woman who wipes Jesus' feet with her tears (Luke 7:36–50) is anonymous. There is no reason to identify her with Mary Magdalene, who is mentioned in Luke 8:2 along with Joanna and others. Mary Magdalene and her friend Joanna are also mentioned in Luke's resurrection narrative (24:9–11). As often happens (for instance, in our "Christmas story" or in popular works such as the musical *Jesus Christ Superstar*), different gospel texts and even different Gospels have been conflated to create a kind of mythology of Mary Magdalene. Describing this process, Ruether writes:

> Although Mary is said to have been healed by Jesus of "seven demons" this kind of healing always refers in the New Testament to some kind of violent illness (epilepsy) and not to sins such as prostitution.... By combining these texts, the Church paints a picture of Mary Magdalene as weeping sinner, thereby displacing her from her original high status as the leader of the faithful remnant of Jesus' apostles who founds the Church's kerygma of the resurrection.[35]

The repentant prostitute may be an important symbol for us to retain in Christian spirituality, but it was most likely *not* Mary Magdalene. Mary Magdalene is the first to whom Jesus appears after the resurrection and the first to be commissioned by Jesus to bring this Good News to the "brothers" (John 20:1–18; Matt. 28:1–7; Mark 16:1–8; and Luke 24:1–11). As such, she is an exalted symbol of women's apostleship.

Junia is the one instance in the New Testament where a woman is actually called by the title "apostle." Not only that, but with her husband, Andronicus, she is "outstanding among the apostles" (Rom. 16:7). Junia and Andronicus are a missionary couple, who were converted before Paul. At the time Romans was written, they, like Paul, are prisoners for their activity. The fact that a woman is explicitly called an apostle was hidden from us for centuries (and still is, in most translations of the Bible) because somewhere along the line male translators or copyists, convinced that no woman could be an apostle, changed her name to "Junias," a masculine form. But the evidence of the church fathers makes it clear that she was indeed "Junia":

> From all the Church Fathers up to about the 12th century...all give the name of either Junia or Julia (a minority).... Origen's view that Andronicus and Junia were among the 72 sent out by Jesus as recorded in Luke 10 is often repeated.... The Fathers cited agree that a woman Junia or Julia...is to be understood here.[36]

Like Mary Magdalene, Junia was clearly called to a life of public witness and preaching.

Women Prophets

Women were also recognized as prophets in the primitive Christian community. In Acts 2:17, Luke has Peter quote the prophet Joel, who tells us that in the new dispensation both "their sons and daughters shall prophesy." In Acts 21:9 there is mention of Philip's four daughters who were all prophets. As we saw in chapter 5, Paul takes it for granted that women are prophets; he just insists that they perform their ministry in a proper fashion (i.e., with their veils on!). The gift of prophecy is second only to apostleship in Paul's estimation (1 Cor. 12:28). The *Didache* of the second century regards prophets as the normal ones to preside at the Eucharist. Presbyters (*presbyteros*, "elders" or "leaders") did so only when there was no authentic prophet present.[37] Ruether tells us that

> the communities of biblical faith never denied that God's Spirit might empower whoever it wills and that this might include women. Prophecy represents the power of freedom and newness of life in which God's word breaks in to speak in judgment on established modes of life and to open up new possibilities.[38]

This freedom of women in the loose structure of the first few decades of Christianity rapidly gives way to the reinstatement of patriarchalism, and women's public ministry in the church is increasingly eclipsed. The role of feminine deacon, however, is one that survived for at least several centuries, albeit with lesser authority.

Women Deacons and Local Church Leaders

There was no way for later translators of the Bible to alter Phoebe's name. It jumps out at us from the first verse of Romans 16. In Greek she is given the title *diakonos*, which is always translated "deacon" or "minister" when it refers to a man. But in her case, it inevitably comes out "deaconess":

> Phoebe receives the titles *diakonos* and *prostasis*. Exegetes take pains to downplay the significance of both titles because they are given to a woman.... The second title of Phoebe, *prostasis*, is usually translated as "helper" or "patroness" even though in the literature of the time it has the connotation of leading officer, president, governor, or superintendent. In 1 Tim. 3:4–5; 5:17, the verb characterizes the functions of the bishop, deacons, or elders. Phoebe had, therefore,

a leadership role in the community of Cenchreae and was a person
with authority for many and for Paul as well.[39]

Gradually, an actual distinction grows between the roles of male deacons
and female "deaconesses" who are reduced to catechizing and baptizing
women and children. But originally it seems that women deacons held a
high place. When the Syrian *Didascalia* was written, sometime before 250
C.E., deacons and deaconesses come right after bishops in the church's
incipient hierarchy, and they are mentioned before presbyters. Female
as well as male deacons were thus seen as ordained members of the
"clergy."[40]

There were a number of other women who are mentioned in the
greetings and farewells of Paul's letters who seem to have been important local church leaders, perhaps even presiders at the gatherings held
in their houses. Among these are Apphia, a leader of the house church at
Colossae (Phil. 2); Nympha, in whose house the church of Laodicea met;
and Lydia, who helps to establish the church in the district of Philippi
(Acts 16:14–15, 40). Women like Lydia were probably fairly well-to-do
and thus had a house large enough to invite others for gatherings and for
the "breaking of the bread." They could help support missionary workers, and as hostesses they undoubtedly exercised significant influence
over their local communities.

We have not yet mentioned Paul's great co-worker, Prisca (or Pris-
cilla), who with her husband, Aquila, was a missionary and founding
member of the churches at both Corinth and at Ephesus. They are referred to in Acts 18:2, 26; Rom. 16:3; 1 Cor. 16:19; and 2 Tim. 4:19.
Thrown out of Rome by the edict of Claudius (c. 49 C.E.), they came first
to Corinth, and later followed Paul to Ephesus, where the young church
met in their house. Was Prisca just her husband's helper? Based on
the fact that Prisca's name is usually mentioned before her husband's,
Schüssler Fiorenza concludes that she must have been the leading figure
in Christian circles.[41]

Early Church Women in Secular Vocations

Although the women discussed above clearly exercised public vocations in their religious communities, should we conclude that Christian
women's vocations should be limited to ministerial ones? In fact, many of
the women we have mentioned also had important economic roles in the
secular sphere. In some cases it was these economic roles that made them
valuable to the Christian community — not just as patrons and house-
leaders, but as women who traveled, or whose employees traveled, and
who could thus act as messengers and liaisons between various early
churches. Lydia was a businesswoman "in the purple-dye trade" (Acts

16:14). She came from the town of Thyatira in Asia Minor, but apparently now owned a house in the city of Philippi, northeast of Greece. Since Thyatira was known as the center of the trade in purple goods, Lydia must have been a commercial agent in Philippi for the industry of Thyatira, probably traveling back and forth occasionally, as her business demanded. We know that Prisca and Aquila were both tentmakers, a trade they shared with Paul himself (Acts 18:3). In 1 Corinthians we read that "Chloe's people" have brought news of Corinth to Paul. She must have been a well-to-do woman with employees who traveled for her business. Phoebe, whose home was in Cenchreae, the port of Corinth, is the bearer of the letter to the Romans. It seems that she also was a well-traveled and independent woman (she was a *prostasis*, or "patron," as well as a deacon) with secular affairs to attend to in Rome.

We don't know much about these women's family lives, although given the culture of the time we can assume that they were all married at one time or another and probably had children. Family responsibilities, in any case, did not prevent them from pursuing either secular careers or a call to ministry. There is never a hint from Luke or Paul that these industrious and influential women were doing anything that was inappropriate to their Christian calling. In fact, quite the opposite is true. Luke and Paul point to these women as sterling examples of early Christian witness.

Hildegard of Bingen:
Healer, Preacher, Musician, and Scholar

If she had been born in the twentieth century she would have been a doctor, a philosopher, or perhaps an astronomer. Born in 1098, she was all of these and much more, under the liberating mantle of being a visionary abbess of a growing German monastery. Hildegard of Bingen has been called "a Renaissance woman, several centuries before the Renaissance" and an "ideal model of the liberated woman."[42] There are other women of the medieval period whom we might have selected as models — queens, saint-reformers, and soldiers — but Hildegard is unique in the way she gave free rein to her keen intellectual curiosity and her considerable creative talents, despite her confinement in the role of cloistered nun. She combined a sense of religious impulsion or mystic vision with practical knowledge and wisdom gained in very ordinary ways. Her writing, music, and preaching influenced the public culture of her time at every level of society from illiterate peasants to emperors and popes.

Hildegard, whose life spans four-fifths of the twelfth century, was the tenth of ten children of aristocratic parents. She was offered to God as a child of eight, apparently as a kind of "tithe." One might argue whether Hildegard was better off than her peers or not: Was it better to be expected to renounce marriage and family life or to end up in a marriage that might well be oppressive and miserable if one's parents happened to make an unfortunate choice. Hildegard probably had little to say about it, but whatever disadvantages there were to her assigned lifestyle, the great advantage was that she was put under the tutelage of the woman hermit, Jutta, and received from her an education that was utterly exceptional for any woman of her day. The women under Jutta's guidance grew gradually to a sizeable monastic community that lived in quarters adjoining the men's monastic community at Disibode. Hildegard apparently learned to read and write Latin and German and she also learned the theology, science, and medicine of her day. Living in the joint monastery of Disibode gave her the chance to know men, understand their natures, and to share many of their interests. This is evident in what might be termed her "psychological" writings — typologies of different kinds of men and different kinds of women.

When Jutta died in 1136, Hildegard was chosen abbess of the women's community. She soon decided to move the community to a new cloister to be built near the town of Bingen. There was considerable resistance to this move, but the demands of space (and perhaps of independence) made it a reasonable one. The move was not completed however until 1151. Except for her various preaching journeys she remained there until her death in 1179.

During these years, first as student, then as mature woman and abbess, Hildegard's curiosity and ability led her in many different directions. There was no question of her faith and piety, but she combined her religious sensitivity with a search for wisdom that made few distinctions (in accordance with her medieval culture) between knowledge of the universe, knowledge of human nature, and knowledge of God. Matthew Fox tells us,

Her interests and accomplishments include science: her books explore cosmology — stones, rocks, trees, plants, birds, fishes, animals, star and winds. They include music: her opera, Ordo Virtutum, is on record and has been playing live by a European group called Sequentia in both Europe and North America, and she wrote about seventy other extant songs. They include theology: her book Scivias [Know the Ways of the Lord] is a study of biblical texts and ecclesial practice combined with personal insight and criticism. They include painting: Scivias, for example, contains thirty-six renditions of her images or visions. They include healing at the personal level: she writes of the appropriate herbs and remedies for psychic and physical ailments — and at the social level: many of her sermons and letters, in particular, take on issues of social disease and injustice. Hildegard was painter and poet, musician and healer, theologian and prophet, mystic and abbess, playwright and social critic.[43]

In addition to incorporating wide scientific knowledge into her theological writings, Hildegard wrote several strictly medical/scientific books. She wrote a medical/scientific encyclopedia, *Nine Books on the Subtleties of Different Kinds of Creatures*, also known as the *Book of Simple Medicine*, or *Physica*. It includes a comprehensive treatment of herbs, of rocks and precious stones, and a bestiary. She also wrote a book on medical diseases and cures known as *Causes and Cures* or the *Book of Compound Medicine*.[44]

By the time of the completion of her first work, *Scivias*, in 1151, Hildegard was already well-known in her part of the world. With a freedom quite unlike what we would expect for a medieval woman, Hildegard engaged in extensive public preaching and teaching:

> Between 1158 and 1159 Hildegard travelled along the Main, preaching at monastic communities in Mainz, Wertheim, Wurzburg, Kitzingen, Ebrach, and Bamberg. Her second trip in 1160 took her to Metz, Krauftal, [and] Trier, where she preached publicly. Within the next three years she visited Boppart, Andernach, Siegburg, and Werden, addressing clergy and people together at Cologne. After 1170 she undertook her fourth and final journey in Swabia, preaching at Roden, Kirchan, Maulbronn, Hirsaw, Kircheim, and Zweifalten.[45]

We can assume from these wide ventures that no one in the contemporary church doubted her vocation to a public ministry among them. Nor did anyone object to her writing medical and scientific works, even though she did not claim any particular divine inspiration for them. No one was going to tell a woman like Hildegard to "pray her prayers," stay at home, or keep quiet.

Yet in this period for a woman to gain such authority and freedom was hardly the normal thing. Hildegard claims visions or "an inner vision" as the source of her impulsion to write and speak. At the beginning of her last book, *The Book of Divine Works*, she describes her call to write it in terms of a heavenly voice:

> It was in the year 1163.... A voice from heaven resounded saying to me: "O wretched creature and daughter of much toil, even though you have been thoroughly seared, so to speak, by countless grave sufferings of the body, the depth of the mysteries of God has completely permeated you. Transmit for the benefit of humanity an accurate account of what you see with your inner eye and what you hear with the inner ear of your soul...."[46]

In fact, it is probable that both her declarations of humility and her insistence on divine inspiration were necessary in order for her writings to be taken with any seriousness. Newman tells us,

> Had she not claimed her gift as a mark of divine authority, no one would have listened to her. Many have suggested that, in an age when the Apostles' command that "no woman is to teach or have authority over men" (1 Tim. 2:12) was rigorously enforced, it was only through visions that a religious or intellectual woman could gain a hearing.[47]

Hildegard's vocation, like most authentic vocations, probably came to her both out of a gradual grasp of her own gifts and identity, and out of her sense of an "inner voice" impelling her to share those gifts with the community. That she struggled to understand and test her vocation, and that it flowed out of her natural gifts and previous training, is evident in her first letter written to the great monastic founder Bernard of Clairvaux:

> I know in Latin text the meaning of the interpretation of the psalms, the gospels, and the other books which are shown to me through this vision. It stirs my heart and soul like a burning flame and teaches me the depth of interpretation. And yet this vision doesn't teach me writings in the German language; these I don't know. I can simply read them but have no ability to analyze them. Please answer me: what do you make of all of this? I am a person who received no schooling about external matters. It is only within, in my soul, that I have been trained. And that is why I speak in such doubt.... Through your work you can show me, if you wish, whether I should say these things openly or guard them in silence. For this vision causes me a lot of concern about the extent to which I should talk about what I have seen and heard.[48]

In the *Book of Divine Works* we find a strange mixture of mystical vision, natural science and cosmology, medical knowledge, and spiritual wisdom. Hildegard used her observations of nature and physiology as the basis for making parallels with the spiritual life. The following selection from this last book gives some indication that her ordinary knowledge was as valuable to her as her visions in shaping what she had to teach:

> If the humors of the organism become unnaturally excited and if they then affect the vessels of the liver, the moistness of these vessels as well as those of the breast will be decreased. And human beings who become dried out in this way will undergo illness. Their phlegm will become parched and poisoned; it thus will ascend to

the brain and cause headaches and eye pains.... For if our thoughts
grow opinionated and obdurate and enter in this way onto empty
byways, we shall oppress justice as a result. It is justice which,
when sprinkled by the dew of the Holy Spirit, ought to germinate
good works through holiness. If our thoughts follow this course,
then the other powers of virtue will be weakened and desiccated
within us.[49]

There are many similar passages in this work. As Allen tells us,

> It is clear that Hildegard associates wisdom with an enlightened use
> of reason to understand one's own nature. This demands a knowl-
> edge of basic physiology, character, medieval elementary science,
> and individual insight.[50]

Hildegard clearly had a public vocation. Was her vocation primarily religious or secular? As we mentioned above such a distinction is hardly
intelligible in the context of medieval Europe. She was certainly called
to know and speak about the natural world and about human nature,
and she did this without apology in her medical, scientific writings. She
was also called to enter fully into the stream of life of her times, meeting
with the Emperor Frederick Barbarossa and criticizing popes and political
leaders in various ways:

> In political affairs Hildegard could take advantage of her aristocratic
> standing and her celebrity to obtain privileges from the great; but
> she could equally well oppose them, qua prophet, in the name of
> God.[51]

Hildegard's music, too, was an important influence in her times. In short,
she lived out a vocation that was at once religious and "of the world."
Despite the limitations of feminine monastic life, she helped to shape the
cultural life of her era.

We mentioned at the beginning of this chapter that several themes
emerge in the lives of the women we are examining. The integration of
self-discovery and divine command is evident in Hildegard's life. So, too,
is the sense of gifts received and the obligation to share them. Implicit in
the great industry of her life is the need to be useful. Finally, we noted
that through their engagement in the public world, these women came to
regard their own gender differently from the way their culture had taught
them. Although she comes long before any explicit theorizing about
women's equality, Hildegard's experiences caused her to consider at some
depth the natures of men and women. Because she had male secretaries
throughout her life, and because she had grown to maturity and worked

as a "nurse-physician" in the infirmary of the joint monastery at Disibode, her theories of men and women's differences and similarities were based on concrete experience. In comparing her writings on men and women to those of St. Thomas Aquinas, Allen finds that Hildegard affirms a theory of masculine/feminine complementarity, while Thomas (about a century later) has a dual theory that affirms equality of all humans on the supernatural plane, but the superiority of men on the natural plane.[52] In addition to her philosophical theory of the sexes, Hildegard's reflection on her experience leads her to recognize the feminine face of God. Calling the feminine aspect of God "Scientia Dei," Hildegard writes:

> She is awesome in terror as the Thunderer's lightning, and gentle in goodness as the sunshine. In her terror and her gentleness she is incomprehensible to men, because of the dread radiance of divinity in her face.[53]

The legacy of this new understanding of her dignity as a woman was not lost on her spiritual daughter, the young nun Elizabeth of Schonau. Elizabeth wrote:

> People are scandalized that in these days the Lord deigns to magnify his great mercy in the frail sex. But why doesn't it cross their minds that a similar thing happened in the days of our fathers when, while men were given to indolence, holy women were filled with the Spirit of God so that they could prophesy, energetically govern the people of God, and even win glorious victories over Israel's enemies. I speak of women like Hilda, Deborah, Judith, Jael, and the like.[54]

Hildegard and Elizabeth knew that they were daughters of Deborah. Like Deborah, they are our foremothers and guides.

Chapter 9

Other Daughters of Deborah:
Four Nineteenth-Century Women

Of all the crying evils in this depraved earth ... the greatest, judged by all the laws of God and of Humanity, is the miserable selfishness of men that keeps women from work. Work, the salvation of the world, the winner of the dreamless sleep and the dreamless thought too, the strengthener of the mind and of the body. ... A girl may go mad with her own soul over needlework, but she could not do so at college, or studying for the bar or for a civil service examination. That is what I demand for myself and for my sisters.

— Alice Meynell at age seventeen

Let us now explore the lives of four women of the nineteenth century whose vocations put them in the forefront of the public life of their time. They represent a spectrum of backgrounds and interests, and their lives collectively span the period from 1792 to 1940. The Grimke sisters came from a Protestant background while Alice Meynell was a convert to Catholicism, and Lillian Wald was formed by the Jewish tradition. Meynell was English, the others were American. Angelina Grimke and Alice Meynell married and had children; Sarah Grimke and Lillian Wald did not. The Grimkes and Meynell were actively religious; Lillian Wald was less so, but all four of them were firmly grounded in a biblical faith and ethic. It is probably not entirely accidental that all of these women came from privileged families. While working-class women may have been less confined by social mores, they were often imprisoned by harsh economic realities, by fear, and by ignorance. The luxuries of education and of time available to upper-middle-class women, as well as the self-confidence that came with their class, made it more likely that they would become nationally influential figures. The stories of the heroines of the nineteenth-century working class remain to be uncovered and told.

142

These four women also differed in their chosen fields of work. Sarah and Angelina Grimke were public lecturers and writers against slavery; Alice Meynell was a poet and journalist; Lillian Wald was a "nurse-practitioner," administrator, and social reformer. What they had in common was a strong conviction that women as well as men had the obligation to be useful, to employ their talents to the fullest, and to live according to their own autonomous conscience.

Sarah and Angelina Grimke

Sarah was the sixth of fourteen children and Angelina, born when Sarah was twelve, was the last. Their parents were well-to-do slaveholders in Charleston, South Carolina, and the girls were raised in affluence amid the services of many slaves. Yet, as they came to maturity, both Sarah and Angelina came to hate the institution of slavery and the cruelties they could not help observing in the system. The Grimke sisters spoke and wrote so much that we have a marvelous record of their development. It is difficult to avoid quoting from their personal writings at some length.

The Grimke girls were given a fairly traditional women's education, but Sarah wanted to learn Latin, Greek, philosophy, and law along with her brothers. She soaked up what she could. This was her first experience of a sense of call. A biographer writes:

> Sarah's mind and spirit were stifled. She felt that her calling was to be a lawyer, and she studied law secretly on her own. Her father is said to have told Sarah that she would have made the greatest jurist in the land — had she not been a woman. She learned very early what it meant to be denied something because of her sex, a lesson that was to shape the course of her life, both in what she did not become and in her life's testimony to the liberty and equality of women.... She wrote... "Had I received the education I wanted and been bred to the profession of the law, a dignity to which I secretly aspired, I might have been a useful member of society, and instead of myself and my property being taken care of, I might have been a protector of the helpless and the unfortunate, a pleader for the poor and the drunk."[1]

During her early twenties, Sarah underwent a period of growing distaste for the gay and frivolous social life expected of young women of her age and class, and growing distaste as well for the slave system that surrounded her. Sarah taught Sunday school to the young Negro slaves and was deeply angered at the law that prohibited her from teaching them to read. Until Sarah was found out and threatened with punishment, she secretly taught her own maid to read. Between 1819 and 1821 she was increasingly attracted to the Quakers whom she had come to know on a trip to Philadelphia, and whose dislike of slavery appealed to her. In 1821 she moved to Philadelphia and joined the Society of Friends Meeting there.

Angelina, sixteen when Sarah left home, underwent a gradual process of self-discovery not unlike Sarah's, although she seemed to be the more confident and extraverted of the two sisters. By 1829 her diary is filled with her active distress at the treatment of slaves in her own town and household. To check on the work of one of her Sunday school students, Angelina had to go to the home of the workhouse master. There she caught glimpses of the inside of the dreaded workhouse, where slaves were sent for whippings or torture on the cruel treadmill by masters "who were too 'delicate' to perform the office themselves."[2] After that she could barely stand to go near the area in which it was situated. She writes,

> These are not things I have heard; no, my own eyes have looked upon them and wept over them....No one can image my feelings walking down that street. It seemed as though I was walking on the very confines of hell. This winter being obliged to pass it to pay a visit to a friend, I suffered so much that I could not get over it for days and wondered how any real Christian could live near such a place.[3]

As distressed as she was about the workhouse, she was perhaps even more upset at the punishment of slaves in her own home. Her brother Henry had a slave named John whom he had recently beaten within Angelina's hearing. When John was again threatened with a beating, he ran away, but Angelina knew he would soon return out of hunger and desperation. She was appalled at the anger and brutality that was stirred up in her brother, as well as at the pain John underwent. After a sleepless night she determined to talk to Henry about it. Approaching her brother gently and affectionately, she broached the subject, and was told that Henry did indeed intend to give John a severe whipping when he returned.[4] Angelina remonstrated with him:

> I said that would be treating him worse than he would treat his horse. He now became excited, and replied that he considered his horse no comparison better than John, and would *not* treat *it* so....I pleaded the cause of humanity....I could not but lift up my voice against his manner of treating John....To my surprise he readily acknowledged that he felt something within him which fully met all I asserted, and that I had harrowed his feelings and made him feel wretched. Much more passed....I left the room in tears.[5]

When John returned the next night, Henry did not punish him, but merely sent him back to his work, and Angelina rejoiced that her words had some effect:

> My heart sings aloud for joy. Dear Henry has good, tender feelings naturally, but a false education has nearly destroyed them.[6]

Soon after this incident Angelina left Charleston to join Sarah in Philadelphia. After a period of charitable and religious work with the Quakers there, the sisters were drawn deeper into the anti-slavery movement. They became disillusioned with the hypocrisy on the subject they encountered in their Quaker group (Negro members were expected to sit separately and discriminated against in other ways) and eventually in 1836 they moved to New York City to work with the American Anti-Slavery Society there. Their deeply-felt vocations had now taken a definite form for them. For the next three or four years the sisters entered upon a career of public lecturing and writing against slavery that brought them both widespread fame and widespread condemnation. Their public lectures sometimes brought mobs out to protest. Although it was not their original intention, they were inevitably drawn into the women's rights controversy.

While Sarah and Angelina's vocations became evident to them in a gradual process of self-discovery, both sisters clearly understood that they were being called by God to the work they were finally to undertake. Sarah writes,

> When [a woman] is engaged in the great work of public reformation ... she must feel, if she feels rightly, that she is fulfilling one of the important duties laid upon her as an accountable human being, and that her character, instead of being "unnatural," is in exact accordance with the will of Him to whom, and to no other, she is responsible for the talents and gifts confided to her.[7]

Being responsible, being accountable, and being useful were phrases that come up often in both Sarah and Angelina's writings. For Angelina, the profound need to be useful led to her discovery that her first-hand experience with slavery, and her ability to speak eloquently about it, were indeed very useful to the anti-slavery campaign. With that discovery came a great sense of relief and joy. Nancy Hardesty connects Angelina's desire to be useful with her conversion experience:

> Angelina Grimke felt this compulsion to be useful from the moment of her conversion in a Presbyterian revival. She felt called to some great mission, though she did not recognize the causes to which she

was to devote her life until much later. In a series of letters to Sarah in 1836, she wrestled with the need to be useful.... "What have we done with the talents committed to us? I sometimes feel frightened to think of how long I was standing idle in the marketplace...." The call to become an antislavery lecturer was just becoming clear to her. Within six months she was writing to her friend Jane Smith (20 January 1837): "How little! how very little I supposed, when I used so often to say 'I wish I was a man that I might go out to lecture' that *I* ever would do such a thing — the idea never crossed my mind that *as a woman* such work would possibly be assigned to me but the Lord...[makes] a way for his people where there seems to be *no* way — Dear Jane, I love the work, I count myself greatly favored in being called to it."[8]

The sense of responsibility to use one's gifts and talents for the good of society was coupled, especially in Sarah's case, with a sense of the impediments that society placed in the way of women's call. She writes:

It is truly marvellous that any woman can rise above the pressure of circumstances which combine to crush her. Nothing can strengthen her to do this...but a call from Jehovah himself. And when the voice of God penetrates the deep recesses of her heart, and commands her to go and cry in the ears of the people, she is ready to exclaim, "Ah, Lord God, behold I cannot speak, for I am a woman."[9]

These obstacles, unwelcome as they were, actually broadened Sarah's own sense of her calling. She could not fulfill her first vocation to work against the institutions of slavery, unless she, at the same time, addressed the situation of women's right to such a vocation:

If in calling us thus publicly to advocate the cause of the down-trodden slave, God has unexpectedly placed us in the forefront of the battle which is to be waged against the rights and responsibilities of woman, it would ill become us to shrink from such a contest.[10]

The Grimkes' call to work against slavery brought them to a new consciousness of women's condition in several ways. First of all they realized that they could not proceed with their own vocations without clearing the way for women's right to speak and teach both men and women. In mid-1837 a "Pastoral Letter" was issued by the Congregationalists in Massachusetts objecting to the Grimke sisters' public anti-slavery activities because they were women. Following this, Sarah and Angelina both wrote to Angelina's future husband, abolitionist Theodore Weld, to insist on the need to address the women's issue. Sarah says,

If we are to do any good in the Anti-Slavery cause, our *right* to labor in it *must* be firmly established.... *We* cannot push Abolitionism forward with all our might *until* we take up the stumbling block out of the road.[11]

Angelina writes to Weld in the same vein,

We *must* meet it [the Pastoral] and meet it *now* and meet it like *women* in the fear of the Lord. They utterly deny *our right* to interfere with this or any other moral reform except in the particular way *they* choose to mark out for us to walk in.... If we surrender the right to speak to the public this year, we must surrender the right to petition next year and the right to *write* the year after that and so on.[12]

A second reason for their concern for the women's issue was the clear parallel they saw to the issue of the oppression of slaves. Not only women's freedom of activity but also their moral autonomy was at stake:

It was when my soul was deeply moved at wrongs of the slave that I first perceived distinctly the subject condition of women. Often when I would ask a sister's signature to an anti-slavery petition, the reply was, I should be rejoiced to sign it, but my husband has forbidden me to have anything to do with it.... I knew that women deferred greatly to the opinions of men, but I had no idea that they were expected to sacrifice their sympathies and their consciences to the opinions of their husbands, fathers, and brothers.[13]

If white women's consciences were subject to men's, how much more were those of black slave women. The sisters were well aware of the common practice of male masters brutally using female slaves for their own pleasure. The oppression of women was inextricably tied up with the oppression of slaves.[14] It was the combination of these three factors that led Sarah to write her series, *Letters on the Equality of the Sexes*, and *The Condition of Women*, published as a pamphlet in 1838, in which she eloquently argues the cause of women, using historical, scriptural, and rational arguments. In one of those she writes,

The Lord Jesus defines the duties of his followers in his Sermon on the Mount.... I follow him through all his precepts, and find him giving the same directions to women as to men, never even referring to the distinction now so strenuously insisted upon between masculine and feminine virtues: this is one of the anti-christian "traditions of men" which are taught instead of the "commandments of

God." Men and women were CREATED EQUAL; they are both moral and accountable beings, and what is *right* for man to do, is *right* for woman.[15]

As the editor of these letters writes,

The moral autonomy of women for which Grimke so ardently argued in the *Letters* was their autonomy to pursue, discover, and fulfill God's design for them.[16]

After Angelina's marriage to Weld in 1838 and the birth of their three children, the sisters retired somewhat from the heat of the fray. Sarah lived with the Welds until her death in 1873, at the ripe age of eighty-one. Although less active they maintained their commitment to abolitionist and women's causes throughout their lifetime. More importantly, their writing and speaking in those few brief years influenced a generation of younger women to recognize and pursue the public vocations to which they already felt called.

Alice Meynell

Alice Thompson Meynell was born in London in 1847, about a half-century after the Grimkes. In some ways, her life seems very peaceful and ordinary in comparison to theirs, for her vocation was less in the world of social reform than in the world of arts and literature. That is not to say that she lived in an ivory tower, for as active Catholic journalists, she and her husband were very much concerned with issues of social justice, in a time when the Catholic church was just beginning to awaken to the crying needs of the modern world.

Alice's father, Thomas, was a scholar and her mother, Christiana, a pianist. Charles Dickens had a fleeting attraction to Christiana and had introduced his friend, Thomas, to her. Dickens remained a family friend during Alice's childhood, much of which was spent in Italy. Thus she was raised in an atmosphere that was exciting, somewhat hectic, and quite cultured. Fortunately, it was not a narrow-minded atmosphere, and thus fostered her own growing independence of thought. She blended in her life the vocations of poet, journalist, mother, and "hub" of an important literary circle that gathered at the Meynell's home. Her capacity for both warm friendships and intelligent artistic criticism made her an inspiration and guide to writers such as Francis Thompson, W. B. Yeats, Coventry Patmore, Robert Browning, Oscar Wilde, Hillaire Belloc, and G. K. Chesterton. It was her husband who printed a poem of the then unknown Thompson, and subsequently he and Alice helped to rescue him from a life of drug dependence, homelessness, and poverty, recognizing his talent as well as his humanity. One biographer writes of Alice:

> She was beautiful, young, a brilliant conversationalist. Her intellectual interests were the reverse of parochial. The culture of the ancient world held her fast, yet she was at the same time what might be called an advanced modern, a feminist, a symbolist, sympathetic toward most of the new political and artistic ideas that germinated so fast in this seminal period.[17]

This rather idyllic picture of Alice, however, contrasts with practical realities that shaped her life, and that make us feel a bond with her today.

Converted to Catholicism along with her mother as a young girl, Alice's sensitivity to both religious and everyday realities found expression in her poetry. After an adolescence spent in relative carefreeness and innocent flirtations, her native seriousness began to assert itself. She had put away her earnestness and her poetry for awhile, but at around age seventeen,

> she was changing again; and yearn though she might for the parties and the gay society of Bonchurch, she was beginning to realise that even that was not enough, that she wanted from life something more, which seemed to be denied her.[18]

It would be ten years before her first book of poetry, *Preludes*, was published, and in that period her own sense of herself and of her vocation matured. It seems to have crystallized by 1873 when she commented on the high standards of art to which she held herself:

> [John Henry Cardinal] Newman can write verses unworthy of himself without a pang because he is a poet fifthly, sixthly, and seventhly in the order of his high vocations. It is far otherwise for me.[19]

But Alice's poetic vocation was, for a time, to take a back seat to her practical vocations as journalist and parent of eight children. Her vocation to befriend, encourage, and challenge other artists and writers was never abandoned. What led her out of her comfortable upper-class life was her romance with Wilfrid Meynell.

Wilfrid Meynell, five years younger than Alice, was a struggling young journalist with no regular position when he wrote an insightful review of Alice's poetry. She asked to meet him, and they fell in love, but her father resisted giving his consent to their marriage until Wilfrid had some significant employment. After a period of difficult negotiations, the

marriage was agreed to, but the two would have to find some way to survive financially. It was a struggle all their lives. Although with the help
of Alice's inheritance from her father, they were eventually able to build
and maintain a comfortable home in which to entertain their friends, they
both had to work hard at their trade, bills were often overdue, clothes
were not the latest fashion, and Francis Thompson commented that the
food at their house was "shocking." Their daughter, Viola, writes in her
biography of Alice of the realities of their work and family life:

> Journalism was the pleasant and constant occupation of both my
> parents; at the time of her marriage it committed its act of con
> fiscation forever of leisure from my mother's life. In the interests
> of bread-winning the worker at will became the worker at every
> demand. . . .
>
> For 18 years the functions of editor, sub-editor, contributor and
> even office-boy [of *The Catholic Register*] kept my father a busy
> man on most days, a harassed man on Thursdays — so that one of
> the things . . . the young family was chiefly aware of was the inde
> scribable effort and struggle against time on those Thursdays, with
> both parents silent and desperate with work. My mother undertook
> any of the odd jobs that were piled too high upon even so quick
> a worker as that editor. She wrote leaders, and reviewed books,
> and read proofs, and translated Papal encyclicals from the Italian.
> (In a letter written later to Coventry Patmore . . . she says: "I have
> just translated for the Register the Pope's letter to the Hungarian
> bishops — without pranks. Sometimes I make His Holiness quote
> our poets!")[20]

At the same time as she was sharing the burden of editing *The Register*
Alice was also contributing regularly to other periodicals including *The
Tablet*, *The Spectator*, and a number of art and literature reviews. The
amounts she earned for these contributions and later from her weekly
columns and books of essays made the difference between penury and
modest comfort for her family. After 1893, with her children beginning to
grow up, Alice returned to her poetry-writing and produced about eight
volumes of poetry, two biographies, and numerous volumes of essays
before her death in 1922. She was invited to be president of the Society
of Woman Journalists in England in 1897 and in 1895 and in 1914 she
was proposed for Poet Laureate of the nation. Calvin Alexander notes,
"On the last occasion it was her sex alone, it seems, which prevented her
from receiving the honor — a bitter blow for so pronounced a feminist."[21]

We have few personal words from Alice about her own inner life and
vocation, but one entry from her diary, written in that significant year
when she was seventeen, expresses her longing for a useful life in which

her womanhood would be no barrier to a full public vocation. It is in
these themes that she is, at heart, so much like the Grimke sisters, and
like her much earlier foremother, Hildegard.

> Answer, O World, man-governed, man-directed, answer for the san-
> ity of your laws and your morals. Of all the crying evils in this
> depraved earth . . . the greatest, judged by all the laws of God and
> of Humanity is the miserable selfishness of men that keeps women
> from work. Work, the salvation of the world, the winner of the
> dreamless sleep and the dreamless thought too, the strengthener of
> the mind and of the body. . . . By work I mean work of the mind as
> well as of the body. . . . A girl may go mad with her own soul over
> needlework, but she could not do so at college, or studying for the
> bar or for a civil service examination. That is what I demand for
> myself and for my sisters.[22]

Stirred by her own desire to work, to use her mind, and to influence
her world, Alice, like the Grimkes, was led to this radical questioning
of women's traditional role. Nothing in her deep personal relationship
with God prevented her from pursuing a public vocation, even while she
and Wilfrid reared eight children. In fact, her faith impelled her to such
activity. She remained an active suffragette throughout her incredibly
full life.

Through their children we know quite a bit about the Meynell's family life. More than any of the other women we are discussing, Alice and
Wilfrid's attempt to live an integrated life of family and work seems similar to our desires today. Alice suffered from migraines throughout her
life, and we have her daughter's account of how the older children would
try to keep the "babies" quiet when she had an attack. Just at the period
when there was the least income and the most bills to pay, there were
small children to attend to in between snatches of work. One of her sons
gives us the following image:

> At her place at the library table the "penciling mamma" (a title
> given her by George Meredith) would sit at her work, the children
> at scrap-books on the floor or perhaps editing a newspaper under
> the table. . . . Blandishment we had little of; we were taken into her
> arms, but briefly; exquisitely fondled, but with economy, as if there
> were work always to be resumed.[23]

Alice was no stranger to child-care problems either. Writing to her husband in his absence she says,

These rascals are pretty troublesome in your absence, but I don't let them stop my work. And between their badnesses they are uncommonly dear. Edith helped me yesterday to control them when visitors came, but the nurse gives up the struggle. She is so spiritless that I shall not regret her so very much. We went on Saturday to Mrs. Cameron's office and I trust she will find me someone.[24]

Supermom, Alice was not. Her biographer writes that at mending, cooking, sewing, and nursing she was rather bad, and her attention to her children was often divided, but in gentleness and affection she was unequalled.[25] Born and bred to live the traditional life of a nineteenth-century upper-class English woman, Alice Meynell led instead the hectic but fulfilling life of a dual-career wife and worker at the cutting edge of her times.

Lillian Wald

Lillian Wald, the founder of the famous settlement house on Henry Street in New York City, was a nurse, administrator, social reformer, and peace activist. She was born in 1867, twenty years after Alice Meynell and while the Grimkes were still alive. But over half of her life takes place in the twentieth century. She is a bridge between the old order where women's place was thought to be more or less securely fixed, and the new order when it had become "unfixed." She was one of the first to forge women's twentieth-century identity.

As the third of four children of a Jewish family whose male ancestors on both sides were merchants, rabbis, and professional men, Lillian's upbringing was fairly conventional. She went to a young woman's boarding school in Rochester, graduated at sixteen, but was turned down for Vassar because she was too young. She never reapplied to a traditional college there or elsewhere. Like the young Grimkes and like Alice Meynell, she spent her young adulthood in the normal, somewhat unserious pursuits of a prosperous young woman of her society. Only when she was twenty-eight, "searching for some more definite purpose" did she decide to go into training to be a nurse at New York Hospital.[26] Of her goal at that time, she writes,

I had little more than an inspiration to be of use in some way or somehow, and going to the hospital seemed the readiest means of realizing my desire.[27]

After graduating from nursing school, she worked at the New York Juvenile Asylum for a year, and then entered the Women's Medical College in the city. In her second year there, 1893, an event occurred that she understood to be the sign of her ultimate vocation, so she never completed her medical degree.

In March of that year, Lillian had been asked to teach a home-nursing course on the East Side. She was in the midst of a bed-making lesson there when a little girl rushed in asking Lillian to come to her mother who had recently given birth. In her account of this in *The House on Henry Street* Lillian writes,

> The child led me on through a tenement hallway, across a court where open and unscreened closets were promiscuously used by men and women, up into a rear tenement, by slimy steps whose accumulated dirt was augmented that day by the mud of the streets, and finally into the sickroom.... The family to which the child led me was neither criminal nor vicious.... Although the family of seven shared their rooms with boarders.... Although the sick woman lay on a wretched, unclean bed, soiled with a hemorrhage two days old, they were not degraded human beings, judged by any measure of moral values.... It would have been some solace if by any conviction of the moral unworthiness of the family I could have defended myself as part of a society which permitted such conditions to exist.[28]

Lillian might have chosen to finish medical school and become one of those pioneering women in the medical profession whose position, while undoubtedly full of challenges, had some clear definition and status. But again, in a decision that integrated self-discovery and some sort of divine or inner impulsion, Lillian knew her vocation to lie elsewhere. Although she does not speak of her decision explicitly as response to a divine command, she uses religious imagery to describe its meaning for her life:

> That morning's experience was a baptism of fire. Deserted were the laboratory and the academic world of the college. I never returned to them. On my way from the sick room to my comfortable student quarters my mind was intent on my own responsibility.... I rejoiced that I had had a training in the care of the sick that in itself would give me an organic relationship to the neighborhood in which this awakening had come....I found myself presenting a plan,...the Ludlow Street experience, resistlessly impelling me to action.[29]

Many years later, just four years before she died in fact, she said that if she were starting over she would do it the same way, "not taking time to worry and wonder about things but just going ahead and doing what

had to be done.... We were driven to it," she said, "... we were driven
to everything we did."[30]

Her plan took shape. Another nurse, Mary Brewster, and she would
move into the neighborhood to give their services as nurses, supported by
financial help from her well-to-do friends. Although Mary Brewster eventually grew ill and had to leave the project, the settlement idea attracted
many young women and grew rapidly. Edward Wagenknecht writes:

> By 1913 the settlement had...seven houses on Henry Street and
> two branches, plus seven vacation homes in the country, with
> ninety-two nurses making 200,000 visits annually, and 3,000 people
> enrolled in clubs and classes. By 1916 the value of their property
> holdings was half a million dollars, and the annual budget for the
> visiting nurse service alone was $150,000. Three years later, the
> thirty-seven residents were being assisted by 101 volunteers and by
> 1932, the visiting nurses would be working out of twenty centers.[31]

Thus, Lillian Wald's vocation grew with the project, from that of simple
nurse, to administrator, fund-raiser, educator, and political advocate. But
all of this was the natural and inevitable outgrowth of her initial response
of compassion to people's concrete needs. Wagenknecht describes the
way in which Wald's public work exposes the unfolding of her own inner
convictions:

> The supreme expression of Lillian Wald's personality was achieved
> in the way the work of the Henry Street settlement developed. Hav-
> ing taken care of this particular case, how could she go away without
> trying to teach the well-meaning but ignorant, often foreign, house-
> wife...that survival itself must depend for her family upon "clean-
> liness, personal hygiene, temperance and good cooking"? How in
> other words, could she avoid undertaking an educational as well
> as...a healing work? That in itself was hard enough, but it was
> not possible to stop there, for even slum homes were not islands.[32]

A boy with an infected scalp led to a campaign for nurses in the public
schools; a retarded or handicapped child led to the request for special
education programs; unhygienic conditions in both home and industry,
often in close proximity, required strict legislation.[33]

> She was startled when the realization came to her that when she
> thought she was only working in the interest of the Eastside babies,
> she was really in politics. By 1921 she was working for the removal
> of outdoor privies, a separate toilet for every tenement family, better

fire protection, and the abolition of cellar dwellings and apartments with no windows.[34]

Lillian came to know about Jane Addams's Hull House in Chicago only after her own foundation on Henry Street was well underway. Lillian and Jane Addams became friends, and like her friend Lillian advocated child labor laws, sought work for the unemployed, and protested American involvement in World War I as a waste of both material and human resources. Her energy and vast care involved her in shaping social policy for her neighborhood, her city, her nation, and her world.

At this point one will hardly be surprised to know that Lillian took the cause of women's rights and women's suffrage as her own. She lived to see women's suffrage in the U.S., of course, but in her book published in 1915, she recalls the state of the suffrage movement in her own Lower East Side at that time:

> The conviction that the extension of democracy should include women has found free expression in our part of the city, and Miss L. L. Dock, a resident of many years, has mobilized Russians, Italians, Irish, and native-born, all the nationalities of our cosmopolitan community for the campaign.... The transition is significant from the position of women among orthodox Jews to the motherly-looking woman who stands on a soap-box at the corner of Henry Street and makes her appeal for the franchise to a respectful group of laboring men. The mere fact that this "mother in Israel" is obliged to work in a factory six days of the week is an argument in itself, but intelligently and interestingly she develops her pleas, and her appeal to the men's reason brings nods of approval.[35]

From Deborah, "a mother in Israel," to Lillian and this woman on a soap-box on Henry Street, women have been called by God to be nurturers of the mind and midwives to their nations as well as to their children. That they did not shrink from their call to be useful, autonomous, and intelligent women is our legacy.

All of the women whose lives we have reflected on in the last few chapters challenge us to carry on their search for a bold and authentic womanhood. In the ferment of contemporary American life, we need to go forward with a strong sense of ourselves and of our unique vocations, just as Deborah and Ruth did, as Prisca and Perpetua did, and as Alice and Lillian did. We also need to go forward together, recognizing that women's experience and women's strengths have not been sufficiently influential in shaping either the outer structures or the inner spirit of our public culture.

There are practical tasks before us that will not be accomplished unless a significant number of us can put aside purely individual dreams, as well as individual fears, and focus on a common dream of love and work. Some of the practical considerations and tasks before us will be discussed in chapters 10 and 11. What we can envision as possible at present, however, is only a fraction of what might be possible if women and men were to pool their creative energies and commit themselves to seeking a more integrated and egalitarian way of life.

Part III

Making a Difference

Chapter 10

Women and the Men in Their Lives

And another thing, when my husband mops, he never does behind the door. I guess we can live with dirt behind the door, but it's not my preference.

The Despair of a Traditional Lifestyle

In chapter 3, we discussed the shared human need we all have to live lives in which we are able to define our uniqueness through our work and affirm our connectedness through our intimate, nurturing relationships. We said that when women are denied work and when men are denied intimacy, both women and men fail to achieve their full human potential and all of us are diminished. The loss that comes from finding oneself able to grow in only one aspect of life is aptly expressed by television talk-show host Phil Donahue in his autobiography. In these excerpts, Donahue, himself a product of the 1950s model of manhood, recounts his realization that, while he had made it by the prevailing standards of his time, his life was far from complete:

> Later I would realize how ill-prepared I was for fatherhood. My energy had been directed toward achieving. . . . I had never been told that children *needed* to be cuddled, *needed* approval and attention, *needed* measured and thoughtful discipline. . . . I thought about my childhood and how nothing, absolutely nothing, was ever said about human relationships. . . . Did our parents' fear of adolescent sex (reinforced as it was by the [Catholic] Church) cause an overkill that left all of us (the boys especially) mortally wounded in other areas of intimacy?[1]

For men like Donahue, the loss comes from not satisfying one's need to express love. For women, the loss most often comes from not satisfying

159

one's need to grow through work. In her book *From Housewife to Heretic*, Sonia Johnson records the tragedy of her mother's life — an intelligent young woman who could have become an administrator, a financier, or an artist:

> The family is a very narrow sphere. It is cruel to bottle up immense talents there. It isn't fair, Mama, what happened to you.... Where is that girl who galloped bareback across the Idaho plains with her hair flying? That she is lost, that her gifts were ignored, spurned and pounded out of her is a cause for grief to those of us who know and love her. But multiply her life by the billions, and try to keep from howling with rage and despair at the impoverishment that women's bondage has wreaked upon the human family.[2]

As we have already seen, when one dares to live a life at odds with traditional expectations, attempting to combine love and work, others are often not only nonsupportive, but sometimes cruel as well. Evidence of the profound constraints on the behavior of women in particular is found in a study of college students conducted a few years ago. In the study, students were asked what they thought happened to a hypothetical young woman named Ann, who at the end of the first term finals, was at the top of her medical school class. The following is an amalgam of paragraphs written by the college students:

> Soon Ann became one of the leading doctors in the world. When she was in France, she met an American man. They both fell in love. Soon they were married. But after they had their first child, Ann turned all her attention to her work. So they got divorced. Ann always was involved in her work. The only people she talked to were fellow doctors and nurses. Soon she got very ill and died. No one even went to her funeral because she was very mean.[3]

Clearly the college students who responded to Ann's career success did not believe she could be equally successful in her personal life. Ann is portrayed as being in danger of a variety of misfortunes when she oversteps the bounds of traditional roles.

The pressures on men who deviate from traditional expectations are just as great. In the few companies that offer paternity leave, for instance, men are often subtly discouraged from taking it. Though not explicit, the message is clear. If they take paternity leave, men are not considered to be serious workers and risk being overlooked for future promotions.

Warren Farrell, author of several books on men and an active feminist himself, points out that men are often prevented from developing high levels of intimacy with their families because of the overwhelming economic pressures they face. As he says,

> Approximately half of married women will... work either part time or full time. If the children are young, she experiences a juggling act. In all but a few cases she earns less than she did before. So the man must earn not only enough for himself, but compensate for her lost income plus supply all the additional income needed to support a child (or children). While she experiences a juggling act, he experiences an intensifying act. She gets paid [because of her husband's financial support] for intimacy; he gets paid for being away from intimacy.[4]

One of the women whom we interviewed understood the societal constraints on men who desire greater intimacy when she said,

> Perhaps deep down, we're all nurturers, but men don't realize it, or they want to be, but don't know how. They've always had the guns, and we've had the dolls. Men want intimacy, but it's not been allowed. They haven't been taught that way or brought up that way, but they want it [intimacy].

Courageous Pioneers: Benefits of Change

Benefits to Individuals

Despite these very real difficulties, when we look at what happens to those people who actually do break away from traditional expectations and move into lifestyles where women and men both love and work, we find very encouraging results. In her book *The Second Stage*, Betty Friedan records some of the unfettering that occurs in the lives of these pioneers:

> Sam, an aerospace engineer in Seattle, told me that the period when his wife "tried to be just a housewife" was the worst time in his marriage. "It was not only her staying home and losing confidence in herself. The pressure was on me, hanging by my fingernails, barely paying the bills each month. But it was crazy. Here I was... suddenly supporting a wife and kids all by myself. It's better now that she's working and bringing some money in."[5]

Friedan interviewed a number of other men from a variety of occupations and educational backgrounds. They all spoke of the improvement in their lives once they were able to participate more fully in relational aspects of life. A doctor, a pilot, and business executives all talked about the same feelings. The doctor told her,

When Ellen finally got up enough nerve to do her own thing —
she's a nurse-midwife now — it was a relief.... I'm coming out of
this, redefining myself, no longer in terms of success or failure as
a doctor (though I still am a doctor) and not as superior or inferior
to her. It was a blow to my ego, but what a relief, to take off my
surgical mask! I'm discovering my own value in the family.[6]

In another study of men who left traditional nine-to-five jobs, Bernard
Lefkowitz found that,

They even enjoyed what they called "passivity" without shame.
... Passivity was not weakness but a state of receptivity, an openness to experience. Above all, they felt a new "wholeness" now
that they were experiencing themselves more vividly in relation to
their children, friends, and open-ended new interests and activities
undertaken for their own pleasure and growth.... They described
their new feeling of "wholeness" as "the pleasure the prisoner takes
in walking across an open field after years of being locked up."[7]

We have already discussed the considerable benefits that come to women
when they are able to respond to the call to contribute their talents
to the community in the public world of work. In addition, there are
also personal, psychological benefits. Working women, as compared to
housewives, are less lonely, less anxious and worried, have fewer sub-
stance abuse problems, feel more worthy as human beings, and report
greater marital satisfaction. Women who have some degree of economic
power through their work also feel better about themselves and have
more power and status within the family and community.[8]

In her book on ethics and moral education, Nel Noddings explores
the effects of fuller integration of love and work on how we care for
others. She describes a man who paid for his mother's care in a nursing
home but never went to see her. He thought that *he* showed that he
cared for his mother by paying her bills; it was his sisters' job to visit
her. Noddings comments,

Women are too often cast as the one-caring; they are the ones who
engage in psychological caring.... However, they are often thought
of as being taken care of by the men who provide the salaries.... If
men and women participate more fully and equally in these two
great worlds [caretaking and genuine caring], both may reap unexpectedly large rewards. Women, with stronger self-images to sustain
them, may care more joyfully in private life and may insist upon
caring in public life as well. Men, participating in the responsi-

bilities of domestic life, may learn its real joys and potential for self-renewal.[9]

Benefits to the Business World

The business world benefits, too, from the presence of women and women's characteristic style of leadership. Friedan (1981) offers the following evidence for the importance of stereotypical feminine characteristics of sensitivity and person-centeredness in management. A study of the distinguishing characteristics of good executives in many types of businesses conducted by Harvard psychologist David McClelland showed that

> too many of the MBA's had been trained in the terms of the old Alpha style of "masculine" aggressiveness, linear-mathematical certainty, computer models, etc. But the most effective executives or human service administrators weren't the ones who were the best on those numerical tests or who were the most aggressive; they were those "competent" and "sensitive" in dealing with people, able to sense their special needs and interests.[10]

Other studies have shown that when negotiating, male managers are likely to be thinking, "I need to come out ahead in this deal, and it's going to be at your expense," and to say something like, "Your price is too high based on what your competitors are charging." Women managers are more likely to be thinking, "Let's find a way to meet both our needs," and to say something like, "I don't suppose you'd consider a slightly lower price."[11] One pair of researchers writes:

> Feminine negotiators tend to visualize the long-term relationship between the people involved when they think about negotiations. Their masculine counterparts tend to visualize a sporting event in which the other person is an opponent who has to be beaten.[12]

The point is that both styles are potentially important for a company. The typical male style is best when the relationship between the two parties is one-time only; they've never seen each other before and probably won't have to deal with each other again. However, when the relationship between the parties needs to continue, as is the case most of the time, the typical female approach is better.

Benefits to Children

We have seen that when women and men both love and work, men feel more fulfilled, women feel more fulfilled, and the business world benefits. But what happens to the traditional sphere of women, the family, and especially the children? Dual-career parents tend to have fewer children than traditional families and to have them later in life.[13] Contrary to popular misconceptions, though, and despite the heavy demands on their time, dual-career parents may spend as much time in one-to-one contact with an individual child as do traditional parents. Traditional mothers are with their children more, but also have to concentrate on their other duties around the house or in the community. Dual-career parents appear to be making an effort to spend exclusive time with their children.

Currently, though, for much of the day, children of dual-career and single-parent families must be cared for by someone other than their parents. In a review of a number of studies on the effects of child care on children's development, Belsky concluded that children cared for in group day-care settings are not harmed in intellectual, social, or emotional development.[14] Some other studies have shown that children of working mothers are more independent and show less stereotyped behavior than children of traditional mothers.[15]

In the future, as more men actively participate in the private sphere of family life, the benefits to children are expected to grow. Psychologists, especially those from the Freudian tradition, have long worried about the effect of single-sex caregivers in a young child's life. In the traditional family, in order to develop healthy sexual identity, boys must *separate* emotionally from their source of care and nurturing (the mother) to identify with the often-absent father. Girls, on the other hand, must form a *bond* with their primary caretaker.

Some people (especially Carol Gilligan) feel that this early dynamic within the family accounts in large part for later patterns of behavior among males and females. For instance, females are more threatened by the "separation" implied in the development of unique identity. Men find the expression of the dependence implied in intimate feelings difficult. Gilligan's points are illustrated by the kinds of stories men and women tell in response to certain kinds of pictures. For instance, one typical man responded to the intimacy portrayed in a picture of a couple sitting by a river next to a low bridge in this way,

> Nick saw his life pass before his eyes.... He knew all along that Sam hated him. Hated him for being rich and especially hated him for being engaged to Mary, Sam's childhood sweetheart. But Nick never realized until now that Mary also hated him and really loved Sam. Yet there they were, the two of them, calmly sitting on a bench in the riverbend, watching Nick drown....[16]

On the other hand, women find the competitive, conflict-filled, win-lose situations often characteristic of the work world threatening. In response to the competition suggested by a picture of two women in white coats working in a laboratory, a typical woman said,

> [Miss Hegstead] is watching Jane Smith, the model student in the class. She always goes over to Jane and comments to the other students that Jane is always doing the experiment right and Jane is the only student who really works hard, etc. Little does Miss Hegstead know that Jane is making some arsenic to put in her afternoon coffee.[17]

In terms of child rearing, the hope is that as men come to play a greater role in the development of young children, boys will have greater chances to identify with care-giving and nurturance, while girls will be encouraged to realize their identity as separate selves. In the long run, both boys and girls should be more comfortable with the range of behaviors necessary for healthy adult life. As Gilligan says, "...We know ourselves as separate only insofar as we live in connection with others.... We experience relationship only insofar as we differentiate other from self."[18]

Benefits to the Marital Relationship

There are a number of studies conducted by social scientists (many of whom are dual-career couples) that give us important information about the marital relationship. Successful marriages among dual-career couples (studied through interviews) are characterized by flexibility in personal style, mobility in career, emotional independence or interdependence, shared interests, and a high degree of self-actualization.[19] Another researcher found that dual-career couples live happier lives when they have careers in the same field, when they are at different points in their careers, when their jobs are flexible in terms of hours, and when they don't have children.[20]

Men and women in dual-career marriages have been found to be more inner-directed than those in traditional marriages.[21] This finding has particular implication for our work. It may be that inner-directed people become that way so as to insulate themselves against criticism from the world around them. But it is also likely that inner-directed people will be better able to understand and reflect on abstract issues of justice and fairness, the first step in effecting changes that will benefit all.

The Challenges of Change

Challenges to the Marital Relationship

While researcher David G. Rice also finds that dual-career couples report happy marriages, he cites the following as common problems among those experiencing difficulties: (1) the wife's resentment that her spouse's career is more important to him than her career is to him; (2) the unequal distribution of homemaking tasks and child-care responsibilities; and (3) sexual limitations (lack of time for sex and little sexual variety).[22] Another researcher, Donna Hodgkins Bernardo, concludes, "Dual-career couples cannot be the 'vanguard of the future' if they continue to jeopardize women's careers by diverting their time and energy to household labor."[23]

Some specific suggestions, gleaned from interviews of dual-career couples, for dealing with the inevitable stresses involved in a such a marriage include:

- ask each other for support

- seek support from other dual-career couples

- limit the number of obligations one accepts

- discuss one's expectations of the other, and one's personal and marital goals

- schedule time alone and time to be together as a couple

- find satisfactory domestic and child-care help outside the family

- ask for work adjustments

- take time to get away together as a couple

- anticipate and plan for emergencies[24]

In order to be most beneficial to the relationship, specific "couple time" should be spent on activities such as eating, playing, and conversing together, rather than on child care, housework, watching television, or community service.[25]

One couple carries out these suggestions by scheduling time for their relationship after the children have gone to bed. The husband describes what they do:

"We participate in a very traditional, very pleasant ritual," he said. "We have tea together. We try to do that three times a week. This might not be every couple's cup of tea," he added, "but partners can create their own way to give the relationship priority."[26]

Challenges to Family Life

The greatest stress in any marital relationship, dual-career or traditional, is the presence of children. Childless marriages (often called child-free marriages) are happier than marriages in which there are children.[27] The profound stress that the presence of children adds to a marriage relationship illustrates clearly that family life and work life are not well integrated. The sad fact that Ann Landers' informal, nonscientific survey of her readers in 1976 showed that 70 percent would not have children if they had the decision to make over again results from the lack of support we provide for families.[28]

In summing up this problem, the president of the Children's Defense Fund, Marian Wright Edelman, says,

[Parents need to] become more vocal in demanding supports for the very important job they're trying to do raising their kids.... They're still the best allies children have.... Our policies must reflect what we value. We don't value parents staying at home, because we don't provide the income supports allowing them to do that and not have their children suffer. On the other hand, when they go to work we don't support them by making sure the kids are taken care of.... We show our kids we love them by how we treat them.[29]

In marriages where there are children, the degree of marital satisfaction declines when the children are born, and often rises again when they become independent. Given these very troubling statistics and their obvious implications for the lives of children, we find that working couples with children do experience less decline in overall marital satisfaction than traditional couples. For working wives, marital satisfaction is higher and marital conflict less in the post-parental period than it is for non-working wives.[30]

While studies of the family lives of working men are much less common than studies of the family lives of working women (the government does not even keep statistics on the number of working fathers), those that do exist are informative. There is generally a curvilinear relationship between marital satisfaction and work success for men, so that men who are either highly successful or highly unsuccessful in their work are least satisfied in their marriages.[31] Perceived failure in his career threatens the primary role of a man in a traditional relationship, providing for his family. For highly successful men, the chief strain on family life is the number of hours they must (or choose to) work.

In general, men tend to work greater numbers of hours than women and to bring work home with them, both factors that cause stress in family life. For women, the primary stress is not as often the total number of

hours worked, but the difficulty of simultaneously satisfying the incompatible responsibilities of work and family, as this example illustrates:

> A family therapist . . . was on the phone counseling a suicidal patient.
> Suddenly, from her office window she saw lightning from a distant
> thunderstorm. It was heading in the direction of the soccer field in
> another town where she knew her son Josh was playing with his
> friends. "I realized my husband and I hadn't arranged to have him
> picked up for another hour and he had no one to take him home
> in the storm," she said. "At that moment, I felt I had to make the
> impossible choice between my patient and my son."[32]

One does wonder where her husband was and if he experienced the
same conflict she did.

Additional information about the differences in the work/family strain
experienced by men and women is provided by a large-scale study of
work and life satisfaction among dual-career couples from five businesses, one university, and one hospital in the St. Louis area.[33] Men
rated themselves significantly higher than women in life satisfaction and
in job involvement. They reported greater levels of self-esteem, a larger
number of hours worked at home on work-related activities, and higher
income. Women rated themselves significantly higher than men in mul-
tiple role stress. The stresses and sources of satisfaction for men and
women in their lives and in their work are the same. It is the ratio of
stresses to satisfaction that differs. Women and men experience job and
life satisfaction for the same reasons, but women receive less job and life
satisfaction than men.

Moving from Coping to Integration

It is clear from the preceding discussion that many men and women
are finding great satisfaction in attempting to live lives in which they
share work and family joys and responsibilities, and yet, as we have
seen throughout this book, significant obstacles and challenges remain.
While men and women may be able to share family and work, they are
not yet able to live truly integrated lives where work enriches family and
family enriches work. For example, when one of us was on an airplane
with her one-year-old daughter, a flight attendant came over and almost
wistfully admired the child. She said that she would like to have a child,
but that she and her husband hadn't figured out how to do it yet. She
wanted to continue flying but couldn't figure out who would care for the
child when she was gone three or four days at a time. Her husband
didn't travel like she did, but was occupied with his career.

For some of us this woman's work schedule might seem attractive.

After all, she could be home full time with her child for eighteen days out of the month. But a "role reversal" in which her husband would be the primary child nurturer, with the help of outside child care, for the days she was gone didn't even occur to this woman. She could easily identify all the situations in which women have been child nurturers in analogous situations when men were gone — to war, to sea, or as salesmen, military servicemen, politicians, or pilots, but because of her expectations of herself as sole care-giver to her child, she felt unable to have a child at all.

We believe that before a real interweaving of work and family experiences and values can occur, substantial changes in work and family attitudes and practices must occur. Suggestions for interim coping measures may make life more pleasant in the short run, but they do not help change an intolerable situation. Further, reliance on coping measures continues to reinforce the view that coping is an appropriate response to an unjust structure. Substantial change in personal attitudes and behavior and in corporate and public policy does not come easily. It is our view that we need to explore ways of sharing our new-found convictions with those we love and with whom we seek an intimate, balanced life. The road ahead is bound to be fraught with frustration and pain. And yet the urge to respond to our call and the sustenance we receive from our personal and spiritual lives will enable us to approach our task with joy, always mindful of the benefits that await us and our children.

As we have seen, the new blend of workplace and family involvement that we envision requires changes in both individual and corporate attitudes and behaviors. In the next chapter we will deal more thoroughly with public policy and corporate change. In the remaining sections of this chapter, we will discuss the changes that must come about on the most basic personal level — within our own hearts and in our relations with those we hold most dear.

Encountering Ourselves

Our first encounter is with ourselves, as we confront our own ambivalent feelings. We must deal with the traditional feminine dilemma of desiring both justice and an absence of conflict. In approaching this dilemma we recognize that real peace never comes without justice. The biblical injunction to be peacemakers found in the Beatitudes requires action, not passivity. The most effective peacemakers (Gandhi, Jesus, Martin Luther King, Jr., Rosa Parks) took insistent, yet nonviolent action in remedying unjust situations.

For too long, women have been threatened by conflict and encouraged to "give in" to keep the peace. But peace is not merely an absence of conflict, particularly when this "absence of conflict" occurs in an environment that is oppressive or abusive. Barbara Harrison, in commenting on books like *The Total Woman* by Marabel Morgan, which encourages women to subordinate themselves to their husband's pleasure and to forgive him no matter what he does, says,

> Female obsequiousness is based on contempt for men and ambivalence and confusion concerning them. [Morgan and others] are happiness merchants who teach us not to confront our human pain and suffering directly, but to learn, through self-deception, to rejoice in our bonds and fetters, and thus to escape the travail and confusion that are an inescapable part of the human condition.[34]

Our willingness to take risks in relationships, confident that we can manage conflict in ways that affirm ourselves and others, depends on our conviction of the rightness of our claims and the obligations of our call. In our study we found a number of women who were confused and wavering in these convictions. In her book *Intimate Strangers*, Lillian Rubin puts it this way,

> When couples who are trying to reorder traditional arrangements in the family live in the large urban centers of the country, there's usually enough social support to take the worst sting out of the criticism they hear. For those who live in the smaller towns and cities across the nation, it's considerably more difficult to sustain the way of life they're trying to build. But, irrespective of where they live, along with the external pressures — and perhaps hanging on so persistently because of them — there are their own internal voices that remind them that they have not yet wholly abandoned the old values themselves.[35]

The pressure to remain in or return to traditional patterns, particularly in times of uncertainty, is very strong. Even though we feel these traditional patterns are unsatisfactory, our socialization fails to provide us with alternatives. Rubin goes on to point out that the ambiguity we feel is most clearly seen when we think about our children, especially our daughters. As she says,

> A woman who seeks to integrate a work identity with mothering lives with a division inside herself — two selves that stir conflict and leave both mother and daughter in a difficult situation. If the daughter turns to a more traditional life than her mother had led, that's no good. If she chooses one that's even more in the vanguard, that doesn't satisfy either. For both options are felt by the mother

to be an implicit statement of her failure; both seem to invalidate not just her struggle for change but her very life itself.[36]

Why is it that we feel this way about our daughters' lives? We know the difficulties we encounter and want to spare our children from them. We want our daughters to be able to experience the fullness of a balanced life, giving up neither the development of their abilities and the contributions they can make to the world, nor the intimacy they can express within their families. We are still not really convinced they can do both because we are not really convinced that we can do both. And yet, we need to develop faith in our daughters and sons and the sons and daughters of others, trusting them to build on the foundation we are able to give them and to develop their own creative solutions to the problems they encounter. We must cultivate in ourselves a sense of hope for and confidence in the generation that will come after us. One of our participants expressed her feelings this way:

> Because we are searching for answers, we are more willing to come up with alternatives than people who aren't being stretched. I think that each of us working in our own realm, and then together as one, has made a big difference. I can tell it. Our struggle has certainly paid off, and it certainly will continue to.

Communicating with Men

The workplace and family changes we are seeking cannot be accomplished solely by a group of women working together, no matter how satisfying and supportive that may be. Although women's solidarity is certainly a key element, change will require the active support not only of the men who love us, but also of the men and women who are threatened by us and afraid.

When relating to our partners, we need to learn better ways of communicating our needs and listening for theirs. Good communication is not automatic; it is a learned skill, empowered by strong convictions and a high level of self-esteem. There are many excellent guides to communication, written for different life situations — couples, managers, parents and children, consumers. Some general principles common to them all are:

1. Stick to the issue at hand. Try not to bring up tangential sins of the past. Don't generalize beyond the specific point at hand ("See, you always . . . ").

2. Practice paraphrasing what the other is saying to check your perception of her/his point. Listen as least as much as you talk.

3. Be sensitive to the feelings that lie behind the verbal statements. Facial expressions and body language give good clues.

4. Talk in ways that affirm rather than attack the other person. Take responsibility for your own feelings and beliefs ("I feel or I think" rather than "You make me...").

5. Learn assertion skills that allow you to stand up for your rights without violating the rights of another. The general steps in a good assertive response are to describe the situation as objectively as possible, relate the feeling associated with the situation, ask for a specific behavior change on the part of the other person, and be ready to compromise in order to assure that the other person's needs are fulfilled as well.

6. Agree to disagree without attacking the personhood of the other. Seek further (professional) help when a true impasse occurs.

Communication requires a certain willingness to become vulnerable before another, to trust the other person enough to risk unguarded exposure. Courage to express our needs in risky situations comes from two sources — well-developed self-esteem (the love we feel for ourselves) and an unwavering belief in the justness of our convictions. As we saw in chapter 4, a spirituality grounded in *agape* love is the foundation not only for our care about other women and men, but also for our own self-esteem.

Mutual Concern at Home

Communication presupposes change as an end product. The change we seek in the relationship between women and men is well-described by Virginia Mollenkott as "mutual submission" (with the emphasis on mutual). Mollenkott finds justification for mutual submission or serving in the life of Christ and in the writings of Paul (see especially 1 Corinthians 11 and 12). About Christian marriage, she says,

> Christian equality is the result of mutual compassion, mutual concern, and mutual and voluntary loving service. The Christian way of relating achieves male-female equality through mutual submission.... There [is] no assumption that either partner is always right or is more important spiritually and hence should have the last word.... Each person is viewed as equally vital and valid in the process of determining God's will for the family. And because of the equal validity, each seeks to serve the other out of love.[37]

Mutual submission means that a couple will really share the tasks that are part of their shared life. He won't merely "help out" with the kids and she merely "help out" with the bills. But she will have equal responsibility for the financial well-being of the family, and he will have equal responsibility for child care and the nurturing of the family.

With respect to the children, it means that he not only takes the children to the pediatrician, to swimming lessons, to the barber, and to buy new shoes, but that he also knows when it's time for the next medical check-up and makes the appointment, initiates the discussion about whether a child could benefit from swimming lessons, notices that the child needs a hair cut, and arranges his Saturday morning to take the children shopping for shoes.[38]

With respect to work, she does not see her work as helping out, but as a mainstay of support for the well-being of the family, and as her responsible contribution to the larger community. Speaking of her personal experience following her husband's illness, Rubin says,

> I never knew what it meant to be responsible for the roof over my own head — let alone over the heads of my loved ones. That's what happens when you're born a girl rather than a boy. . . . For the first time, I was in the position that men know so well: If I didn't go to work today, there would be no money tomorrow. . . . It was only when the responsibility of supporting the family was dropped onto my shoulders that I could comprehend how oppressive a responsibility that is.[39]

Some couples find that role-reversal helps them experience dramatically the world of the other person and begin to appreciate the extent of gender-dependent expectations in our society. They agree for a specific period of time (an hour, a day, a week) to switch roles. He does everything she usually does (and says), and she does everything he usually does (and says). One woman told us,

> In our family, it would mean that I play catch with the kids after school while he cooks dinner. He would help with homework and find out what the kids need for the next day. I'd read stories to the kids, then go off to play basketball or back to work. He'd write to family members and say nurturing things to the neighbors. I'd turn down the heat, turn off the lights, and worry about the car inspection coming up.

This exercise is almost always eye-opening for both participants. And if the realities of life or lack of cooperation from one's partner make this exercise impossible, that in itself is further food for thought.

Experiencing the life of the other and helping that person to experience our life require that both of us be willing to give up some of the
control we have over our life. We have to allow our partner to approach
tasks that are new to him by bringing his own personality and creativity
to play. We have to allow him to do things differently from the way we
would do them, and even to make mistakes. Perhaps we have to lower
our standards for housekeeping, laundry, and meals, at least temporarily.
   One of our participants put it this way,

> When I'm not home for supper my husband always fixes the kids'
> spaghetti for supper. Usually they have corn or canned pears to
> go with it. At least I've progressed enough not to plan and fix
> everything up for them before I go, but I still worry a little about
> their nutrition. It's OK once in a while, but I'd hate for them to eat
> like that all the time. And another thing, when my husband mops,
> he never does behind the door. I guess we can live with dirt behind
> the door, but it's not my preference.

Especially in this transition time, women have to be willing to live with
less than perfect housekeeping and child-care behavior by men. Most
men have not been raised to know automatically how to do these things.
If we constantly tell them how to do something or criticize their efforts,
they are not likely to be too enthusiastic about trying. Perhaps we will
have to tell ourselves that the kids can take vitamins and we can sacrifice
our best sweater washed in hot water for the sake of the development
of men in the family. Surely men have something valuable to teach us
about family nurturance just as we have something valuable to teach
them about workplace practices.

Mutual Concern at Work

A spiritually-based mutual serving between women and men is important
in the work world as well as at home. Changing many of the practices that would make possible a better integration of work and family
life depend on the understanding and commitment of one's immediate
supervisor and co-workers. Here too we need honest and courageous
communication. Courageous communication in the workplace means we
are willing to acknowledge and overcome our insecurities about not being
taken seriously when we speak out in defense of women's rights. Part
of the problem derives from our own ambivalent feelings about our dual
commitment to family and work, and part from societal and workplace
discrimination against women.
   One woman we know was on spring break. When she has a break
from teaching, she always tries to do something special with her children.

(This of course produces guilt, because she also needs to be working on research and writing during teaching breaks.) She recalls,

> I arranged to have lunch with my daughter, a neighbor, and the neighbor's daughter at the local Dairy Queen. While we were eating lunch, the dean of my husband's college walked in. I didn't know this man well and was not sure he knew what I did professionally. I was worried that he would think I was a homemaker and dismiss me. I was torn between my desire not to devalue the importance of spending time with my child and my friend, and my desire to be taken for a serious professional. I was not confident that the dean could see me parenting a child and still assume that I was a professional. For the same reason, I very infrequently take my children to the office. Keeping my private and professional lives separate is my way of assuring that I keep my professional credibility. My husband, on the other hand, more often takes the children to his office. Many of the students and cleaning personnel know the children well. My husband is well respected. Evidence of his private life in the professional world does not hurt his professional standing.

A participant pointed out that women especially are criticized for taking time off work for family responsibilities:

> If you look at the time that a president is out on the golf course weekly — during the middle of the day they disappear to go play golf — nobody says, where's this forty-hour week now? But if a woman took that same amount of time to do something that to her was important and involved family, the thing would be that she's goofing off.

In the same vein,

> When one of us was in graduate school, she and the other students had desks outside the faculty offices. One male faculty member complained that the "girls" talked too much and disturbed his work. The only woman faculty member (in a thirty-member department) told him she would speak to us only after he stopped reliving the week-end sports events with the male students, a habit he had which bothered her work.

It is important to realize that when women are accused of wasting time at work, they may really be engaged in tension-relieving activities that are merely different from the ones men engage in. Women who talk about what is important to them at work (their children, home decorating) are seen as disturbing others, whereas men who talk about the things that are important to them (sports events) are engaging in normative behavior.

In our work situations, we also have to insist on our right to flexibility, especially when that flexibility has no negative effect on the operations of the company.

> One woman very tentatively asked her department chair if it would be possible not to schedule a class for her on a particular afternoon because of her child-care responsibilities. He is known to have arranged his teaching schedule to fit his family and professional responsibilities, but told her that she would just have to take whatever schedule she got.

Unless the corporation has a policy allowing for flexible schedules, her only recourse is to appeal to him on a personal level. But women can share these experiences with each other and move for change in a way suggested by one of our participants:

> My personality sort of tends to say, OK, this is an institutional problem; these are the people who are interested in it; let's get together and do something about it. And it's effective, but it means building community, consensus, constituency, developing a plan, going to your supervisor and saying, "Now these are the kinds of things we can do, and we're willing to do this, that, and the other. What are you willing to do for us?" And until more people start doing that, the force of inertia will keep everything exactly the way it is.

Reweaving Life

There's an educational film we once saw called *The Fable of He and She*.[40] In it, a series of unexpected events resulted in the women (called she-mels) being separated from the men (called hardy-bars) and children by a vast stretch of water. Before the split, hardy-bars and she-mels had worked contently in their separate spheres, but now they were forced to enter the realm of the other gender if they were to survive. After initial controversy and several false starts, they managed quite well. But they managed in different ways. Thanks to two courageous individuals, hardy-bars developed new dishes that sounded disgusting but were really nutritious and quite tasty. They built a different kind of swing to soothe the babies. Meanwhile, the she-mels designed new forms of architecture and built the tools they needed for construction. As is only possible in fables, the islands came together again and the hardy-bars, children, and she-mels were reunited. They did not immediately go back to their former roles. They began to share their insights and responsibility for care and production within the community. Their individual lives and their community were immeasurably enriched when the creative abilities of all of the members were encouraged to blossom, when spheres of influence were not rigidly separated, but woven together into the variegated tapestry that was their community.

So in the end, we are faced with a task that is often a lonely one, played out in the innermost recesses of our hearts and in the times when we share most intimately the life of another. And yet these private tasks are being multiplied by the millions. If the sharing of these personal struggles can lead to solidarity among women and men, the re-creation of a balance of work and family life will be genuinely possible. Values of intimacy and connectedness *can* become public virtues. We have begun to taste the fullness of humanity lived in communion with others and the taste is so sweet that there is no turning back. Internal and external obstacles will be placed in our paths, but we will overcome even these. And together we will build a new life, for other women's daughters, and for other men's sons.

Chapter 11

Ourselves, Our Daughters, and Our Sons: Concrete Tasks for the Future

In this family, they're both professionals. She's a teacher; he's a dentist. This means that his income potential probably is at least three times greater than hers. . . . What's sensible about the wage disparity between dentists and teachers? . . . Isn't it at least as important to educate our children as it is to fix their teeth? — Lillian Rubin

For all those who work for the sake of their own families and for the sake of the family of humankind, and who are committed to integrating the private sphere of the family with the public sphere of work, change in traditional family and workplace structure is vital. The subtle and overt resistance from business and professional communities highly invested in the traditional family/work pattern is personally frustrating and corporately harmful to our continued development as a society. To the extent that each individual is shaped by and feels loyalty to these business and professional communities, we too resist (or are unable to envision) necessary change.

In this chapter we will consider current business/professional attitudes and practices that interfere with a communion of private and public life, examine interim strategies that have been proposed to affect greater work and family integration, and end with a vision for a future in which human potential is realized in an environment committed to family nurturance and humane work. The creativity and determined leadership necessary to bring this vision to life are only just beginning to take form. They are rooted in our ability to see work and family as the "whole" of adult life rather than as separate, disconnected parts.

178

Current Attitudes and Practices

When Patricia Schroeder, Democratic representative from Denver, announced her decision not to seek the Democratic nomination for the presidency in 1988, she said that she couldn't turn every encounter between people into a photo opportunity, she couldn't lose contact with the needs of the people she represents.[1] After Walter Mondale and Geraldine Ferraro lost the 1984 presidential election, Jeanne Kirkpatrick was asked why more women did not enter politics. She said that in addition to overt discrimination against women in politics, women are not willing to give up family and private life to the extent required in political life. Schroeder and Kirkpatrick, representatives of very different political perspectives, both felt the same thing, the reluctance of women to enter a political arena dominated by a traditional masculine value system and lifestyle. Business and professional life, especially at the higher levels, is no less governed by male patterns of behavior and the life experiences of men.

Work Patterns

Currently the workplace does not encourage multi-dimensional lives or easy transitions between work and family roles over the course of a worker's lifetime. The typical pattern is for twelve to twenty years of education followed by forty to fifty years of uninterrupted work, then mandatory retirement.[2] In the first fifteen years of the traditional work pattern, the trajectory of one's career is set. Hence, from about ages twenty-five to forty, one is expected to prove one's worth to the company or profession by working fifty- to sixty-hour weeks, being available nights and weekends, and being willing to travel or relocate. These are also the prime child-bearing and child-rearing years for parents.

For women, work patterns are often quite different. Although there is less uniformity among women, two patterns are relatively common. Some women marry and have children relatively early in life, often interrupting their education or career to do so. If they work for pay while the children are young, it is usually in a less demanding position, often part time. At around age thirty-five, once the children are in school, these women return to job training, education, or their previous careers, realizing that thirty years or so of work life remains. However, in career advancement and salary they are about ten years behind, and often never recover those lost years.

Other women continue their education and early career without interruption. When they reach age thirty or so, the biological clock begins to tick loudly. Being highly competent individuals, they often enter a pregnancy confident that they can handle the added stress of a child.

They may be able to dismiss the remnants of guilt as they drop the child off with the sitter. They may have a spouse who shares household and child-care responsibilities. But they don't often anticipate the fatigue of the pregnancy and post-partum period or the feelings they have after the child is born. For most of these women, having a child means at least a psychological interruption of their career, even if they continue to work full time.

A woman we know went to law school several years after college. At thirty she was married, had passed the bar, and had a job with a prestigious law firm in a large city. She hated it and after two years moved to another firm. Even though the new job was a struggle, she and her husband decided they couldn't delay childbearing much longer. At thirty-five she became pregnant. She was a little surprised when nausea and fatigue in her first trimester caused her to close her door and nap for two hours in the afternoon. Since the baby was born she has been torn between wanting to continue her career and wanting to spend time with her child. She is unsure what path her career will take.

Of course not everyone's work life follows these demanding but relatively predictable patterns. For many of us, our work lives and those of our spouses have been characterized by dissatisfaction at our place of work, job changes, starting over at the bottom, branching out on our own, and periods of unemployment. These events, too, usually happen in the first years of work life, compounding and lengthening the years of insecurity and stress. Some would say women who want to combine career and family should follow the "mommy-career-track," admitting that they are not serious, committed professionals and thus not eligible for promotion to the highest levels of the company. Once again we see women's experiences defined as problematic for companies. No one speaks of "daddy-tracks." In fact, the appropriate response to our changing life-patterns would be to acknowledge that both men and women have added responsibilities in the home sphere for the prime child-rearing years and to change the expectations of career progress accordingly.

Decisions not to "buy into" the present competitive model of career advancement can be an admirable witness — even prophetic. But the cost is great. Material sacrifices are very real, but even more profound is the fact that individuals who choose to blaze a new trail, perhaps among the wisest and most caring individuals, are usually not able to reach positions of power and influence where they could become change agents for others.

Work Culture

Higher education and specific job-training programs are also dominated by traditional male behavior — aggression, competitiveness, hierarchical management models, a win-lose decision making style. People advance in their careers through informal sponsorship arrangements, often known as the "old boys network." The social-emotional bonding that takes place in work settings is frequently accomplished in male-only social clubs or activities. Management models and behaviors clearly show the impact of the male sports experience in shaping work culture. A team of social psychologists writes,

> Males become familiar with competitive games at an early age. When they encounter unfamiliar situations later on, they try to understand them in terms of what is familiar. As a result, many types of relationships are described in sports terms, from "making a big hit" in a business presentation to "scoring" on a date. Unfortunately, such metaphors shape the way males think about relationships in unhelpful ways. . . . Sports contests are episodic by nature; they are either won or lost, so meeting mutual needs is inappropriate; any tactics that do not violate explicit rules are permissible and the other person is defined as an opponent rather than a potential ally in solving a mutual problem.[3]

Family Care

In order for women to take their rightful place in the world of work and professional life, changes in the culture of work are necessary. At the same time, responsibility for nurturing the family must be seen as a duty critical to our society and embraced by all — men, childless couples, and public policy makers. As Andolsen says,

> Children are not the sole property of the parents who conceived them. Nor should the woman who gives birth to a child be considered naturally responsible for that child's total care. Children are society's future; therefore society is responsible for the well-being of children. . . . Social programs need to be devised which assist families in coping with illness, disability or aging without placing undue burdens on the female members of the household. . . . The virtue of justice challenges us to strive to distribute domestic burdens equitably. Justice for wage-earning women requires not solely a fair division of chores among family members, but also greater support for domestic life.[4]

The greatest impediment to women's continued progress is our continuing responsibility for domestic chores and child care. Women at all occupational levels report inadequate time for meeting home and work responsibilities.[5]

Any distribution of family responsibilities which leaves the wage-earning women with the major share of household tasks violates the norm of justice. . . . Fair treatment of salaried women within the family requires significant social change, as well as personal commitment from household partners.[6]

One of our participants felt the burden of household responsibility very keenly when she said,

What's happening is that we just had a big family meeting about this two weeks ago because I was ready to walk. I can't handle this any more. He says, "I'll cut the grass." At the end of January there's not much grass to cut. So I kept a list of everything I did and he did for three days. Then I said to him, "I'm losing my mind."

As women move into the paid labor force, it is essential either for men to move equally into the unpaid labor force at home, or for alternatives fair to all to be found.

Interim Strategies

In the meantime, practical, interim alternatives have been suggested. Unfortunately, these accommodations are often based on old, faulty assumptions — that the individual woman is responsible for making personal changes that will enable her to cope better with societal and family expectations of her. These personal solutions continue to limit women's contributions to and advancement in professional life, as well as obligating her to continue disproportionate responsibility for the family. Further, they consign men to the economic sphere of life, denying them and their families their full participation in the nurturance of others. Let us turn now to the specific solutions that have been offered in response to the dilemma one faces trying to balance career and family and assess their real impact on increasing men's participation in the family and women's participation in the workplace.

Part-Time Work

One of the strategies most frequently adopted by women is to seek part-time employment. In our study, 55 percent of the women said they would prefer to work less than full time, given proportionate pay and opportunity for status and advancement in the workplace. National estimates are that about 25 percent of women in the paid work force currently work part time.[7] Conversely, few men work part time; nearly eighty percent of part-time workers are women.[8]

Many women are attracted to part-time work as a direct result of the unfair burden of child and family care resting on their shoulders. Others want to spend more time with their families than traditional full-time work allows. In either case, the cost of part-time work to one's professional development is very great. Part-time positions are generally rare in high-status positions unless the worker has already proved her value by dedicated, traditional, full-time work. (This is particularly true at higher administrative levels.) Additionally, the part-time person's contributions may not be taken seriously, as it is presumed she is less committed to her work. Important policy-setting meetings are scheduled without regard to the part-time worker's schedule, and often without her knowledge. If she wishes to participate, she does so on her own time.

Opportunities for advancement and access to powerful channels of influence within the profession are less available to the part-time worker. Financial and other benefits are rarely proportional to the number of hours worked. At one hospital with which we are familiar, nurses who wish to work part time are placed on a "casual schedule," emphasizing in a not-so-subtle way the status afforded them by the hospital. Although these women work twenty-four hours a week, they receive no medical or retirement benefits and are not allowed to return to a full-time position. In part-time positions such as these, time off and financial support for participation in professional meetings and continuing education are rare. Part-time workers are afforded little job security, often being the first to be laid off in times of economic hardship.

Temporary part-time workers (those hired by the company for non-continuous positions, not those who work for a temporary agency) enjoy even less status within the workplace. Laurel Walum has identified three types of workers that businesses need: the decision-makers; the cogs, who carry out the decisions; and the temporaries, who assist the cogs. Women fill the vast number of temporary positions. Their lower status is reinforced in part by the cogs (mostly men), who resent their own position with respect to the decision-makers, but feel superior to the temporaries.[9] Temporary workers generally have low wages, few or no benefits, little control over their work environments, minimal social relationships with their co-workers, and alienated attitudes with respect to their jobs.[10]

Despite the difficulties part-time workers face, they do provide great benefits to their employers. One study showed that part-time workers do 89 percent of the work that regular full-time workers do (though they get far less than 89 percent of full-time salary and benefits) and have one-third the turnover rate.[11] With new models that reflect care and commitment to the worker's needs, part-time work could be beneficial to the employee as well as to the employer. But part-time positions will be a helpful solution to the work-family dilemma only when workplace structures and attitudes change to support part-time workers, and when

part-time work is seen as a viable alternative for men, and at all levels
of employment.

One of the institutions we know recognized the valuable contributions
made by part-time workers and instituted a specific policy for them. Part-
time employees are given pay and benefits proportionate to the fraction
of full-time they work. In addition, they can be promoted, vote on policy
matters, and serve on decision-making committees. So far, this program
appeals mostly to women with young children, men of retirement age,
and women and men who wish to hold an additional part-time position
(usually as a consultant). The commitment of these workers will assure
the program's continuance.

Working at Home

Sometimes women who feel the pressure of family concerns choose to
work at home, perhaps on computer terminals connected to the office. Besides having to deal with the unpredictable demands of children, at-home
workers are cut off from informal channels of communication, mutual
support, and power in the workplace.

On the other hand, work at home might be seen as a temporary solution, especially in small companies. A law office of which we are aware
had three attorneys and two legal secretaries. One of the secretaries had
a child. The company paid her full salary during a three-month maternity
leave. In return she agreed to do as much work as she could at home,
in order to help the office cope with her absence. The other secretary
also agreed to take on extra work at the office (anticipating the return
favor when she had a baby). This temporary arrangement required care
for and trust between all the people involved. This is clearly an interim
strategy, the best solution possible at the present time, but not ideal for
either of the secretaries involved, or for the attorneys.

Flextime

Flextime, varying one's hours at work around a common core, may make
scheduling of child care and family maintenance activities (such as wait-
ing for deliveries and repair people) easier, but it generally does not
involve a lesser time commitment to work, and may in fact be harder
on the family. One study of the work patterns of dual-career couples
showed that families with young children are especially likely to use the
concept of flextime in arranging the hours they work.[12] On the average,
a dual-career couple spends 16.95 hours a day at work (8.2 hours for
the wife, and 8.8 hours for the husband). But in families with children
under six years of age, both parents are gone only 6.13 hours a day.
Working couples with young children schedule their work time this way

to minimize external child-care needs and costs. Nevertheless these arrangements have a profound impact on the time the family unit and the couple have to spend together.

For example, if she works 7:00 a.m. to 3:30 p.m., and he works 10:00 a.m. to 6:30 p.m., they are working a total of about seventeen hours a day, and at least one of them is home all but six hours a day (7–10 and 3:30–6:30). For about ten hours a day, the family is not together as a total unit. In our example, the whole family would be together from 6:30 until they went to bed. Allowing for supper, baths, laundry, bed-time stories, and church or community activities, this couple would be lucky to have an hour a day together. On the other hand, if both worked 8:30–5:00, the family would be together an additional three hours per day, but they would also need three more hours of child care.

Hiring Domestic Help

The following scenario is only a dream for most working women:

> When Matthew was born, his parents' answer to the child-care question was to hire a live-in au pair as well as a housekeeper who worked three days a week. Later [they] replaced the au pair with a governess.... For the past year and a half a daily housekeeper has been taking care of the cleaning, laundry, shopping, and cooking.[13]

At a just wage, most women cannot afford domestic help, especially in addition to the cost of child care. In a major urban center, full-time child care for two preschool children costs about $1200–1400 a month. That total is equivalent to the take-home pay of many social workers, church workers, and educators, to say nothing of the salaries of many non-professionals. Only families with incomes over $50,000 can really afford child care, much less domestic help.

In addition, middle-class women are often caught in a moral-economic dilemma. Domestic and child-care workers who are hired by women struggling with their own low wages work for even lower wages and fewer benefits. Unjust wages for domestic and child-care workers exploit these women and reflect the lack of value we place on child care. Informal arrangements that are not reported to the government deny domestic workers and immigrants the protection of social security. In addition, the fact that virtually all domestic workers are women contributes to the presumption that domestic work is the just responsibility of wives or their substitutes.

The few women who have chosen to stay at home with their children are overburdened with requests from the school, brownie and cub scout troops, and the church for the volunteer activities that were once more widely shared. Some at-home women, sensitive to the criticism they have received, are reluctant to help working women who are perceived to have denied motherhood and homemaking, forsaking children and community service for the apparently more rewarding world of work. The unfortunate bitterness that sometimes surfaces between homemaking women and women who work outside the home is part of the legacy of Sarah and Hagar — a resentment stemming from the strains both groups of women feel trying to survive in a world that is not truly supportive of women in either the public or private sphere. If we can move beyond our differences and see our common need for a culture that esteems both women's productive and reproductive work, perhaps we can reach a new level of solidarity.

Time Management

Articles and books that advise women to manage their time better and treatment programs that advocate training for more effective anxiety-management skills are insulting to women, already notoriously efficient time managers. They also presume that women have an obligation to "cope" with an unjust situation.

Job-Sharing

Job-sharing is a remedy with a certain appeal. Two (or more) people, either related or not, share the responsibilities and benefits of a single job. Couples who share a position — mostly professionals such as ministers, professors, and administrators — have been found to divide child-care responsibilities more equitably, to have more leisure time, to report an increased satisfaction with their work lives, to have a lower absenteeism rate, to cooperate well, and to have an enhanced sex life.[14] As we noted in chapter 2, when men and women work together, they enjoy more intimacy with each other, emotionally, spiritually, and physically. On the negative side, though, the family's income is less than if both partners worked at full-time jobs. Promotion and tenure rights are ambiguous at best, and if one of the job-share partners quits, filling that position may be difficult for the company. In short, job-sharing shows some promise for some persons in special circumstances (couples in the same, high-paid profession), but to date is too rare and complex to have been thoroughly studied.

Visionary Models

The mandate we present for the future calls for both attitudinal and be-havioral changes that must come about on a number of levels. First, changes must come from deep within the heart and mind of an individual willing to give up the security of the status quo for the promise of a better future, maybe not even for herself, but for her daughters and sons, or even for her friend's daughters and sons. As we have suggested previously, shaping our lives by the virtues of courage, self-esteem, and a self-giving solidarity with others will enable us to be agents of transformation.

Changes must also come in the relationships of couples seeking to find a richer commitment and intimacy through true sharing of their lives. Changes must come from small businesses willing to take a chance on the good-will of their employees by experimenting with creative solutions to human problems, and from large corporations willing to examine how they might move from controlling the family life of their employees to allowing family needs to control corporate policies. Changes must come from the educational systems that train future adults. Finally, governmental regulations must ensure the rights of both women and men to full and mutual participation in their families and in their work.

In the last chapter we dealt with individual and family changes. In this final chapter we will concentrate on changes that must come in the larger social institutions. These changes, of course, require the personal commitment of a number of individuals and families with the courage to challenge the old and familiar for the new and uncertain.

Child-Rearing and Education

Early Childhood: We need to consider carefully the attitudes and behaviors that are shaped in the earliest years of life. One of the most often asked and presumably most important question at birth is the gender of the child. Friends and relatives begin immediately to define the baby in terms of its gender by the toys and clothes they bring, by the way they hold the child, and by the things they say to the child. Very few baby girls receive baseball bats and gloves while still in the hospital; very few boys receive dolls, ever.

At a local hospital the custom is to wrap newborn girls in pink blankets and newborn boys in blue blankets. Not too long ago, there were more baby boys than blue blankets. Hospital personnel had to start wrapping baby boys in pink blankets. Such an uproar! The hospital had to purchase more blue blankets to calm the babies' friends and relatives.

As we described in chapter 10, the pain that Phil Donahue and Sonia Johnson's mother felt in later life has its roots in the way children are treated at home and at school.

Elementary and Secondary Education: In school, girls need to be encouraged to study and develop their abilities in math and science while boys study and develop their abilities in literature and art. When girls get to college, they will be free to enter majors like engineering and medicine only if they have a good math and science background. These interests and aptitudes are nurtured in elementary school and before by the experiences and reading material we offer our children. An investigation of current textbooks and pleasure books written for children will show some important progress in these areas. At least the days of Dick and Jane have given way to women doctors and astronauts, if not male nurses and secretaries.

As girls and boys seek their unique identities in adolescence, opportunities for exploration and development of personal gifts and interests, free from gender stereotyping, are essential. Churches and synagogues should be especially attuned to helping young people discern a basic vocational direction that integrates their public and private hopes and dreams.

Higher Education: The role of higher education is to conduct basic and applied research into questions of human concern, to educate students and those outside the scholarly community regarding the results of research, to engage in a dialogue about fundamental human values, and to model a progressive vision in institutional policies. Specifically in a college or university, there should be opportunities:

1. *To discuss with students the issue of economic and gender justice, interpersonal mutuality, individualism versus civic virtue, and the need to reintegrate the public and private spheres of life.*

All these issues crucial to human development need to be discussed broadly across the curriculum, not relegated to specific ethics course or parts of courses. These issues also need to be connected to specific and concrete implications for the business and professional worlds. In church-related schools, there may be a stronger mandate to discuss the religious and spiritual foundation of our commitment to civic virtue and to an integrated life. In these settings, there should be a sense of work as "calling," with both private and public dimensions.

2. *To teach and in other ways help to develop in women students the skills that will enable them to exercise power directly, effectively, and justly — skills of public speaking, persuasion, assertion, and critical thinking.*

These skill goals must be accomplished in ways that respect the relational strengths of women. Women who have genuine personal power and self-esteem will be able to fill positions of authority by resorting neither to authoritarian nor to indirect, manipulative methods of management.

3. *To encourage and support interdisciplinary study of human problems, particularly on issues pertaining to the integration of family life and career, and the interplay of the public and private spheres of life.*

The spiritual and ethical concerns of religious studies and philosophy need to be in active dialogue with the realities of economics and business. Research in history and data gathered in the social sciences can enlighten and facilitate the dialogue. Where this cannot be done effectively in public education, it should be done in the forum of church education.

4. *To demand that researchers consider the experience of women as integral to the human experience and not as an aberration.*

The commitment to women as normative affects not only the interpretation of research results, but also the framing of research questions and the design of research methodology.

Employment Practices

Job Entry and Recruitment: Following college graduation, as women and men move on to further study or to positions of employment, additional changes are needed. Often positions are not advertised, and if they are, it is only to satisfy the letter of the (equal opportunity) law. Higher level positions are especially likely to be offered on the basis of protégé sponsorship, through the "old boys network." Men in influential positions hesitate to sponsor women because of negative attitudes toward women workers ("She'll get pregnant and quit" or "She's one of those women's libbers"). Perhaps some of you have seen, as we have, a chief executive officer who time and time again calls up his old cronies or former (male) students and asks whom they would recommend for a position. These "cronies" are frequently brought in at a salary far greater than the salaries of those already in the company, creating ill will among employees.

We believe it is important for workers to develop watchdog groups to monitor an institution's hiring practices. It is up to employees to identify the unfair practices they see and to gather necessary data. Employees should operate as a group to minimize retaliation to an individual, then seek support from professional or governmental sources. For example, in higher education, the American Association of University Professors has the power to censure institutions with unfair labor practices. The federal government can provide support through the Equal Opportunity Office. The courage to act in ways that carry significant personal risk comes from our inner convictions that what we are doing is right — for ourselves and for other women's daughters.

Promotion and Advancement: Within a company, we need increased opportunities for women to advance. Currently, even in professions dominated by women workers (nursing, social work, teaching, and librarianship), administrative positions and positions of power in the associated professional organizations are controlled by men.[15] Among companies judged to be the best for women (more on that later), the greatest number of women board members is three out of thirteen. These three women are on the board of Avon, a company that produces products mostly for women.

Changes that benefit women (and men and families) have come mostly in companies that have women in powerful decision-making positions. We must work to increase the number of women in top-level administrative positions and on boards of directors. Churches can provide important models. In the church to which one of us belongs (Christian Church, Disciples of Christ) members of the national board are carefully and intentionally selected to represent the widest and fairest constituency. In addition, the constitutions of the Boards of Overseas and Homeland Ministries mandate equal numbers of women and men board members.

Linda Carpenter, who works as an industrial consultant to large companies, provides some helpful information to those who wish to bring about change in the workplace.[16] She says one can get further by focusing on the cost to the corporation (rather than to women) of certain business practices. Companies interested in hiring the best people need to look at the data on entering workers. Women constitute 44 percent of the workforce. Fifty-three percent of recent college graduates are women. Eighty-five percent of professional women go back to work following the birth of a baby. The average employee holds 10.5 jobs in a lifetime. Both men and women consider issues such as paternity leave, health care, leisure time, opportunities for lateral as well as upward movement, opportunities for nearby spouse employment, and work hours required, when deciding to take a particular job. Companies that continue to concentrate on traditional recruitment and retention practices will not have the workers they need for the future.

Carpenter also invokes the 80/20 rule. She says that in working for change it is crucial to be efficient. Don't waste time trying to change policies that have a relatively small impact on the lives of workers. Instead, look for the 20 percent of company policy that will change 80 percent of the company's behavior. In looking for the crucial 20 percent, observe and monitor actual company behavior, not written policy. For instance, measures that make it more possible for women with families to hold management positions might affect a great deal of a company's future behavior. Finally, structure solutions to fit the habitual response of the company. If in times of crisis top administrators habitually turn to an executive committee for advice, make sure that sympathetic women and men are members of the executive committee.

Wages: The wage differential between men and women continues to interfere with the continued progress of women in the work world. Perhaps we have progressed some from the colonial period when 30–50 percent of what a man made for the same work was considered appropriate pay for women, to the present day, when women make about 70 percent of what men make. But many people still claim that this wage differential is accounted for by the fact that women "choose" low-paying jobs. In reality, one-third to one-half of the pay difference between men and women is due to the fact that women are paid less than men for the *same* job.[17] As one of our participants, an accountant, said,

> If a man spent as much time as I do with the professional tasks, he would be in the very top category of earnings — $200,000 a year. I make less than $50,000 even with extra summer employment.

A part of the discrepancy does come from the fact that women are concentrated in low-paying jobs (or that jobs in which women are concentrated are low-paying). Unequal monetary reward for jobs that require the same skill, effort, and responsibility causes a host of related problems. Women who must support their children have great difficulty and often are forced to live in poverty. When a wife makes substantially less than her husband, even for comparable work, she has less status in the family. Her career is considered to be less important when it comes to decisions about where to move and how to divide household responsibilities. Unfair salaries may account in large part for the unfair distribution of household tasks.[18] The answer, of course, is comparable pay. Lillian Rubin illustrates the importance of the concept of comparable pay this way.

> In this family, they're both professionals. She's a teacher; he's a dentist. This means that his income potential probably is at least three times greater than hers.... What's sensible about the wage disparity between dentists and teachers? Don't they both do work that's socially valuable? Isn't it at least as important to educate our children as it is to fix their teeth?... The disparity lies in the fact that one is dominantly women's work, the other, men's. We might notice, too, that such differences permeate the entire wage structure of our economy — that we, as a society, have systematically devalued the work women do, thereby justifying this inequality.[19]

It is generally not the value of the work but the gender of the worker that determines the wage.

Traditionally unionization has helped workers deal with unfair wages. Here again, though, women are at a disadvantage. It is considered selfish and even unethical for workers to unionize (and especially to strike) in the very fields dominated by women (service professions such as public school teaching and nursing). Because women are concentrated in positions where they care for the welfare of others, union activities are not considered an appropriate alternative for them. The recent success of the Harvard Technical and Clerical Workers Union, mentioned above in chapter 5, is a hopeful example of women's leadership and solidarity making a difference. The concern of its membership for a rich and complex life, rather than for a narrowly-defined "success" is indicative of the integrative insight women bring to the work world.

Women who choose to remain in the home, either temporarily or permanently, need financial protection as well. They need to be assured of social security and other retirement and health benefits independently of their husbands. As we well know, a husband can leave, taking not only his wife's immediate financial security, but her long-term security as well.

Corporate Personnel Policy: There are a number of companies that are beginning to establish policies and adopt corporate attitudes that will lead to a better integration of public and private life. In 1986, *Working Mother* magazine identified the thirty best companies for working mothers.[20] According to their definition, companies good for women were characterized by: decreased reliance on traditional hierarchical styles of management and more reliance on democratic management; decreased rigidity in personnel practices and more willingness to try innovative ideas; less authoritarian and more intuitive, consensus-based decision-making models; and greater compassion (more attention to employee and community needs) in corporate policies. Specifically, these companies offer good pay, fair benefits, and good opportunities for women to advance. Among them were companies that offered: sabbaticals for study and research, a summer camp program for school-age children, aid to workers wishing to adopt children, college loans for workers and their dependents, lenient transfer policies with specific help for the spouse trying to find a position in the new community, wellness programs, employee profit sharing, and, in one case, take-out dinners.

In 1987 *Ms. Magazine* reported a similar survey. The criteria for this survey included: the availability of flextime, job-sharing, maternity and paternity leave, and child-care resources; the number of women directors, top executives, officials, and managers; the number of women among the highest paid; the position of the highest-ranking woman; the companies' policies on sexual preference, sexual harassment, and purchases from women-owned businesses.[21] The seven companies that made both the *Ms.* and *Working Mother* lists were Campbell Soup, General Motors, IBM, Kellogg, Pillsbury, Procter & Gamble, and Xerox. These companies represent the best we currently offer workers. But most of us don't work for these huge companies. In our view we still have far to go.

Some people are concerned about the profitability of companies with policies specifically designed to be helpful to families. Rosabeth Moss Kanter reported on a study of the financial performance of companies with specific policies for serving the public and a history of putting these policies into practice. The report concluded that,

[After instituting such policies, these companies] showed a 10.3 percent growth in profits compounded over 30 years — better than... the growth of the Gross National Product, which rose at a 7.8 percent rate during the same period....Equally impressive were the results for the shareholder....For the 30 years studied, a $30,000 investment spread evenly over the companies would have been worth five times what an equal amount would have earned invested in a composite of the Dow Jones.[22]

It is clear that policies that are good for women, men, and families are also good for business. The authors of both survey articles suggest that we rate our employers on the same criteria, and work to change the areas in which they are particularly weak.

Issues to Consider in Workplace Change

We found that our respondents had difficulty imagining the sorts of changes in the workplace that would be helpful to them and would undoubtedly benefit from information about what other companies are doing. The following questions are ones we encountered in our research. As we seek positions and as we serve on personnel and welfare committees, these questions can give us direction for change.

1. Are there opportunities for part-time work and job-sharing at higher levels of management?[23]

2. Are frequent transfers of employees necessary? Are workers allowed to refuse transfers without penalty?

Today one-third to one-half of executives asked to transfer are refusing because the transfer would interfere with the spouse's position![24] When transfers are necessary, companies should assist spouses in finding a position in the new community by advertising all jobs within a company in the same ad and actively soliciting applications from dual-career couples.[25] Different companies can also cooperate in finding jobs for spouses. Perhaps assisting in this task is a worthwhile activity for chambers of commerce.

3. Are there creative alternatives to frequent travel, such as the use of conference calls and computer-generated data transfer? Are workers allowed compensatory time off for travel?

4. Is overtime discouraged by basing promotion on reasonable workloads with no extra consideration given for excessive overtime work?

Workaholics who neglect their family responsibilities should be denied promotions rather than rewarded for unhealthy behavior.

5. Do personal benefits for workers include the services of an errand person for employees (like the handicapped man, Benny, on "L.A. Law") and employee assistance programs and support groups for those experiencing stress?[26]

6. *Can the traditional pattern of work be altered to allow for periods of education, work, and rest? Could workers "bank" credit for later time off or release from responsibilities?*[27] *Would a spiral model of work characterized by upward movement with pauses along the way to attend to family-personal needs be possible?*[28]

The patterns of our personal lives could be quite compatible with American work life if we simply acknowledged that for the approximately three to eight years of childbearing and preschool, the professional lives of the parents would be limited. For example, let's imagine a high school English teacher who has finished his M.A. and six years of successful teaching at age twenty-nine. He and his wife begin their family. He works half time for seven years so she can finish her internship and begin her medical career full time. At thirty-six, with his second child starting kindergarten, he resumes full-time teaching. She establishes a group practice where she can work somewhat regular and limited hours.

7. *Is one's position and salary guaranteed following maternity or paternity leaves, leaves to care for sick relatives, and leave to care for an adopted child?*

A study conducted by the Institute for Women's Policy Research for the American Association of University Women showed that lack of parental leave costs workers (who are taxpayers) $715 million each year in lost wages. The Government Accounting Office estimates it would cost employers $102 million to provide parental leave.[29]

8. *Do work and school schedules conform so that parents can more easily care for children?*[30] *Do the schools provide supervision early enough in the morning so that parents can get to work on time? Are school children transported to their after-school care?*

9. *Are women granted equal access to land, capital, technology, and credit?*[31]

Some fear that corporate policy changes will negatively affect a company's profit margin and thus our gross national product. The best evidence we have is that these fears are unfounded. But we do need to be sensitive to our responsibility to an employer who takes a risk on us and our sisters. To help assure the success of workplace changes we must engage in our most productive work and encourage others to do so as well. If we ask for justice, we must act justly ourselves. This aspect of a "public spirituality" recognizes that when we act thoughtlessly or dishonestly in our workplaces we multiply the damage to the cause of women's progress far more than the immediate repercussions to our institutions. Columnist Ellen Goodman makes an important related point:

There is a real tension between our wants and what we want from others. Nobody wants to be married to [or to be] a doctor who works weekends and makes house calls at 2 a.m. But every patient would like to find one. No one admires a lawyer who spends vacations and weekends with a briefcase, except, of course, the client. We all agree that a politician should spend private time with his [or her] family. And we all want him [or her] to speak at our banquet.[32]

Public Policy

Of course all these changes in corporate policy and the behavior of employers are informed by changes in our attitudes about the rights women have to work in the public realm and to shape public culture. Change rests on the conviction that women are called to contribute their talents to the common good and that their work and their influence are necessary to the continued development of the country. Discrimination against women may be obvious (unequal pay for the same work) or more subtle, but equally damaging (companies do not train women for higher-level positions because they are perceived as not really serious about a career or are considered to be on the "mommy-track"). The attitudes and myths that underlie subtle discrimination must be addressed as forcefully and clearly as overtly unfair practices are.

The presumption that traditional male patterns of work, styles of management, and life experiences are the most efficient and should form the basis for the world of work is simply not true. The separation of reproductive and nurturing work from productive work harms all of us. Further, the assumption that the traditional 1950s model of family life and structure is necessary for businesses to be competitive is not supported by careful study.

And yet, attitude change often lags far behind behavior change. If one concentrates on attitudes among the rank and file, one has a long battle to fight. If, rather, visions and attitudes are firmly established among the leaders, they can push for changes necessary to a fuller integration of life for all. Psychologist Uma Sekaran reminds us:

As early civil rights legislation has indicated, attitudes are an important part of the movement toward equality and opportunity for groups, but attitudes often follow rather than precede behavioral adaptations of both individuals and organizations and institutions. For this reason, the political institution — and its active identification, monitoring, and enforcement of equity — is a critical area for intervention in the movement toward equality for women in work and society.[33]

Or as a former president is purported to have put it, "if you have them by the balls, their hearts and minds are sure to follow."

We have the following specific suggestions for public policy changes.

1. *Seek new models of political life that respect the importance of the family in human life.*

Limiting campaign spending and the length of campaigns is a first step. Programs such as Feminization of Power, founded by Eleanor Smeel, former president of NOW, encourage women to run for public office, then provide financial and sophisticated political support for their efforts. This program has identified lack of financial support early in the campaign as the primary factor that lessens women's chances of being elected to public office. In response, they have established the Emily Fund (Early Money Is Like Yeast. It helps the dough rise.).

2. *Provide financial and other political support for pro-family, pro-workplace change candidates. Form and support watchdog groups that assess the platforms and voting behavior of current representatives. Organize letter-writing and phone campaigns to express pro-family views.*

3. *Develop family-centered laws regarding public support for child care for all children (infants included), and for paternity and maternity leave.*

Before the 1988 presidential nominations, all the candidates were invited to a panel discussion on child care sponsored by the Child Care Action Campaign. No one came. Panel moderator Patricia Schroeder said,

> The candidates really don't understand child care because political marriages are the last traditional marriages in America.... Intellectually they understand it, but it's not a gut issue for them.[34]

We need to make child care a gut issue for men as well as for women. Our political leaders must understand that appropriations that help poor people afford child care are only a tiny step in the right direction. Availability and quality of child care, as well as affordability for all families, are issues that must be addressed in legislation. Promises made in the 1988 presidential campaign have yet to be fulfilled.

European models of pro-family governmental policies provide good resources for us. In reporting on the conclusions of the Family Policy Panel of the Economic Policy Council of the United Nations Association of the USA, a group established to sponsor involvement of private companies in international economic matters, Sylvia Hewlett found France to have the most progressive policies. French policy represents a national consensus that unites right-wing political groups with the Catholic church, Socialist party, and labor unions. It not only supports single and working parents, but traditional families as well.

> [The panel] liked the French mind set, which regards motherhood as "a social function similar to military service for men, that had

to be financially supported by the whole community." One panel member remembered that twenty years ago, when he did National Guard duty, he had no trouble getting a six-month paid leave from his job as a junior executive with a Madison Avenue advertising firm. He told the panel that giving a child a good start in life was probably just as important to the nation as a tour of military duty.[35]

Anna-Greta Leijon, Minister of Labor in Sweden and a guest speaker at a Family Policy Panel meeting, contrasted this to United States family policy, illustrated by Jesse Helms's proposed 1981 family protection bill:

[This bill] sought to get rid of sex education, eliminate birth control information, and repeal federal wife and child abuse laws in the name of supporting the family.[36]

4. *Provide grant or seed money for corporations beginning imaginative or "model" programs, especially for small organizations attempting innovative policies.*

For instance, the capital might be provided for constructing a child-care facility, which the organization would then agree to staff and maintain in a 50-50 partnership with those who use it.

The Role of Churches and Synagogues

Since public policy change is inevitably grounded in the religious and ethical values of our society, churches and other humanitarian organizations bear a special responsibility to lead the way by their own practices. We have the following specific suggestions for religious organizations.

1. *Grant women access to all positions of spiritual and administrative leadership within the church, including ordination.*

When women are denied these crucial leadership roles, not only are their particular contributions lost, but all women continue to be relegated to "other, abnormal, less-than holy" status. Both women and men need the unique spiritual resources of women leaders.

2. *Develop study materials to assist groups of people considering issues presented here in the context of their own faith development.*

3. *Explore alternate fund-raising techniques. Replace labor-intensive fund-raising efforts (like bake sales) with pledges by highly-paid, two-income families.*

This approach not only reduces the guilt of dual-career families who don't have the time to bake the goodies, sit at the sale, then buy back the goodies, but also reduces the burden on the few people who are not working outside the home.

4. Develop programs and services that meet the actual needs of people.
Church leaders need to consider what their programs and policies say
about the kinds of families that are welcome and valued in the church.
For instance, if women's programs meet only during the day, or if only
women are welcomed at day-time programs, the message is that working
women are not valued, and that men at home during the day are an
aberration. On the other hand, churches that offer quality child care, meal
programs for the elderly, and shelters for the abused and homeless give
an entirely different message to the community and to their members.

*5. Remain vigilant in assessing the values that govern the corporate be-
havior of churches and synagogues. Look for more profound ways to remain
faithful to the agape ethic by encouraging the redefinition of virtue for men
and women, a redefinition in which interpersonal and civic virtues are balanced components of a public spirituality.*

*6. Stimulate creative and visionary thinking about the future that rec-
ognizes that in the design of God there is neither Jew nor Greek, male nor
female, slave nor free.*

Conclusion

That women have had difficulty envisioning and working toward change
is both understandable and problematic. For too long, women have been
pitted against each other by schools, churches, and employers. Solidarity
is difficult. Issues of class and race are intertwined with issues of gender
fairness. Women don't have much time to agitate for change when they
are barely surviving in their families and careers. Finally, there is not
a generic woman's experience or set of woman's needs. We live in a
pluralistic society characterized by a multitude of experiences and needs.

There is, however, a commonality among us that transcends the individual. The issue is ultimately one of simple human justice. On what
basis will decisions be made in our world? Will it be on the basis of
accumulated power, or gender, or money, or will it be on the basis of an
agapeic ethic that considers the greatest good for all? Will we work for
the integration of public work and private care so that all of us, women,
men, and children, will be able to enjoy a fuller, richer, more productive life, lived out in the context of our deepest personal beliefs and in
community with all our fellow humans?

Notes

Introduction

1. The first stage of our research consisted of a survey sent to a randomly-selected sample of 286 professional and semi-professional women in the state of West Virginia. We received 153 responses, a 53.5 percent return rate. The respondents included women in business (21 percent), higher education (30 percent), psychology (19 percent), nursing (15 percent), and other professions such as social service, medicine, and law (15 percent). Their average age was 39.9 years (with a range from 22 to 65 years). Sixty-nine percent were currently married and 56 percent had dependent children. Seventeen percent had less than a bachelor's degree as the highest degree held, 11 percent had a bachelor's, 48 percent had a master's, and 24 percent had a doctorate. The survey instrument included 53 Likert-type items (agree-disagree on a scale of 1–7). We also solicited and received 21 responses from men who were spouses of women in the sample.

Although this was a small and self-selected sample it provided us with some interesting comparative data. After initial analysis of the survey data we conducted four group interviews with a total of about 40 women, and the personal comments we quote come from those interviews. We did not collect information on race or ethnic background on our surveys, but judging from those who participated in our interviews most of our respondents were relatively successful white women. The demographics of our state limit the ethnic and racial diversity available to us among middle-class professional women. A study of women in a large urban area would undoubtedly provide a better balance. Further design and demographic details not discussed in this book are available from the authors.

Chapter 1
Careers and Families among American Women: Can We Do Both?

1. Sylvia Ann Hewlett, *A Lesser Life: The Myth of Women's Liberation in America* (New York: William Morrow, 1986), p. 16.

2. Parker J. Palmer, *The Company of Strangers: Christians and the Renewal of America's Public Life* (New York: Crossroad, 1981), pp. 22, 31.

3. Ida Withers Harrison, *Forty Years of Service: A History of the Christian Woman's Board of Missions 1874–1914* (privately published), p. 17.

4. Rosalind Rosenberg, *Beyond Separate Spheres: Intellectual Roots of Modern Feminism* (New Haven: Yale University, 1982), p. 177.

5. Agnes N. O'Connell and Nancy F. Russo, *Models of Achievement; Reflections of Eminent Women in Psychology* (New York: Columbia University Press, 1983).

6. R. Rowan, "How Harvard's Women MBA's are Managing," *Fortune* 108 (1983), pp. 58–72.

7. Barbara Basler, "Putting a Career on Hold," *New York Times Magazine* (December 7, 1986), p. 152.

8. Debra R. Kaufman, "Associational Ties in Academe: Some Male and Female Differences," *Sex Roles* 4 (1978), pp. 9–21.

9. Hewlett, *A Lesser Life*, p. 407, n. 10.

10. Mary Kay Blakely, "Calling All Working Fathers," *Ms.* 15 (December 1986), p. 33.

11. M. A. Ferber and J. W. Loeb, "Performance, Rewards, and Perception of Sex Discrimination Among Male and Female Faculty," *American Journal of Sociology* 78 (1973), pp. 996–997.

12. Nijole V. Benokraitis, "Employment Problems of Women: Federal Government Examples." In Karen Wolk Feinstein, ed., *Working Women and Families* (Beverly Hills, Calif.: Sage, 1979), pp. 223–246.

13. Kaufman, "Associational Ties in Academe," 1978.

14. Rebecca B. Bryson, Jeff B. Bryson, Mark H. Licht, and Barbara G. Licht, "The Professional Pair: Husband and Wife Psychologists," *American Psychologist* 31 (1976), pp. 10–16.

15. Thomas W. Martin, Kenneth J. Berry, and R. Brooke Jacobsen, "The Impact of Dual-Career Marriages on Female Professional Careers: An Empirical Test of a Parsonian Hypothesis," *Journal of Marriage and Family* 37 (1975), pp. 734–742.

16. Phyllis Bronstein, Leora Black, Joyce Pfennig, and Adele White, "Getting Academic Jobs: Are Women Equally Qualified — And Equally Successful?" *American Psychologist* 41 (1986), pp. 318–322.

17. J. Centra and N. Kuykendall, *Women, Men, and the Doctorate* (Princeton, N.J.: Educational Testing Service, September 1974).

18. Spencer Rich, "The Vanishing Family: A Myth," *Louisville Courier-Journal*, October 18, 1987.

19. Beverly Johnson and Elizabeth Waldman, "Most Women Who Maintain Families Receive Poor Labor Market Returns," *Monthly Labor Review* 106 (December 1983), p. 31.

20. U.S. Bureau of the Census, *Current Population Reports: Household and Family Characteristics*, March 1983 (Washington, 1984), p. 6. Cited in Barbara H. Andolsen, "A Woman's Work Is Never Done." In Barbara H. Andolsen, Christine E. Gudorf, and Mary D. Pellauer, eds., *Women's Consciousness, Women's Conscience* (San Francisco: Harper & Row, 1987), pp. 4, 6.

21. Rhona Rappoport and Robert N. Rappoport, "The Dual Career Family," *Human Relations* 22 (1969), p. 3.

22. Myra Strober, "Bringing Women into Management: Basic Strategies." In F. E. Gordon and M. M. Strober, eds., *Bringing Women into Management* (New York: McGraw-Hill, 1975). Laurel Richardson Walum, *The Dynamics of Sex and Gender: A Sociological Perspective* (Chicago: Rand McNally, 1977). Mary Frank Fox and Sharlene Hesse-Biber, *Women at Work* (Palo Alto, Calif.: Mayfield, 1984).

23. Andolsen, "A Woman's Work Is Never Done," p. 16.

24. Joanna Stratton, *Pioneer Women: Voices from the Kansas Frontier* (New York: Simon & Schuster, 1981), p. 57. Quoted in Hewlett, *A Lesser Life*, p. 235.

25. Jean E. Friedman and William G. Shade, *Our American Sisters: Women in American Life and Thought* (Lexington, Mass.: D. C. Heath, 1982), p. 13.

26. Rappoport and Rappoport, "The Dual Career Family," p. 4.

27. Gerda Lerner, "The Family and the Mill Girl: Changes in the Status of Women in the Age of Jackson." In Friedman and Shade, *Our American Sisters*, pp. 183–195.

28. Ida Withers Harrison, *The Christian Woman's Board of Missions 1874–1919*, p. 19.

29. Friedman and Shade, *Our American Sisters*, p. 178.

30. Indeed women have often brought their private moral sensitivities to bear on oppressive social situations, and raised these concerns within their church communities. See chapters 6 and 9 for specific examples.

31. Harrison, *Forty Years of Service*, pp. 27–28.

32. Ibid., p. 27.

33. Hewlett, *A Lesser Life*, p. 151.

34. Ruth S. Cowan, "Two Washes in the Morning and a Bridge Party at Night: The

American Housewife Between the Wars." In Friedman and Shade, *Our American Sisters*, p. 522.

35. Ibid., 527. For much of the above material we are indebted to the work of Friedman and Shade and their colleagues. After reading their "you can't put it down" book, we had a "click" experience. No wonder we had never liked history before. It had never been about us. Imagine a group of people thinking that the lives and experiences of women were so important that they wrote a book about us. We only hope our children have the pleasure of reading a book like this in their history classes.

Chapter 2
The Women's Movement and Family:
A Historical View

1. California Federal Savings and Loan Association et al. versus Mark Guerra, Director, Department of Fair Employment and Housing et al.

2. Sylvia Ann Hewlett, *A Lesser Life: The Myth of Women's Liberation in America* (New York: William Morrow, 1986), p. 50.

3. Elizabeth Griffith, *In Her Own Right: The Life of Elizabeth Cady Stanton* (New York: Oxford University Press, 1984), p. 54. Quoted in Hewlett, *A Lesser Life*, p. 151.

4. Betty Friedan, *The Feminine Mystique* (New York: Dell, 1963), p. 82.

5. Lucy Stone, "Extemporaneous Remarks at a National Women's Rights Convention in Cincinnati, Ohio." In Miriam Schneir, *Feminism: The Essential Historical Writings* (New York: Random House, 1972), pp. 106–107.

6. Hewlett, *A Lesser Life*.

7. Ibid., p. 150.

8. Sarah Grimke, "On the Condition of Women." In Elizabeth Ann Bartlett, ed., *Letters on the Equality of the Sexes* (New Haven: Yale University Press, 1988), p. 130.

9. Miriam Schneir, *Feminism: The Essential Historical Writings* (New York: Random House, 1972), p. 76.

10. Ida Withers Harrison, *The Christian Woman's Board of Missions 1874–1919* (no city: no publisher, no date), p. 20.

11. Nancy F. Cott, *The Grounding of Modern Feminism* (New Haven: Yale University Press, 1987), p. 17.

12. W. L. O'Neill, *Everyone Was Brave: The Rise and Fall of Feminism in America* (Chicago: Quadrangle, 1969), p. 21. Quoted in Maren Lockwood Carden, "The Women's Movement and the Family: A Socio-Historical Analysis of Constraints on Social Change." In Beth B. Hess and Marvin B. Sussman, *Women and the Family: Two Decades of Change* (New York: Harworth, 1984), p. 10.

13. Carden, "The Women's Movement and the Family," pp. 9–10.

14. Ellen Carol DuBois, *Elizabeth Cady Stanton/Susan B. Anthony Correspondence, Writings, Speeches* (New York: Schocken, 1981), pp. 50–51. Quoted in Cott, *The Grounding of Modern Feminism*, p. 19.

15. Jane Frohock, *The Lily* 8, 23 (1 December, 1856). Quoted in Cott, *The Grounding of Modern Feminism*, p. 19.

16. Cott, *The Grounding of Modern Feminism*, p. 19.

17. Mari Jo Buhle, *Women and American Socialism* (Urbana, Ill.: University of Illinois Press, 1981), p. 68. Quoted in Cott, *The Grounding of Modern Feminism*, p. 20.

18. Shulamith Firestone, *The Dialectic of Sex* (New York: William Morrow, 1970), p. 25. Quoted in Hewlett, *A Lesser Life*, p. 152.

19. Cott, *The Grounding of Modern Feminism*, p. 91.

20. Schneir, *Feminism: The Essential Historical Writings*, p. 306.

21. Friedan, *The Feminine Mystique*, pp. 60–61.

22. Simone de Beauvoir, *The Second Sex* (New York: Random House, 1952), pp. 586, 587–588.

23. Schneir, *Feminism: The Essential Historical Writings*, p. 322.

24. Phyllis Chessler, *Women and Madness* (Garden City, N.Y.: Doubleday, 1972), pp. 243–244. Quoted in Hewlett, *A Lesser Life*, p. 157.

25. Hewlett, *A Lesser Life*, pp. 157–158.

26. David Bouchier, *The Feminist Challenge: The Movement for Women's Liberation in Britain and the United States* (New York: Schocken, 1984), p. 45. Quoted in Hewlett, *A Lesser Life*, p. 159.

27. Anne Bowen Follis, *I'm Not a Women's Libber, But...* (Nashville: Abingdon, 1981), pp. 50–51.

28. Kathleen Newland, *The Sisterhood of Man* (New York: W. W. Norton, 1979), p. 19.

29. Ibid., pp. 19–22.

30. Hewlett, *A Lesser Life*, p. 185.

31. Ibid., p. 188.

32. Ruth Murray Brown, "In Defense of Traditional Values: The Anti-Feminist Movement." In Hess and Sussman, *Women and the Family*, p. 24.

33. Brown, "In Defense of Traditional Values," p. 27.

34. Jean Elshtain, "Feminism, Family and Community," *Dissent* 12 (Fall 1982), pp. 442–449, 447.

35. Erich Fromm, *The Art of Loving* (New York: Harper & Row, 1956), p. 17.

36. Ibid., p. 22.

37. Quoted in Richard M. Ryckman, *Theories of Personality* (Monterey, Calif.: Brooks/Cole, 1985), p. 148.

38. Elshtain, "Feminism, Family and Community," p. 442.

39. Follis, *I'm Not a Women's Libber, But...*, p. 88.

40. Betty Friedan, *The Second Stage* (New York: Summit Books, 1981), pp. 86–87.

41. Angela Miles, "Integrative Feminism," *Fireweed*, pp. 55–81, 57.

42. Ibid., p. 66.

43. Schneir, *Feminism: The Essential Historical Writings*, p. v.

Chapter 3
New Work Attitudes, New Family Patterns:
Where We Find Ourselves Today

1. U.S. Department of Labor, Women's Bureau, *Facts on U.S. Working Women* (Washington, D.C., July 1985), p. 1.

2. Robert N. Bellah, Richard Madsen, William M. Sullivan, Ann Swidler, and Steven M. Tipton, *Habits of the Heart: Individualism and Commitment in American Life* (Berkeley: University of California Press, 1985), p. 288.

3. Rosemary R. Ruether, quoted in Barbara Hilkert Andolsen, "Agape in Feminist Ethics," *Journal of Religious Ethics* 9 (Spring 1981), p. 76.

4. U.S. Department of Labor, *Facts*, p. 4.

5. J. H. Pleck, "The Work-Family Problem: Overloading the System." In B. L. Furisha and B. H. Goldman, eds., *Outsiders on the Inside: Women and Organizations* (Englewood Cliffs, N.J.: Prentice-Hall, 1981), pp. 239–254. See also S. W. Pyke and S. P. Kahill, "Sex Differences in Characteristics Presumed Relevant to Professional Productivity," *Psychology of Women Quarterly* 8 (1983), pp. 189–192, and Kathy Weingarten, "The Employment Pattern of Professional Couples and Their Distribution of Involvement in the Family," *Psychology of Women Quarterly* 3 (1978), pp. 43–52.

6. Heidi I. Hartman, "The Family as the Locus of Gender, Class and Political Study: The Example of Housework," *Signs* 6 (Spring 1981), p. 379. Wanda Minge-Klevana, "Does Labor Time Decrease with Industrialization? A Survey of Time Allocation Studies," *Current Anthropology* 21 (June 1980), p. 285. Jo Ann Vanek, "Time Spent in Housework," *Scientific American* (November 1974), p. 120. Barbara H. Andolsen, "A Woman's Work Is Never

Done," In Barbara H. Andolsen, Christine E. Gudorf, and Mary D. Pellauer, eds., *Women's Consciousness, Women's Conscience* (San Francisco: Harper & Row, 1987), p. 5.

7. Carol Tavris and Carole Offir, *The Longest War: Sex Differences in Perspective* (New York: Harcourt Brace Jovanovich, 1977).

8. Paula Englander-Golden and Glenn Barton, "Sex Differences in Absence from Work: A Reinterpretation," *Psychology of Women Quarterly* 8 (1983), pp. 185–188.

9. Benson Rosen, Thomas H. Jerdee, and Thomas L. Prestwich, "Dual-Career Marital Adjustment: Potential Effects of Discriminatory Managerial Attitudes," *Journal of Marriage and the Family* 37 (1975), pp. 565–572.

10. Sey Chassler, "Men Listening," *Ms.* 13 (1984), pp. 51–100.

11. Catherine Faver, "Women, Career Orientation, and Employment," *Psychology of Women Quarterly* 8 (1983), pp. 193–197.

12. Sylvia Ann Hewlett, *A Lesser Life: The Myth of Women's Liberation in America* (New York: William Morrow, 1986), p. 402.

13. Marilyn Parker, Steven Peltier, and Patricia Wolleat, "Understanding Dual Career Couples," *The Personnel and Guidance Journal* 60 (September 1981), pp. 14–18.

14. Jay Cocks, "How Long Til Equality?" *Time* (July 12, 1982), pp. 20–29.

15. Carol Tavris and Carole Wade, *The Longest War: Sex Differences in Perspective* (San Diego: Harcourt Brace Jovanovich, 1984), p. 27.

16. Diana Pearce and Harriette McAdoo, *Women and Children: Alone and in Poverty* (Washington, D.C.: Center for National Policy Review, 1981), p. 1.

17. Ibid.

18. Sigmund Freud, *An Outline of Psychoanalysis*, J. Strachey, ed. and trans. (New York: W. W. Norton, 1969).

19. Abraham H. Maslow, *Motivation and Personality* (New York: Van Nostrand, 1970).

20. Erich Fromm, *The Sane Society* (New York: Holt, Rinehart, and Winston, 1955).

21. Richard M. Ryckman, *Theories of Personality* (Monterey, Calif.: Brooks/Cole, 1982).

22. Abraham H. Maslow, *Toward a Psychology of Being* (New York: Van Nostrand, 1962).

23. P. C. Sexton, "Women and Work," *U.S. Department of Labor, Employment and Training Administration*, R and D Monograph 46 (1977).

24. A. C. Bebbington, "The Function of Stress in the Establishment of the Dual-Career Family," *Journal of Marriage and the Family* 35 (August 1973), pp. 530–537.

25. Irene H. Frieze, Jacquelynne E. Parsons, Paula B. Johnson, Diane N. Ruble, and G. I. Zellman, *Women and Sex Roles: A Social Psychological Perspective* (New York: W. W. Norton, 1978).

26. Parker J. Palmer, *The Company of Strangers: Christians and the Renewal of America's Public Life* (New York: Crossroad, 1981).

27. Hewlett, *A Lesser Life*, pp. 399–400.

28. Janet Hunt and Larry Hunt, "Dilemmas and Contradictions of Status: The Case of the Dual-Career Family," *Social Problems* 24 (April 1977).

29. Mary Frank Fox and Sharlene Hesse-Biber, *Women at Work* (Palo Alto, Calif.: Mayfield, 1984), p. 148.

Chapter 4
Other Women's Daughters:
Individualism and Relatedness among Working Women

1. Robert N. Bellah, Richard Madsen, William M. Sullivan, Ann Swidler, and Steven M. Tipton, *Habits of the Heart: Individualism and Commitment in American Life* (Berkeley: University of California Press, 1985), p. 167. See also Bellah's description of the therapeutic and managerial mentalities in U.S. society today, pp. 44–48.

2. Barbara Hilkert Andolsen, "Agape in Feminist Ethics," *Journal of Religious Ethics* 9 (Spring 1981), p. 77. In this article Andolsen treats the work of theologians such as Anders Nygren, Gene Outka, and Martin D'Arcy. See also the landmark article by Valerie Saiving,

"The Human Situation: A Feminine View," originally published in *Journal of Religion* (April 1960), and reprinted in *Womanspirit Rising*, C. P. Christ and J. Plaskow, eds. (San Francisco: Harper & Row, 1979), and Carol Gilligan's *In a Different Voice* (Cambridge: Harvard University Press, 1982), pp. 128ff.

3. The Greek verb *agapao* translated the Hebrew verb *'aheb* in the Septuagint (Greek translation of the Hebrew Bible) and the noun *agape* stands for the Hebrew noun *'ahabah*.

4. Philip S. Watson, "Preface" to Anders Nygren, *Agape and Eros* (New York: Harper & Row, 1969), p. xvi.

5. Ibid., p. xxii.

6. *New International Dictionary of the Bible*, p. 544.

7. Ibid.

8. Martin D'Arcy, *The Mind and Heart of Love* (New York: Meridian Books, 1959), p. 348.

9. Gene Outka, *Agape: An Ethical Analysis* (New Haven: Yale University Press, 1972), p. 290.

10. Paul Ramsey, quoted in D'Arcy, *The Mind and Heart of Love*, p. 279.

11. Quoted in Gilligan, *In a Different Voice*, p. 128.

12. Andolsen, "Agape," pp. 75–76.

13. Rosemary R. Ruether, quoted in Andolsen, "Agape," p. 76.

14. Ruether, "Feminist Theology and Spirituality" in *Christian Feminism*, Judith L. Weidman, ed. (San Francisco: Harper & Row, 1984), p. 23.

15. Bellah et al., *Habits of the Heart*, p. 111.

16. Suzanne Gordon, "Why 'Working Girls' Doesn't Work," *Boston Globe*, January 8, 1989.

17. Linda Gordon, "Why 19th Century Feminists Did Not Support Birth Control and 20th Century Feminists Do: Feminism, Reproduction, and the Family," in *Rethinking the Family: Some Feminist Questions*, Barrie Thorne, ed. (New York: Longman, 1982), p. 50.

18. Andolsen, "Agape," p. 76.

19. Ibid., p. 79.

20. Sara Ruddick, "Maternal Thinking," in *Rethinking the Family*, pp. 84–85.

21. Alice Walker, *The Color Purple* (New York: Harcourt Brace Jovanovich, 1982), pp. 37–38.

22. Ibid., pp. 41–43.

23. Mary O'Brien, *The Politics of Reproduction* (Boston: Routledge and Kegan Paul, 1981), p. 15.

24. Hilary Rose, "Hand, Brain, and Heart: A Feminist Epistemology for the Natural Sciences." *Signs* (Autumn 1983), p. 83.

25. Angela Miles, "Integrative Feminism" *Fireweed*, p. 56.

26. O'Brien, *The Politics of Reproduction*, p. 210.

27. Ruddick, "Maternal Thinking," p. 89.

28. Ibid., p. 90.

29. Clare B. Fischer, "Liberating Work," in *Christian Feminism*, p. 120.

30. Ibid., p. 121.

31. The 1978 Pregnancy Discrimination Act requires that women be entitled to at least the same benefits for pregnancy leave as for any disability, and that they not be fired or required to take an unpaid leave just because they are pregnant.

Chapter 5
Rediscovering a Public Spirituality

1. Barbara Andolsen, Christine Gudorf, and Mary Pellauer, eds., *Women's Consciousness, Women's Conscience* (San Francisco: Harper & Row, 1985), p. xii.

2. Robert N. Bellah, Richard Madsen, William M. Sullivan, Ann Swidler, and Steven M. Tipton, *Habits of the Heart: Individualism and Commitment in American Life* (Berkeley: University of California Press, 1985), p. 16.

3. Ibid., p. 109.

4. Ibid., p. 111.

5. Suzanne Gordon, "Why 'Working Girls' Doesn't Work," *Boston Globe*, January 8, 1989.

6. Bellah et al., *Habits of the Heart*, p. 45.

7. Ibid.

8. Ibid., p. 48.

9. Gordon, "Working Girls."

10. Bellah et al., *Habits of the Heart*, pp. 194–195.

11. Ibid., p. 167.

12. *The Jerusalem Bible* (Garden City, N.Y.: Doubleday, 1966). All subsequent translations in this chapter are from this version. However, we have taken the liberty of changing the proper name "Yahweh," used in this translation, to the more commonly used terminology, "the Lord God." Sexist language in scriptural passages has not been changed. To do so would raise innumerable questions of culture as well as grammar that cannot be resolved without a thorough reexamination of the whole text.

13. Bellah et al., *Habits of the Heart*, p. 38.

14. Parker J. Palmer, *The Company of Strangers: Christians and the Renewal of America's Public Life* (New York: Crossroad, 1981), pp. 18–19.

15. Ibid., p. 22.

16. Ibid., p. 24

17. Ibid.

18. Ibid., pp. 22, 31.

19. Sylvia Ann Hewlett, *A Lesser Life: The Myth of Women's Liberation in America* (New York: William Morrow, 1986), p. 151.

20. Ibid., p. 37.

Chapter 6
Biblical Roots for a New Spirituality for Women

1. Shelly Finson, "Feminist Spirituality within the Framework of Feminist Consciousness," *Studies in Religion* (Winter 1987), p. 73.

2. Elisabeth Schüssler Fiorenza, "Women in the Early Christian Movement," in *Womanspirit Rising: A Feminist Reader in Religion*, Carol P. Christ and Judith Plaskow, eds. (New York: Harper & Row, 1979), p. 84.

3. Katharine Doob Sakenfeld, "Feminist Uses of Biblical Materials," in *Feminist Interpretation of the Bible*, Letty Russell, ed. (Philadelphia: Westminster, 1985), p. 55.

4. Mary Ann Tolbert, "Defining the Problem: The Bible and Feminist Hermeneutics," *Semeia* 28 (1983), p. 120.

5. Cf. Virginia Ramey Mollenkott, *Women, Men, and the Bible* (Nashville: Abingdon, 1977), pp. 108–120.

6. Ibid., pp. 108, 118.

7. Ruether, "Feminist Interpretation: A Method of Correlation," in *Feminist Interpretation of the Bible*, pp. 112–113.

8. Elisabeth Schüssler Fiorenza, "The Will to Choose or to Reject: Continuing our Critical Work," in *Feminist Interpretation of the Bible*, p. 130.

9. Tolbert, "Defining the Problem," p. 120.

10. Schüssler Fiorenza, "Women in the Early Christian Movement," pp. 86–87.

11. Cf. Schüssler Fiorenza, *Bread Not Stone: The Challenge of Feminist Biblical Interpretation* (Boston: Beacon, 1985).

12. Schüssler Fiorenza, "The Will to Choose or to Reject," p. 134.

13. Ibid., p. 133.

14. Schüssler Fiorenza, "A Feminist Critical Interpretation for Liberation: Martha and Mary: Luke 1:38-42," *Religion & Intellectual Life*, vol. 3, no. 2 (Winter 1986), p. 24.

15. Ruether, "Feminist Interpretation," p. 117.

16. Ibid., p. 118.

17. Sakenfeld, "Feminist Uses of Biblical Materials," p. 56.

18. Michael Rosenzweig, "A Helper Equal to Him," *Judaism*, vol. 35, no. 3 (Summer 1986), p. 277.

19. Ibid., pp. 278–279.

20. Phyllis Trible, *God and the Rhetoric of Sexuality* (Philadelphia: Fortress, 1978), pp. 12ff. See Duane Christensen, "Huldah and the Men of Anathoth: Women in Leadership in the Deuteronomic History," *Society of Biblical Literature Seminar Papers* 23 (1984), p. 399. We are deeply in debt to scholars like Phyllis Trible for helping us see that Adam was not in fact a male figure as such until after woman was removed from him in the creation of Eve. Thus the familiar arguments for the subordination of women based on the order of creation have no actual basis in the biblical text. Male and female are created together as Adam is transformed in the story of Genesis 2 — from "humankind," on the one hand, to the male counterpart of a remarkable "help-mate" who is in fact Adam's equal.

21. Elizabeth Clark, "The Old Testament," in Elizabeth Clark and Herbert Richardson, eds., *Women and Religion: A Feminist Sourcebook of Christian Thought* (New York: Harper & Row, 1977), p. 29.

22. Leonard Swidler, *Biblical Affirmations of Women* (Philadelphia: Westminster Press, 1979).

23. Christensen, "Huldah and the Men of Anathoth," p. 403.

24. Schüssler Fiorenza, "Women in the Early Christian Movement," p. 87.

25. Ben Witherington III, *Women in the Ministry of Jesus* (New York: Cambridge University Press, 1984), p. 127.

26. Mollenkott, *Women, Men and the Bible*, p. 119.

27. Elisabeth Schüssler Fiorenza, *In Memory of Her* (New York: Crossroad, 1984), pp. 169–170, 245ff.

28. *The Oxford Annotated Bible*, Revised Standard Version (New York: Oxford University Press, 1973). Further citations from Scripture in this chapter and in later chapters will be identified in the text as RSV or JB (Jerusalem Bible).

29. Schüssler Fiorenza, "Women in the Early Christian Movement," p. 88.

30. For a full discussion of Pauline authorship see W. G. Kummel, *Introduction to the New Testament* (Nashville: Abingdon, 1975), pp. 315–387, or other scholarly introductions to the New Testament.

31. William O. Walker, Jr., "The 'Theology of Woman's Place' and the 'Paulinist' Tradition," *Semeia* 28 (1983), p. 111.

32. Constance Parvey, "The Theology and Leadership of Women in the New Testament," in *Religion and Sexism*, Rosemary Radford Ruether, ed. (New York: Simon and Schuster, 1974), p. 136.

33. Krister Stendahl, *The Bible and the Role of Women*, trans. Emilie T. Sander (Philadelphia: Fortress Press, 1966), p. 34.

34. Ibid., p. 35.

35. Monique Dumais, "Pour que les noces aient lieu entre Dieu et les femmes," *Studies in Religion*, vol. 16, no. 1 (Winter 1987), p. 64. Translation is our own.

36. See Virginia Ramey Mollenkott, *The Divine Feminine* (New York: Crossroad, 1987). We are indebted to Mollenkott's work for systematically calling our attention to many of the biblical passages that we quote below.

37. Ibid., p. 5.

38. Ibid.

39. Ibid., p. 112.

40. Ibid.

41. Julian of Norwich, *Showings*, trans. by Edmund Colledge and James Walsh (New York: Paulist, 1978), pp. 299, 301.

42. Ibid., p. 296.

43. See Mollenkott, *The Divine Feminine*, pp. 97–105, for a discussion of this.
44. Ibid., pp. 36–43.
45. Ibid., p. 37.

Chapter 7
A Spirituality of Self-Esteem and Social Communion

1. Shelly Finson, "Feminist Spirituality within the Framework of Feminist Consciousness," *Studies in Religion* (Winter 1987), p. 71.
2. Joann Wolski Conn, "Issues in Women's Spirituality," in *Women's Spirituality*, ed. Joann Wolski Conn (New York: Paulist, 1986), p. 11.
3. Sarai and Abram's names are changed to Sarah and Abraham when God makes the covenant promising them their own child. See Genesis 17:5–15.
4. A Tamar different from David's daughter, raped by her half-brother Amnon.
5. It is intriguing that a standard commentary such as *Jerome Biblical Commentary* has a hard time figuring out why this story is put here at all. It couldn't be because this woman was interesting! See *Jerome Biblical Commentary* (Englewood Cliffs, N.J.: Prentice Hall, 1968), section 146 on Gen. 38:1–30.
6. Claudia V. Camp, "The Wise Women of 2 Samuel: A Role Model for Women in Early Israel?," *Catholic Biblical Quarterly* 43 (January 1981), p. 17. See note 8.
7. Ibid., p. 18.
8. Sharon Ringe, "A Gentile Woman's Story," in *Feminist Interpretation of the Bible*, Letty Russell, ed. (Philadelphia: Westminster, 1985), p. 69.
9. Ibid., pp. 65–72.
10. Ibid., pp. 71–72.
11. Ibid., p. 72.
12. Fran Ferder, "Zeal for Your House Consumes Me: Dealing with Anger as a Woman in the Church," *Miriam's Song*, Talks given at the Women in the Church Conference, Washington, D.C., 1987 (Hyattsville, Md.: Quixote Center, 1987), pp. 11–13.
13. Ibid., p. 15.
14. Ibid.
15. Ibid., p. 13.
16. Ibid., p. 14.
17. See also Michael Carroll, "Myth, Methodology and Transformation in the Old Testament: The Stories of Esther, Judith and Susanna," *Studies in Religion*, vol. 12, no. 3 (1983), p. 305.
18. Frieda C. Hyman, "The Education of a Queen," *Judaism*, vol. 35, no. 1 (Winter 1986), p. 79.
19. Ibid., p. 80.
20. Ibid., p. 83.
21. Ibid., p. 82.
22. Rosemary Radford Ruether, "Foremothers of WomanChurch," in *Womanguides: Readings toward a Feminist Theology* (Boston: Beacon, 1985), p. 179.
23. *The Passion of Saints Perpetua and Felicitas*, vol. 3, in Roberts and Donaldson, *Ante-Nicene Fathers*, quoted in Ruether, *Womanguides*, pp. 190–191.
24. Ibid., pp. 191–192.
25. Ibid., p. 192.
26. Ibid.
27. Ibid.
28. John F. Craghan, "Esther, Judith and Ruth: Paradigms for Human Liberation," *Biblical Theology Bulletin*, vol. 12, no. 1 (1982), p. 14.
29. Finson, "Feminist Spirituality within the Framework of Feminist Consciousness," p. 72.

Chapter 8
Daughters of Deborah:
Rediscovering Women's Public Vocation

1. *De Vidius* 8:49–50, *Patrologia cursus completus: series latina*, 16:363 (Paris: J.-P. Migne, 1841–1864).
2. National Catholic Conference of Bishops. "Partners in the Mystery of Redemption: First Draft of the U.S. Bishops' Pastoral Response to Women's Concerns for Church and Society." *Origins* 17:45 (April 21, 1988), p. 773.
3. Ibid., p. 775.
4. Robert G. Middleton, "Revising the Concept of Vocation for the Industrial Age," *Christian Century* (October 29, 1986), pp. 943–945.
5. Steven Murphy, "Resistance in the Professions," *Religion & Intellectual Life* 4 (Spring 1987), pp. 71–80.
6. Robert Merrihew Adams, "Vocation," *Faith and Philosophy*, vol. 4, no. 4 (October 1987), pp. 448–462.
7. Ibid., p. 454.
8. Ibid., p. 455.
9. Ibid., p. 462, note 14.
10. Dorothy Sayers, *Creed or Chaos* (New York: Harcourt Brace, 1949), pp. 54–55.
11. Adams, "Vocation," p. 456.
12. Middleton, "Revising the Concept of Vocation for the Industrial Age," p. 944.
13. Robert N. Bellah, Richard Madsen, William M. Sullivan, Ann Swidler, and Steven M. Tipton, *Habits of the Heart: Individualism and Commitment in American Life* (Berkeley: University of California Press, 1985), p. 66, emphasis added.
14. General Secretariat of the Synod of Bishops, "Working Paper for the 1987 Synod of Bishops on the Vocation and Mission of the Laity," *Origins* 17:1 (May 21, 1987), pp. 1–19.
15. National Public Radio, August 19, 1988.
16. Kathleen Lentz, "Commitment to Calling: The Image of Education," *Religion & Intellectual Life* 4 (Spring 1987), pp. 59–70.
17. Robert N. Bellah and William M. Sullivan, "The Professions and the Common Good: Vocation/Profession/Career," *Religion & Intellectual Life* 4 (Spring 1987), pp. 4–20.
18. Ruth A. Tucker, "Working Mothers," *Christianity Today* (July 15, 1988), pp. 17–21.
19. "Partners in the Mystery of Redemption," p. 787.
20. "The Role of Women in Contemporary Society," *The Pope Speaks* 69 (December 8, 1974), p. 316, quoted in ibid., p. 763.
21. "Unity in the Work of Service," 1987 Address to the San Francisco Laity, quoted in "Partners in the Mystery of Redemption," ibid.
22. "Partners in the Mystery of Redemption," p. 763.
23. Tucker, "Working Mothers," p. 19.
24. Ibid., p. 21.
25. "Partners in the Mystery of Redemption," p. 767.
26. Ibid., pp. 773, 776.
27. Adams, "Vocation," pp. 459, 461.
28. Ben Witherington III, *Women in the Ministry of Jesus* (New York: Cambridge University Press, 1984), p. 9.
29. Pam Scalise, "Women in Ministry: Reclaiming Our Old Testament Heritage," *Review and Expositor*, vol. 83, no. 1 (1986), pp. 7–13.
30. Claudia V. Camp, "The Wise Women of 2 Samuel: A Role Model for Women in Early Israel?," *Catholic Biblical Quarterly* 43 (January 1981), p. 14.
31. Scalise, "Women in Ministry," p. 9.
32. Ibid., p. 10.
33. Elisabeth Schüssler Fiorenza, "Women in the Early Christian Movement," in *Wom-*

anspirit Rising: A Feminist Reader in Religion, Carol P. Christ and Judith Plaskow, eds. (New York: Harper & Row, 1979), p. 89.

34. Ibid., p. 90.

35. Rosemary Radford Ruether, "Foremothers of WomanChurch," in *Womanguides: Readings toward a Feminist Theology* (Boston: Beacon, 1985), p. 178.

36. Ray R. Schulz. "Romans 16:7: Junia or Junias?," *Expository Times* 98 (January 1987), pp. 108–110.

37. Ruether, *Womanguides,* p. 180.

38. Ibid., p. 175.

39. Schüssler Fiorenza, "Women in the Early Christian Movement," p. 92.

40. Karl H. Schelke, *The Spirit and the Bride: Women in the Bible,* trans. Matthew J. O'Connell (Collegeville: Liturgical Press, 1977), p. 158.

41. Schüssler Fiorenza, "Women in the Early Christian Movement," p. 92.

42. Joseph McLellan, "Recordings: Hildegard in the Spotlight," *Washington Post,* March 30, 1986, quoted in Matthew Fox, ed., *The Book of Divine Works* (Santa Fe, N.M.: Bear & Co., 1987), p. ix.

43. Ibid.

44. Barbara Newman, *Sister of Wisdom: St. Hildegard's Theology of the Feminine* (Berkeley: University of California Press, 1987), p. 10.

45. Barbara Newman, "Divine Power Made Perfect in Weakness," *Medieval Religious Women* (Kalamazoo, Mich.: Cistercian Publications, 1965), p. 28, note 4.

46. Hildegard of Bingen, *The Book of Divine Works,* Matthew Fox, ed., p. 5.

47. Newman, *Sister of Wisdom,* p. 34.

48. Hildegard of Bingen, "Letter to Bernard of Clairvaux (1147)," trans. Ronald Miller, in Matthew Fox, ed., *The Book of Divine Works,* p. 271.

49. *Book of Divine Works,* p. 74.

50. Prudence Allen, "Two Medieval Views on Women's Identity," *Studies in Religion,* vol. 16, no. 1 (1987), pp. 22–36.

51. Newman, *Sister of Wisdom,* p. 13.

52. Allen, "Two Medieval Views on Women's Identity," pp. 30–35.

53. Hildegard, *Scivia,* quoted in ibid., p. 22.

54. Elizabeth of Schonau, quoted in Newman, *Sister of Wisdom,* p. 39.

Chapter 9
Other Daughters of Deborah:
Four Nineteenth-Century Women

1. Elizabeth Ann Bartlett, intro. to Sarah Grimke, *Letters on the Equality of the Sexes* (New Haven: Yale University Press, 1988), quoting her.

2. Gerda Lerner, *The Grimke Sisters from South Carolina: Rebels against Slavery* (Boston: Houghton Mifflin, 1967), p. 78.

3. Ibid.

4. Ibid., p. 80.

5. Angelina Grimke's diary (February 6, 1829), quoted in Lerner, *The Grimke Sisters from South Carolina,* p. 81.

6. Ibid., February 7, 1829.

7. Sarah Grimke, *Letters on the Equality of the Sexes,* Elizabeth Ann Bartlett, ed. (New Haven: Yale University Press, 1988), p. 41.

8. Nancy A. Hardesty, *Women Called to Witness: Evangelical Feminism in the 19th Century* (Nashville: Abingdon, 1984), p. 107.

9. Ibid., p. 88.

10. S. Grimke, "Letter to Amos Phelps" (August 3, 1937), quoted in Hardesty, *Women Called to Witness,* p. 121.

11. S. Grimke, "Letter to Theodore Weld" (August 20, 1937), quoted in ibid.

12. A. Grimke, "Letter to Theodore Weld" (August 20, 1937), quoted in ibid., p. 91.

13. S. Grimke, "The Condition of Women," in *Letters*, p. 130.

14. Bartlett, intro. to Grimke, *Letters*, p. 18.

15. S. Grimke, *Letters*, p. 38.

16. Bartlett, intro. to Grimke, *Letters*, p. 22.

17. Calvert Alexander, *The Catholic Literary Revival* (Milwaukee: Bruce, 1935), p. 114.

18. June Badeni, *The Slender Tree: A Life of Alice Meynell* (Cornwall: Tabb House, 1981), p. 27.

19. Alice Meynell, manuscript of her notebook, 1873, quoted in Badeni, *The Slender Tree*, p. 50.

20. Viola Meynell, *Alice Meynell: A Memoir* (New York: Scribners, 1929), pp. 60, 65.

21. Alexander, *The Catholic Literary Revival*, p. 128.

22. Alice Meynell, manuscript of her diary, 1865, quoted in Badeni, *The Slender Tree*, p. 28.

23. Alexander, *The Catholic Literary Revival*, p. 127, quoting Everard Meynell.

24. Alice Meynell, "Letter to Wilfrid Meynell," quoted in Badeni, *The Slender Tree*, p. 85.

25. Badeni, *The Slender Tree*, p. 85.

26. Edward Wagenknecht, *Daughters of the Covenant: Portraits of Six Jewish Women* (Amherst: University of Massachusetts Press, 1983), p. 101.

27. Lillian Wald, *The House on Henry Street* (New York: Holt and Co., 1915), p. 1.

28. Ibid., pp. 6–7.

29. Ibid., p. 7.

30. Quoted in Wagenknecht, *Daughters of the Covenant*, pp. 98–99.

31. Wagenknecht, *Daughters of the Covenant*, p. 102.

32. Ibid., p. 110.

33. Ibid.

34. Ibid., p. 112.

35. Wald, *The House on Henry Street*, pp. 266–268.

Chapter 10
Women and the Men in their Lives

1. Phil Donahue and Company, *My Own Story: Donahue* (New York: Simon and Schuster, 1979), pp. 104–105.

2. Sonia Johnson, *From Housewife to Heretic* (Garden City, N.Y.: Anchor Books, 1983), pp. 62–63. Sonia Johnson was excommunicated from the Mormon Church. Although church officials cite other reasons, Johnson believes she was excommunicated as a result of her support for the Equal Rights Amendment.

3. Lynn Monahan, Deanna Kuhn, and Phillip Shaver, "Intrapsychic Versus Cultural Explanations for the 'Fear of Success' Motive," *Journal of Personality and Social Psychology*, vol. 29, no. 1 (1974), pp. 60–64.

4. Warren Farrell, "Economics Feared, Not Intimacy," *The Wheeling Intelligencer* 136, 117, January 1988.

5. Betty Friedan, *The Second Stage* (New York: Summit Books, 1981), p. 128.

6. Ibid., p. 129.

7. Ibid., p. 139.

8. Veronica F. Nieva, "Work and Family Linkages." In Laurie Larwood, Ann H. Stromberg, and Barbara Gutek, *Women and Work: An Annual Review*, vol. 1 (Beverly Hills, Calif.: Sage, 1985), pp. 162–190. Laurel Richardson Walum, *The Dynamics of Sex and Gender: A Sociological Perspective* (Chicago: Rand McNally, 1977). Irene H. Frieze, Jacquelynne E. Parsons, Paula B. Johnson, Diane N. Ruble, and G. I. Zellman, *Women and Sex Roles: A Social Psychological Perspective* (New York: W. W. Norton, 1978).

9. Nel Noddings, *Caring: A Feminine Approach to Ethics and Moral Education* (Berkeley: University of California Press, 1984), p. 127.

10. Friedan, *The Second Stage*, p. 270.
11. Leonard Greenhalgh and R. W. Gilkey, "Our Game, Your Rules: Developing Effective Negotiating Approaches." In Lynda L. Moore, *Not as Far as You Think: The Realities of Working Women* (Lexington, Mass.: D. C. Heath, 1986), pp. 135–148.
12. Ibid., p. 140.
13. M. F. Maples, "Dual Career Marriages: Elements for Potential Success," *The Personnel and Guidance Journal* 60 (1981), pp. 19–23.
14. Jay Belsky and L. Steinberg, "The Effects of Day Care: A Critical Review," *Child Development* 49 (1978), p. 929.
15. Frieze et al., *Women and Sex Roles*.
16. Carol Gilligan, *In a Different Voice* (Cambridge, Mass.: Harvard University Press, 1982), p. 40.
17. Ibid., p. 42.
18. Ibid., p. 63.
19. Maples, "Dual Career Marriages."
20. Francine S. Hall and Douglas T. Hall, *Two Career Couples* (Reading, Mass.: Addison-Wesley, 1979). We might guess that the lower satisfaction occurring in dual-career marriages with children testifies to the dearth of adequate arrangements for children of working parents and the stresses created by little workplace support of family life. We will discuss this point in greater detail later.
21. Willa R. Huser and Claude W. Grant, "A Study of Husbands and Wives from Dual-Career and Traditional Families," *Psychology of Women Quarterly*, vol. 3, no. 1 (Fall 1978), pp. 78-89.
22. David G. Rice, *Dual-Career Marriage: Conflict and Treatment* (London: Colliers MacMillan, 1979).
23. Eleanor Grant, "The Housework Gap," *Psychology Today*, vol. 22, no. 1 (January 1988), p. 10.
24. Marilyn Parker, Steven Peltier, and Patricia Wolleat, "Understanding Dual Career Couples," *The Personnel and Guidance Journal* 60 (1981), pp. 14–18.
25. Vincent Bozzi, "Time and Togetherness," *Psychology Today*, vol. 22, no. 1 (January 1988), p. 10.
26. Glenn Collins, "Two-Career Couples: A Delicate Balance," *New York Times*, December 3, 1987.
27. Juanita Williams, *Psychology of Women: Behavior in a Biosocial Context* (New York: W. W. Norton, 1977), pp. 285–317.
28. Marjory Roberts, "America's Counselor," *Psychology Today*, vol. 21, no. 12 (December 1987), p. 80.
29. Marilyn Gardner, "Protecting Our Most Important Assets," *Christian Science Monitor* 79, November 5, 1987.
30. Frieze et al., *Women and Sex Roles*.
31. Nieva, "Work and Family Linkages."
32. Collins, "Two-Career Couples."
33. Uma Sekaran, "Factors Influencing the Quality of Life in Dual-Career Families," *Journal of Occupational Psychology* 56 (1983), pp. 161–174.
34. Quoted in Virginia Ramey Mollenkott, *Women, Men and the Bible* (Nashville: Abingdon, 1977), p. 48.
35. Lillian Rubin, *Intimate Strangers: Men and Women Together* (New York: Harper & Row, 1984), p. 31.
36. Ibid., p. 189.
37. Mollenkott, *Women, Men and the Bible*, pp. 33, 27–28.
38. Rubin, *Intimate Strangers*.
39. Ibid., pp. 22–24.
40. Elliot Noyes, Jr., *The Fable of He and She* (New York: Learning Corporation of America, 1974).

Chapter 11
Ourselves, Our Daughters, and Our Sons:
Concrete Tasks for the Future

1. "All Things Considered," National Public Radio, September 29, 1987.

2. Alan Pifer, "Women Working: Toward a New Society." In Karen Wolk Feinstein, *Working Women and Families* (Beverly Hills, Calif.: Sage, 1979), pp. 13–34.

3. Leonard Greenhalgh and R. W. Gilkey, "Our Games, Your Rules: Developing Effective Negotiating Approaches." In Lynda L. Moore, *Not as Far as You Think: The Realities of Working Women* (Lexington, Mass.: D. C. Heath, 1986), pp. 135–148.

4. Barbara Hilkert Andolsen, Christine E. Gudorf, and Mary D. Pellauer, *Women's Consciousness, Women's Conscience* (San Francisco: Harper & Row, 1985), p. 18.

5. Steven Nock and Paul W. Kingston, "The Family Work Day," *Journal of Marriage and the Family* 46 (1984), pp. 333–343.

6. Barbara Hilkert Andolsen, "A Woman's Work Is Never Done: Unpaid Household Labor as a Social Justice Issue." In Andolsen et al., *Women's Consciousness*, p. 3.

7. Ralph E. Smith, "Hours Rigidity: Effects on the Labor Market Status of Women." In Feinstein, *Working Women and Families*, pp. 211–222.

8. Denise Polit, "Nontraditional Work Schedules for Women." In Feinstein, *Working Women and Families*, pp. 195–210.

9. Laurel Richardson Walum, *The Dynamics of Sex and Gender: A Sociological Perspective* (Chicago: Rand McNally, 1977), pp. 153–166.

10. Margaret L. Anderson, *Thinking about Women: Sociological and Feminist Perspectives* (New York: Macmillan, 1983).

11. Polit, "Nontraditional Work Schedules for Women."

12. Nock and Kingston, "The Family Work Day."

13. Jacqueline Giambanco, "Concerned Mother, Successful Attorney, Expert Delegator," *Working Woman* (December 1987), p. 118.

14. William Arkin and L. R. Dobrofsky, "Job-Sharing Couples." In Feinstein, *Working Women and Families*, pp. 159–176.

15. Mary Frank Fox and Sharlene Hesse-Biber, *Women at Work* (Palo Alto, Calif.: Mayfield, 1984).

16. Linda Carpenter, "Sex Role Stereotyping: Organizational and Individual Costs," presentation at the Association for Women in Psychology, Bethesda, March 14, 1988.

17. Kathleen Newland, *The Sisterhood of Man* (New York: W. W. Norton, 1979).

18. Fox and Hesse-Biber, *Women at Work*.

19. Lillian Rubin, *Intimate Strangers: Men and Women Together* (New York: Harper & Row, 1984), p. 32.

20. Milton Moskowitz and Carol N. Townsend, "The Thirty Best Companies for Working Mothers," *Working Mother* (August 25–28, 1986), pp. 109–112.

21. Rosalyn B. Will and Steven D. Lydenberg, "20 Corporations that Listen to Women," *Ms.* 16 (November 1987), pp. 45–52.

22. Ibid., p. 49.

23. Fox and Hesse-Biber, *Women at Work*.

24. Carpenter, "Sex Role Stereotyping."

25. Donna M. Stringer-Moore, "Impact of Dual Career Couples on Employers: Problems and Solutions," *Public Personnel Management Journal* 10 (1981), pp. 393–401.

26. Stringer-Moore, "Impact of Dual Career Couples on Employers."

27. Pifer, "Women Working: Toward a New Society."

28. Polit, "Nontraditional Work Schedules for Women."

29. "Lack of Maternity, Medical Leave Cost U.S. $715 Million Each Year," *Wheeling News-Register*, March 14, 1988.

30. Halcyone H. Bohen and Anamaria Viveros-Long, "Balancing Jobs and Family Life."

In Patricia Vaydanoff, ed., *Work and Family: Changing Roles of Men and Women* (Palo Alto, Calif.: Mayfield, 1984), pp. 320–329.

31. Newland, *The Sisterhood of Man.*

32. Ellen Goodman, "Points to Ponder," *Reader's Digest* 131 (November 1987), p. 230.

33. Fox and Hesse-Biber, *Women at Work*, p. 220.

34. "Who Cares about Day Care?" *Newsweek*, March 28, 1988, p. 73.

35. Sylvia Ann Hewlett, *A Lesser Life: The Myth of Women's Liberation in America* (New York: William Morrow, 1986), p. 374.

36. Ibid., p. 375.

Index

Also from Meyer • Stone Books ...

AGAINST MACHISMO
Rubem Alves, Leonardo Boff, Gustavo Gutiérrez, José Míguez Bonino, Juan Luis Segundo ... and Others Talk About the Struggle of Women

Interviews by Elsa Tamez

"At last, a book that draws male Latin American liberation theologians into dialogue! These interviews provide important insight into the links between liberation and feminist theologies."
— Letty M. Russell

"...a very important contribution. While some of the feminist theologians in the United States are not conscious of the class dimensions of our work, some liberation theologians seem not to be aware of the theoretical achievements of a feminist theology of liberation. Elsa Tamez is to be commended for initiating this dialogue."

— Elisabeth Schüssler Fiorenza

"...encouraging, creative responses to the probing questions of an incisive and caring interlocutor. The results will mean a lot of changed attitudes in North America as well."
— Robert McAfee Brown

Elsa Tamez is Professor of Biblical Studies at the Seminario Bíblico Latino-americano in Costa Rica.

Theology/ Feminist Studies   160 pp.

Hardcover: $24.95 (ISBN 0-940989-13-1)
Paperback: $9.95 (ISBN 0-940989-12-3)

WOMANPRAYER, WOMANSONG
Resources for Ritual

Miriam Therese Winter

Illustrated by Meinrad Craighead

" . . . a groundbreaking contribution to the church of our day. While drawing on Scripture and affirming God's self-revelation in Jesus Christ, this exciting book addresses the urgent need for ritual that incorporates women's experience. Feminine biblical images of God are recovered; feminine pronouns for God are supplied; valiant women are remembered; the church year is reinterpreted to highlight women's experience; and oppression and violence against women in Scripture and society are exposed. I have been searching for alternatives to hierarchical, coercive, male images of God that are at the same time faithful to the Christian revelation. I have found a rich resource here!"

— Ruth Duck, Editor, *Everflowing Streams*

"With Miriam Therese Winter's *WomanPrayer, WomanSong*, the feminist movement in the Christian community goes beyond the critique of patriarchal bias in religion and begins a new phase. Through a new religious encounter with the Mother-spirit of God, a new religious culture begins to develop that also renews the liberating grace and power of biblical faith. For the first time the church prays and sings the ancient story of creation and redemption through women's creative imagination."

— Rosemary Radford Ruether

"By drawing on tradition to challenge tradition, this book models how a feminist hermeneutic can revitalize tradition. The preface, liturgies, and songs reveal a sophisticated theological mind blessed with the gift of poetic expression."

— Thomas Troeger, Professor of Preaching and Parish Ministry, Colgate Rochester Divinity School, Bexley Hall-Crozer Seminary

Miriam Therese Winter is Professor of Liturgy, Worship, and Spirituality at Hartford Seminary, Hartford, Connecticut. She is the author of *Why Sing? Toward a Theology of Catholic Church Music.*

Feminist Studies/Liturgy   264 pp.

Paperback: $14.95 (ISBN 0-940989-00-X)

NEW EYES FOR READING

Biblical and Theological Reflections by Women from the Third World

Bärbel von Wartenberg-Potter and John Pobee

New Eyes for Reading is a Third World contribution to women's theology. The reflections included in the book are by women from Africa, Asia, and Latin America. As these women read the Bible and look at their role in church and society with new eyes, they gain new insights, experience a new freedom, and come to a new commitment. Their contributions are part of an ongoing dialogue between women in the ecumenical movement about their responsibility to further the ecumenical debate and to renew their own churches.

"Pobee and von Wartenberg-Potter provide the reader with a broad and fresh introduction to biblical and theological reflections by women from the Third World. One of the remarkable features of this book is that the reader soon becomes sympathetically and critically aware of the opinions of women from Africa, Asia, and Latin America, and the resilience of their spirits. Even when these reflections 'emerge from the wounds that hurt, the scars that do not disappear, the stories that have no ending,' the women dream and hope."   — *Wellsprings*

Bärbel von Wartenberg-Potter is a Lutheran pastor from West Germany. She teaches at the United Theological College of the West Indies in Kingston, Jamaica. **John Pobee** is associate director of the Program on Theological Education, World Council of Churches.

Theology/ Feminist Studies   96 pp.

Paperback: $7.95 (ISBN 0-940989-07-7)

MORE THAN WORDS
Prayer and Ritual for Inclusive Communities

Janet Schaffran and Pat Kozak

"*More Than Words* is a wonderful combination of prayers, songs, and entire worship services that reflect the spirituality of many different peoples and cultures. It uses inclusive language and a rich diversity of images of God with a deep sensitivity to the gospel call of justice and peace. We have been privileged to be part of several worship services using this marvelous resource."
— Jim and Kathy McGinnis, The Institute for Peace and Justice

"Thirty multi-cultural liturgies are a good start for communities that want to connect justice and spirituality in an inclusive style. It includes introductory materials on symbols and pluralism that will help groups branch out on their own and create new models." — *Waterwheel*

Janet Schaffran is Campus Minister at Walsh College, Canton, Ohio.
Pat Kozak is a graduate student at Pacific School of Religion in Berkeley, Calif.

Feminist Studies/Liturgy   192 pp.

Spiral: $11.95 (ISBN 0-940989-33-6)
Paperback: $7.95 (ISBN 0-940989-30-1)

Order from your bookstore
or from
Meyer • Stone Books
2014 South Yost Avenue
Bloomington, IN 47403
Tel.: 800-937-0313